George Herbert Mead

The Making of a Social Pragmatist

Gary A. Cook

University of Illinois Press   *Urbana and Chicago*

© 1993 by the Board of Trustees of the University of Illinois
Manufactured in the United States of America
I 2 3 4 5 C P 5 4 3 2 I

This book is printed on acid-free paper.

Library of Congress Cataloging-in-Publication Data
Cook, Gary A., 1939–
    George Herbert Mead : the making of a social pragmatist / Gary A.
Cook.
        p. cm.
    Includes bibliographical references and index.
    ISBN 0-252-01969-5. – ISBN 0-252-06272-8 (pbk.)
    1. Mead, George Herbert, 1863–1931.   2. Sociologists–United
States–Biography.   3. Sociology–United States–History.   4. Social
psychology–United States–History.   I. Title.
HM22.U62M433   1993
301'.092–dc20   92-22923
                                                              CIP

To the memory of my parents

Contents

Acknowledgments   ix

Bibliographical Abbreviations   xi

Introduction   xiii

1. Early Life and Letters: Part 1   1

2. Early Life and Letters: Part 2   20

3. From Hegelianism to Social Psychology   37

4. The Development of Mead's Social Psychology   48

5. Behaviorism and Mead's Mature Social Psychology   67

6. Taking the Attitude or the Role of the Other   78

7. Mead and the City of Chicago: Social and Educational Reform   99

8. Moral Reconstruction and the Social Self   115

9. Whitehead's Influence on Mead's Later Thought   138

10. Mead's Social Pragmatism   161

Epilogue: Mead and the Hutchins Controversy   183

Notes   195

Bibliography   215

Index   227

Acknowledgments

Generous research and travel grants from Beloit College, the University of Chicago, and the Humanities Program of the Associated Colleges of the Midwest/Great Lakes Colleges of America enabled me to make numerous trips to various libraries in the course of my work on this book. The National Endowment for the Humanities helped support my writing with a Summer Stipend for the summer of 1987.

Most of the archival research for the biographical portions of this book was done in the Department of Special Collections at the Regenstein Library of the University of Chicago. Members of the library staff in that department were invariably congenial as they helped me locate and obtain needed copies of relevant materials. In addition, I am indebted for similar assistance to staff members at the following libraries: the Beloit College Library, the Williston Memorial Library at Mount Holyoke College, the Bentley Historical Library of the University of Michigan, the Chicago Historical Society Library, the Houghton Library of Harvard University, the Newberry Library of Chicago, the Oberlin College Library, and the Special Collections Department in the Library of Health Sciences at the University of Illinois at Chicago.

Two outstanding graduates of Beloit College, Susan Cook and Randy Bell, helped me search out and obtain copies of materials in the Bentley Historical Library and the Graduate Library at the University of Michigan. Randy, in particular, deserves thanks for the hours she spent paging through microfilm copies of the *Michigan Daily* dating from the early 1890s when G. H. Mead taught at Michigan as an instructor under the chairmanship of John Dewey.

David Heesen of the Beloit College secretarial services department is really the second author of this book. With unfailing good humor, he typed successive drafts of almost every chapter during the past several summers. No one else I know can navigate the keys of a computer so rapidly and accurately while listening alternately to operatic arias and broadcasts of Chicago Cubs baseball games!

Professor Darnell Rucker, whose book *The Chicago Pragmatists* was one of the main inspirations for my work on Mead, kindly shared with me some of the materials he had obtained in his research. Similarly, Professor Van Meter Ames shared with me notes he had taken while a student in several of Mead's courses at the University of Chicago. These notes have since been deposited in the George Herbert Mead Papers housed in the Department of Special Collections at the Regenstein Library of the University of Chicago.

Professors William L. Kolb, Hans Joas, and Peter H. Hare read the entire manuscript and offered me helpful critical comments. Their encouragement and their knowledgeable suggestions did much to make this a better book than it would otherwise have been. I am also indebted to Professor Joas for permission to use the excellent bibliography in his *G. H. Mead: A Contemporary Re-examination of His Thought* as a basis for my own chronological listing of Mead's writings.

For permission to quote from unpublished manuscripts, I thank Irene Tufts Mead and the Department of Special Collections at the Regenstein Library of the University of Chicago. Chapters 4 and 9 were published previously in the *Transactions of the Charles S. Peirce Society*. Chapter 5 was published in the *Journal of the History of the Behavioral Sciences*. I am indebted to the editors of both these journals for permission to make use of this material in the present work.

Finally, I thank my wife, Marilyn, for her patient understanding throughout the long duration of this project. She picked up the pieces and kept the home fires burning whenever I vanished into the library to do research and writing. For all this and for her unshakable confidence that I would finally finish, I owe more gratitude than I can express.

Bibliographical Abbreviations

ESP   John W. Petras, ed. *George Herbert Mead: Essays on His Social Philosophy.* New York: Teachers College Press, 1968.

LE   Student notes on G. H. Mead's lectures in the University of Chicago course elementary ethics, autumn quarter, 1927. These notes are in the George Herbert Mead Papers, box VII, folders 3 and 4, the Department of Special Collections, the Regenstein Library, the University of Chicago.

MSS   George Herbert Mead, *Mind, Self and Society.* Edited by Charles W. Morris. Chicago: University of Chicago Press, 1934.

MT   George Herbert Mead, *Movements of Thought in the Nineteenth Century.* Edited by Merritt H. Moore. Chicago: University of Chicago Press, 1936.

PA   George Herbert Mead, *The Philosophy of the Act.* Edited by Charles W. Morris et al. Chicago: University of Chicago Press, 1938.

PP   George Herbert Mead, *The Philosophy of the Present.* Edited by Arthur E. Murphy. La Salle, Ill.: Open Court Publishing Co., 1932.

SW   George Herbert Mead, *Selected Writings.* Edited by Andrew J. Reck. Indianapolis: Bobbs-Merrill, 1964.

Introduction

The work of the American philosopher and social psychologist George
Herbert Mead (1863–1931) has been the object of growing scholarly
interest from several different quarters in recent years. Sociologists and
historians of the social sciences have been debating the legitimacy of his
long-standing honorary status as one of the founding fathers of symbolic interactionism in American sociology; they have devoted attention not only to his social psychological ideas but also to such matters
as his influence upon the Chicago School of sociology and his involvement in Progressive social reform.[1] Meanwhile, philosophers have increasingly come to regard him as one of the canonical figures in the
history of American pragmatism; they have sought to specify his contributions to the pragmatic tradition and to assess the relevance of these
contributions for issues of current concern.[2] And, in addition, certain
German thinkers have begun to investigate Mead's writings with an
eye to suggestions bearing upon their own research in the areas of
philosophical psychology and critical social theory.[3]

Despite the increasing attention being paid to his work, however,
Mead's thought remains to this day an only partially explored territory.
This is due in large measure to the often fragmentary character of his
writings: "I am vastly depressed by my inability to write what I want
to," he lamented in a letter to his daughter-in-law late in his career.
"The distance between what I want and what I can is so unbridgeable.
It is an ancient theme."[4] Perhaps because of this inability, or because of
what his long-time friend and colleague John Dewey called "a certain
diffidence which restrained George Mead from much publication,"[5] he
never published a systematic treatment of his many social psychological and philosophical insights. Anyone who wishes to do justice to the
full scope and coherence of Mead's intellect must therefore struggle to

discern unifying threads running through the numerous short essays and reviews he published during his lifetime; he or she must further attempt to identify and find linkages between the central themes in a small mountain of additional materials consisting mainly of unfinished manuscripts, correspondence, and student notes from Mead's most important courses at the University of Chicago.

It is just this sort of scholarly inquiry that I have undertaken in the present study. My approach here is essentially that of an intellectual historian: I am primarily concerned to elucidate the meaning and coherence of Mead's key ideas, and I seek to accomplish this by locating these ideas within a well-documented account of his development as both a thinker and a practitioner of educational and social reform. Thus, I begin my discussion of Mead's thought in chapters 1 and 2 by looking carefully at his early life and letters. Here I trace the initial stages of his intellectual development, from his undergraduate education at Oberlin College through the beginning of his professional career as an instructor at the University of Michigan. These two largely biographical chapters show what can be gleaned from historical documents about the formative influence of Mead's early encounters with such important teachers and colleagues as Josiah Royce, George Herbert Palmer, William James, Wilhelm Dilthey, and John Dewey. The next several chapters are devoted to the development of what I take to be the core of Mead's thought, his social psychology. In these chapters I follow Mead's transition from an early Deweyan version of Hegelianism to an interest in social psychology (chapter 3), examine the deployment of his distinctive social psychological ideas in a series of essays he published early in his career at the University of Chicago (chapter 4), and consider the culmination of these ideas in his mature social psychological writings and lectures (chapters 5 and 6). Mead's social philosophy and ethics are taken up in chapters 7 and 8; the former chapter deals with his involvement in social and educational reform activities in the city of Chicago, while the latter surveys the development of his ideas on ethics and moral psychology. The next two chapters address the continuing development of Mead's thought in the years following 1920: chapter 9 examines the various ways in which the writings of Alfred North Whitehead influenced the development of Mead's later thought, and chapter 10 seeks to supply an overview of Mead's social pragmatism, especially as this relates to his mature understanding of experience, nature, and knowledge. Finally, the epilogue offers a biographical account of the end of Mead's career at the University of Chicago, focusing upon his involvement in a controversy between the department of philosophy and Robert Maynard Hutchins—a controversy that resulted in the virtual demise of the Chicago School of pragmatism.

Although I shall occasionally refer to the secondary literature on Mead's thought in the course of this study, I make no attempt to survey this literature in a systematic fashion. Nor do I attempt to assess the various ways in which Mead's teaching and writing have influenced subsequent creative work in sociology and philosophy. Rather, my concern here is to dig deeply into Mead's own writings and related historical materials that shed light upon his intellectual development. Since these primary documents are a heterogeneous lot, it may be helpful to alert the reader in advance to some of their salient features and also to indicate how they are to be utilized in what follows.

Let me begin with the materials in the George Herbert Mead Papers at the Department of Special Collections at the Regenstein Library of the University of Chicago. Of the many unpublished documents included in this collection, I have found particularly helpful Mead's early letters, which provide information about his years as an undergraduate at Oberlin College, his years of graduate study at Harvard, Leipzig, and Berlin, and the beginnings of his relationship with John Dewey at the University of Michigan: the treatment of this period of his intellectual development found in chapters 1 and 2 is based in large part upon his long correspondence with an Oberlin friend and subsequent intellectual companion, Henry Northrup Castle. Similarly, letters Mead wrote during the 1920s to his daughter-in-law, Irene Tufts Mead, were a source of information helpful in tracing the influence of Alfred North Whitehead's writings upon Mead's later thought. With very few exceptions, all of the better manuscripts (as opposed to personal correspondence) contained in the Mead Papers have been published in the posthumous volumes of Mead's works to be mentioned later; hence I have seldom had occasion to cite these manuscripts in their unpublished form. The Mead Papers also include a variety of student notes taken in Mead's courses at the University of Chicago. But, again, the best of these have been posthumously published, and the others contain little that is relevant for my purposes; consequently I have cited these unpublished student notes only in one or two cases. In addition, the Department of Special Collections at the Regenstein Library houses several other collections containing materials related to Mead's career.

I have drawn from the Henry Northrup Castle Papers in chapters 1 and 2 and also from the collection entitled Presidents' Papers ca. 1925–1945 in the epilogue dealing with the controversy between Hutchins and the Chicago department of philosophy in the years immediately preceding Mead's death.

A second, and extremely important, category of Mead documents consists of the essays and book reviews Mead published in various periodicals. The bibliography of his writings includes over ninety such items, at least forty of which are fairly substantive in character. For a number of years these documents were largely overlooked in scholarly discussions of Mead's thought, perhaps because they were not readily accessible. But many of these publications have now been reprinted in two anthologies of Mead's essays edited, respectively, by Andrew J. Reck[6] and John W. Petras.[7] I have relied heavily on these essays throughout my book, and for two reasons. First, unlike much of Mead's posthumously published work, they bear definite dates—a consideration of some importance when one is trying to trace the development of an author's thought. Second, in contrast to student lecture notes and fragmentary manuscripts posthumously edited by others, these documents were given their finishing touches by Mead himself; presumably, therefore, they represent what he took to be his best work at the time of their submission for publication.

A third category of documents pertaining to Mead's intellectual development consists of official records of his remarks and actions as a member of various organizations. In chapter 7, for instance, where I explore his involvement in organizations dedicated to social and educational reform, I draw upon such records as the University of Chicago Settlement Board Minutes[8] and the *Bulletins* of the City Club of Chicago.[9] These documents enable me to pin down with considerable specificity the nature and dates of Mead's reform activities.

Lastly, there are the four volumes of Mead's work published in the decade following his death in 1931. The first of these posthumous volumes, *The Philosophy of the Present* (1932), was edited by Arthur E. Murphy, one of Mead's colleagues at the University of Chicago, and was published by the Open Court Publishing Company as part of its series of Carus Lectures. Approximately half of this volume consists of Murphy's edited version of three Carus Lectures delivered by Mead at the Pacific Division meeting of the American Philosophical Association in December 1930. The remainder of the volume includes related material drawn from several previously unpublished (and undated) manuscripts and from two essays published in the late 1920s. In chapter 9, I try to show how the new ideas Mead tentatively explores here—especially in the portion of *The Philosophy of the Present* based upon the 1930 Carus Lectures—grew out of his earlier work.

Three additional posthumous volumes of Mead's work were published by the University of Chicago Press during the 1930s, due mainly to the efforts of Mead's son and daughter-in-law. Convinced that Mead's lectures and manuscripts were of sufficient importance to deserve a wider audience, Henry and Irene Tufts Mead secured the services of Charles W. Morris and Merritt Hadden Moore to undertake the task of selecting and editing suitable portions of Mead's unpublished work for posthumous publication.[10] From this editorial project there eventually issued two volumes based upon student notes taken in Mead's courses, *Mind, Self and Society* (1934) and *Movements of Thought in the Nineteenth Century* (1936), and a third volume containing previously unpublished manuscripts and fragments, *The Philosophy of the Act* (1938).

The well-known *Mind, Self and Society*, as Charles Morris indicates in his editorial preface, is based upon student notes taken in several different offerings of Mead's course on advanced social psychology during the years from 1927 to 1930. After rearranging and rewriting these notes, Morris added a number of undated items he labeled supplementary essays. The most important of these, "Fragments on Ethics," is derived from a set of student notes taken in Mead's course on elementary ethics offered during the autumn quarter of 1927.[11] I have made some use of this volume in chapters 5 and 6, where I consider Mead's mature social psychology, as well as in chapters 8 and 10, dealing with the development of Mead's views on ethics and his social pragmatism. But, in general, I have preferred to rest my analysis of his social psychology, ethics, and pragmatism upon the more secure ground of materials actually written by Mead rather than upon reconstructions of student notes.

Movements of Thought in the Nineteenth Century is based primarily upon student notes taken in Mead's offering of the course by that name during the spring quarter of 1928. In addition, it contains some material from student notes taken in Mead's course on the philosophy of Bergson in the summer quarter of 1927. For the most part, I have not found his discussions of nineteenth-century intellectual history to be particularly useful for my study. But Mead also ventures into such areas as the philosophy of science, pragmatism, behaviorism, and social psychology in the course of these lectures. And while he discusses all of these topics more fully in other places, his remarks in this volume sometimes help to clarify his mature views with respect to them. Hence, I have occasionally drawn relevant information from this work in connection with my treatment of these matters in the later chapters of my book.

Of all the posthumously published volumes of Mead's work, the most problematic for the purposes of the present study is *The Philosophy of the Act*. It is problematic not because of the diversity of the many previously unpublished manuscripts and fragments it contains, but because all of these are undated. Professor Harold Orbach of Kansas State University is currently attempting to date these items on the basis of various evidence, including the typescript and paper used in the original manuscripts; until the results of this enterprise have been made available, however, we can do no better than to use the content of the most important of these manuscripts as a basis for assigning them an approximate place in the chronology of Mead's work. One very helpful clue in this regard is provided by the influence of Whitehead. As I show in chapter 9, Mead did not begin to read the writings of Whitehead until the summer of 1921, and he did not begin to make references to Whitehead's ideas in his publications until 1925. Hence, we may safely infer that any of Mead's undated manuscripts that refer to Whitehead's works or that employ Whiteheadian terminology (and there are many such manuscripts included in *The Philosophy of the Act*) were composed no earlier than 1921 and probably somewhat later. I rely upon this clue in my selection of items from this volume to supplement my use of Mead's dated publications when I deal in chapters 9 and 10 with his philosophical explorations during the final decade of his life.

One further comment about the posthumously published volumes of Mead's work is in order before bringing this introduction to a close. David L. Miller has edited an additional volume of Mead's previously unpublished work under the title *The Individual and the Social Self*, published by the University of Chicago Press in 1982. The main body of this volume consists of Miller's edited version of two sets of student notes taken in Mead's courses on social psychology and preserved among the Mead Papers at the Regenstein Library. Miller identifies the first of these as being from Mead's course of 1914 (although, in fact, it dates from the fall quarter of 1912); the second set of notes was taken in

Mead's course on advanced social psychology during the winter quarter of 1927. In addition, the volume includes an undated twenty-page manuscript that Miller has entitled "Consciousness, Mind, the Self, and Scientific Objects," and an appendix of commentary on Mead's work by an author Miller is unable to identify.[12] None of these documents, as far as I can see, adds much substance to the materials already mentioned above—although the student notes presented here do provide a helpful supplement to those used in the composition of *Mind, Self and Society*. But, again, I have chosen to rest my analysis of Mead's social psychology primarily upon relevant essays he published in various journals rather than upon reconstructions of student notes; thus I have seldom cited Miller's volume in my examination of Mead's intellectual development.

Chapter I

Early Life and Letters: Part I

George Herbert Mead was born on February 27, 1863, in South Hadley, Massachusetts. His father, Hiram Mead, was a graduate of Middlebury College in Vermont and of the Andover Seminary in Massachusetts. After serving as pastor of Congregational churches in South Hadley and Nashua, New Hampshire, Hiram Mead was appointed in 1869 to the chair of Sacred Rhetoric and Pastoral Theology at the Oberlin Theological Seminary in Oberlin, Ohio. He remained in this post until his death in 1881.[1] George Mead's mother, Elizabeth Storrs Mead, was educated at Mount Holyoke Seminary, and prior to her marriage she taught for several years at schools in Northampton and Andover. After her husband's death, Elizabeth Mead became an instructor of English composition for two years at Oberlin College, taught from 1883 to 1889 at Abbot Academy in Andover, Massachusetts, and served as president of Mount Holyoke Seminary and College from 1890 until her retirement in 1900. She died in 1917.[2]

While little information is available concerning Mead's earliest years, we are fortunate to possess a number of historical documents that shed light on the period extending from his study at Oberlin College to the beginning of his professional career as a teacher and scholar. Due to the foresight of the Mead and Castle families, ninety-five letters written by George Herbert Mead to his close friend Henry Northrup Castle during the years 1883–95 have been preserved at the Regenstein Library of the University of Chicago. In addition, this library houses an even larger collection of letters written by Castle during the same period to Mead and members of the Castle family.[3] Because most of the letters in these two collections are unpublished, I shall quote extended passages from them in this chapter and the next. With related documents, the Mead-Castle correspondence enables us to trace the main stages in Mead's early intellectual development. This correspondence also records the story of a friendship that did much to stimulate and sustain Mead's intellectual life as he moved from Oberlin College, through public school teaching, surveying, and tutoring, to further study at Harvard and Berlin, and finally to teaching positions at the universities of Michigan and Chicago.

The Oberlin Years (1877–83)

George Mead first became acquainted with Henry Castle in 1877 when both were second-year students in the preparatory department associated with Oberlin College. Mead had entered the preparatory department in 1876 and matriculated as a freshman at Oberlin College in 1879. Castle, whose father was one of the founders of the Castle & Cooke Company of Hawaii, came to Oberlin from Honolulu in 1877.[4] He studied in the preparatory department for two years and, then, after an interim year spent in Hawaii and Europe, entered Oberlin College in the fall of 1880. Mead and Castle graduated together in the Oberlin class of 1883.

Although Mead first met Castle in 1877, the two did not become close friends until 1882 when both were college juniors. Mead, writing his recollections of Castle twenty years later, recalled the intellectual side of their friendship at this initial stage: "It was in the last term of the junior and throughout the senior years, that our common interest in philosophical matters bound us most closely together. In these we stood perhaps upon a common level, though he had much the keener mind of the two. But in literature I followed him, and awoke to the glories of English poetry because of the direction he gave to my reading. The English poets remain for me so permeated with my friendship for him, that I never read them now without a return to the passion of those days, and that passion is indissolubly bound up with our friendship."[5]

The "common interest in philosophical matters" to which Mead refers originated with their joint participation in one of the required courses in the Oberlin curriculum of the day. The course was mental philosophy, and it was apparently based upon Noah Porter's textbook *The Elements of Intellectual Science* (1871).[6] A letter Castle wrote home during May 1882 mentions the course and gives us a glimpse of the two friends' first serious exposure to the field of philosophy.

> I am becoming immensely interested in philosophy. I have had incipient longings after it for a good while back, but I heroically determined to withstand them until my Senior year, when I would be able to understand what I read better. But this term we have "Mental," which has proved the last straw. It is ever so interesting, and quite hard. I am reading in connection with it Hamilton's *Metaphysics*. Of course I don't understand it all, but I take in enough to make it very enjoyable reading. I am going to read this sort of stuff now pretty steadily until I graduate, so that before I read German philosophy, I may know something about the English. Hamilton is a good man to begin with. He is very clear, and is very pious and orthodox. We have lots of fun in Porter (Mental Philosophy), catechizing the Professor and arguing with him. I presume I told you that I read *Edwards on the Will*, last short vacation. I also read Carpenter's *Mental Physiology*, as a preparation for Porter. I think I shall read next in this line Bain's *Mind and Body*.[7]

To this contemporary report by Castle we can add Mead's later recollection of the same period as one in which he and Henry were ignorant but exuberant in their approach to philosophy.

> We knew next to nothing of the history of philosophy, nor of any systems but that of the dogmatic Scottish school, together with something of the English psychologists. We had nothing really constructive, for the aim of the philosophy taught was to do away with the need of any and all speculation. Against this dogma we sought weapons largely in our own consciousness; and in the mere discovery that we had there all the problems of thoughts, and all their possibilities of solutions, we passed suddenly into another new world that was even more our own than was literature. I remember the time and place—the spring of '82, on the way to the class in *Porter*—when and where I demonstrated to Henry's and my satisfaction that no dogmatic philosophy was possible. The statement is dry enough; but the sudden awakening to an inner consciousness that could know no law that was not its own, was

an experience that was as profound as any religious conversion could be. It is identified in memory with all the indefinite promise of spring.[8]

The fall of 1882 marked the beginning of the senior year for Mead and Castle. Castle's sister, Helen Kingsbury Castle (later to become Mrs. George Mead), came to study at Oberlin and roomed with Henry at the home of an aunt. This was also the year in which Castle and Mead shared the task of editing the student newspaper, the *Oberlin Review*. "It will be a wonder if George Mead and I do not run the *Review* into the ground before the end of the year," Castle observed to his parents. "We do not trouble to cater to the popular taste, and with our lofty transcendental ideas, and superlative scorn of all things practical, it will be strange indeed if we do not have the whole establishment in the ditch, with ourselves as well."[9] Both Mead and Castle apparently found their editorship to be a heady experience. It is evident, at any rate, that they had been in harness only a short time when their newspaper work began to have an impact upon their still hazy plans for the future. "George Mead and I want to start a literary paper in New York," Castle reported in October. "That is our favorite dream."[10]

The two friends' uncompromising approach to the editorship of the *Oberlin Review* was accompanied by an increasingly aggressive approach to the study of philosophy and the bating of their favorite teachers, Professor John M. Ellis and Oberlin President James H. Fairchild. (Both Ellis and Fairchild were graduates of Oberlin College and the Oberlin theological department. Combining Christian piety with a commitment to the Scottish philosophical tradition promulgated in America by such writers as James McCosh and Noah Porter, they argued for the freedom of the will, the doctrine of immediate perception or natural realism, and the theory that experience is structured by a priori intuitions or self-evident principles of common sense.[11]) Mead later recalled that he and Castle turned their classes in philosophy into a "series of running fights with the professor": "It was a new and magnificent game, a sort of border warfare, in which we feared no serious invasions of our own territory. The enemy was bound to a defensive system, and we congratulated ourselves on many a successful incursion."[12] Castle, writing to his parents in the fall of 1882, provides a contemporary account of these skirmishes: "I wonder what Prof. Ellis thinks of George and myself. He must regard us as a perfect nuisance, because hardly a day passes in Mental Philosophy when we do not start a discussion with him. We have lots of fun too, asking questions of Pres. Fairchild, who has our Bible class. He, however, is inclined to bulldoze a little. He has a great delight in getting the laugh on one— more delight in that, in fact, than in settling our difficulties. We all like the President, however, very much indeed. This is an interesting year. We have finished Porter, and Prof. Ellis is giving us lectures on the Intuitions." [13]

The theory of intuitions was one of the facets of the Scottish philosophy about which Mead and Castle were inclined to be skeptical. But they were even more uneasy with the doctrine of free will championed by Professors Ellis and Fairchild. Indeed, according to Castle's letters, this doctrine was perhaps chief among those with which he and Mead struggled during their senior year.

> Prof. Ellis, in his lectures on Psychology, has just reached the subject of the Will, so that now we propose to have some fun questioning and arguing with him. The subject of the Freedom of the Will perhaps monopolizes more of the attention of two or three of us than any other whatever. We are in the habit of considering the logical argument against the Freedom of the Will as unanswerable, and so of course we are anxious to hear what Professor Ellis can say against it. We have read Jonathan Edwards and do not believe that he can be answered, or at least that he has been answered yet. . . . Sir William Hamilton admits that the doctrine of Free Will involves us in logical contradictions, but he falls back on the testimony of consciousness. Pres. Fairchild does the same, though he may not admit what Hamilton does. I was going to prove to him one morning by quoting some laws of logic that the Will could not be free, but he got out of it by stating that the Will wasn't subject to the laws of logic. I began the first skirmish with Prof. Ellis this A.M. That was merely a prelude to the coming battle. [14]

Mead and Castle thus achieved a measure of intellectual independence in their last two years at Oberlin College: they argued freely with their professors and questioned many of the doctrines they were being taught. But they had yet to develop any positive philosophical position of their own, and they were hesitant to abandon the religious attitudes and beliefs they had brought with them to Oberlin. As Mead put it later, "the most serious intellectual effort of these two years was the discussion—'still beginning, never ending'—of the doctrine of the Church. . . . We remained, in appearance, skeptical; but we had no higher criticism to rationalize Christianity, and we knew personally of no profound moral life outside the dogma of the Church. In the end, as in the beginning, we were baffled." [15]

Teaching, Surveying, and Tutoring (1883–87)

Mead's letters to Castle begin in the summer of 1883, following the graduation of both from Oberlin, and continue on a regular basis until the two friends meet again to share rooms in Cambridge, Massachusetts, in the fall of 1887. His letters of this period are filled with a great deal of soul searching about a possible mission in life as he tries his hand successively, but not always successfully, at school teaching, surveying, and serving as a private tutor for boys preparing for college studies. In addition, the letters record Mead's initial struggles with the philosophy of Immanuel Kant and his continuing reflections upon philosophical ideas he and Castle had begun to discuss at Oberlin.

Mead spent much of the summer of 1883 in Oberlin, pursuing leads for possible employment in the fall. In September he wrote Castle, who had returned home to Honolulu, that his search had finally been successful: he had landed a teaching job in nearby Berlin Heights, a position to which he was looking forward with considerable trepidation.

> I have not the slightest confidence in my abilities to pass the examination [required for a teaching certificate] or maintain discipline or to inspire enthusiasm in my scholars or to satisfy the school board. I shall have $50.00 a month for the Fall term at least and then if the Board like me I shall get the school for the rest of the year and receive $600.00. . . . We are slightly differently situated my friend. I have 10 years work before me at least before I begin studying for any profession or fitting for any calling in life at all. For I must see that my mother does not want a cent. By that time I calculate to have her fortune sufficiently increased to allow my striking for Germany, and by that time I shall expect to support myself by literary work and shall fit myself for a Professorship

and strike off into literature a la Lowell. It's going to be a tough tug but I feel on the whole rather invigorated by the prospect if I can only get a start.[16]

A few weeks later Mead wrote to Castle again, observing that he was still on the job at Berlin Heights, "so that so much can be said in favor of my having been a success but not much more and you will appreciate my not caring to write further upon a painful topic." He had passed his certification examination and claimed to be enjoying teaching, but he was clearly having a difficult time adjusting to the transition from the pious atmosphere of Oberlin College to life in Berlin Heights: "I have been considerably transformed since I came here from Oberlin. . . . I have had a truly missionary spirit raised within me. For this town is dead spiritually. . . . The boys in the town are all going to the devil with a vengeance. Three saloons are in full working order and they spend their evenings under the influences of these hot houses of his Satanic Majesty. . . . Of course you understand that I use the terms of spiritual life as they now exist though I do not in the slightest change my sentiment, but the necessity of a spiritual life of some kind remains as much without as with Christianity, and as Christianity seems to be the only religion that can reach the common people I shall work in connection with this."[17]

Several subsequent letters shed further light upon Mead's intellectual and emotional life during this period. He was, first of all, reading Kant's *Prolegomena* and first *Critique* and professed to "having a great attraction toward Kant lately."[18] Second, he was reflecting on the question of free will that he and Henry had discussed at Oberlin. Mead confessed that "although I think that the arguments on the whole are against freedom of the will, I find that my feelings do not suit that state of the case and so like a poor feminine devotee I follow my feelings and not my beliefs."[19] Third, and most important, he was struggling mightily with his religious feelings: "I can't tell you old boy what temptations of the most insidious and perplexing kind I have had to resist to keep from becoming a Christian with no reference to my reason but out of deference to my sensibilities." He had, he feared, "too much reason and too little strength to be a Christian, and too little reason and too much sentiment to be a philosopher."[20]

Mead's religious struggles were no doubt exacerbated by difficulties he was experiencing in his work as a schoolteacher. At any rate, the longer he was in Berlin Heights, the more intense these struggles seemed to become. Thus on February 23, 1884, he wrote to Castle that "I have been [in] a most confused state lately. I have been trying to get strength for my work and some light in the miserable darkness, and greater power in working for others in Christianity. I have been praying and reading the Bible. . . . To be sure I do not know that there is a God. And more fundamentally still I do not even believe in the intuitions. But if I can pursue religion as I do other matters I can find surety enough and perhaps coming years will bring a confidence in the intuitions which I do not now possess. But beyond a determination to do the right as I see it, to follow what light I can get, I am utterly at sea." [21]

Perhaps fortunately for Mead's peace of mind the decision concerning his future in Berlin Heights was taken out of his hands. Just two weeks after the preceding remarks were written, and six months after he had signed on as a schoolteacher, he was back home in Oberlin without a job: "Well old Boy the game is played. The school dwindled down to 8 scholars and the board came to the conclusion that they could not afford to maintain it any longer, and so I am back in Oberlin looking for a place." [22]

Mead remained in Oberlin for about two months, while he looked for another job and wrote frequently to Castle concerning his continuing philosophical and religious struggles. He was, he reported, "wallowing in the depth of agnosticism" and could not seem to find his way philosophically to any settled beliefs. [23] Looking ahead to the future, he now found himself vacillating between two options. On some occasions he spoke as if the Christian ministry might be a serious possibility for him: "If I only could get a strong character [and] some settled beliefs I could find more pleasure in the ministry than anywhere else in the world." [24] More frequently, he longed for a career in philosophy and literature:

> If I could only be convinced that my mission did really lie in philosophical criticism and Literature I could give myself to the study with my whole heart. But I am continually confronted with [the] idea that I should make a poor weak writer, a mere literary hack who in his best estate would be only hired to review recent German productions in philosophy or else would become art critic for some daily. Now such a life of inaction I must not lead. But on the other hand my nature resents the idea of settling my views

in haste and forgetting all philosophy. . . . Well I am pretty certain that I shall get me out in the world soon and do what work I can for souls, reserve some time for metaphysics, and let Providence, if there is one, lead me to the work it has destined me for.[25]

Mead did, in fact, get himself "out in the world" in short order, but not in any capacity that had much to do with either philosophy or the saving of souls. Early in April 1884 he began work as a member of a crew surveying in northeastern Minnesota for an extension of the Wisconsin Central Railroad. The work, he reported to Henry, was "out of doors and healthful, but unfortunately I am associated with an engineer and axeman who smoke, drink, [and] swear like troopers."[26] Clearly Mead's life in Oberlin, and even his experience in Berlin Heights, had not prepared him for such colleagues! The drunken behavior of the engineer, in particular, increasingly repulsed Mead as the summer wore on. The engineer's quarrels, he remarked, kept the camp in a constant uproar. And "a drunken man howling right outside of your tent would destroy the concentration of Socrates."[27]

Despite such distractions and the demands of his surveying work, Mead wrote Castle that he was reading poetry whenever he got a chance and also continuing his study of Kant: "I have read the *Prolegomena* all day, not very comprehendingly but with an increasing sense of the power of Kant's mind. I am not hampered by my feeble knowledge of the psychology and logic of his time or indeed any time. I am now going to begin the *Critique* again and like a railroad train struggling with a steep grade gain all the momentum possible from what I can master."[28] Mead's references to Kant during this period do not indicate that he succeeded in mastering much of the first *Critique*. But they do show that he found in Kant an analysis of sense experience more to his liking than what he had been taught at Oberlin. In comparison to Kant's discussion of perception in the transcendental aesthetic of the first *Critique,* the orthodox Scottish doctrine of immediate perception now struck Mead as woefully inadequate. That doctrine, he contended, implausibly attributed the perception of the extension of physical objects to one faculty of the mind and the perception of space itself to another faculty. In addition, it held that space was perceived by the same faculty responsible for the intuition of the infinite and the absolute. This division of the intuitions in orthodox philosophy, Mead proclaimed, was "a piece of philosophic slothfulness" to which

Kant's analysis was greatly superior.[29] At the same time, Mead was not at all satisfied with what he called Kant's agnosticism, i.e., the view that knowledge is restricted to phenomena structured by the forms and categories of the mind and that things cannot be known as they are in themselves: "Certain feelings set in certain forms or categories afford us our only *cognitions*!! It is the most depressing philosophy that I have met with rendered more so by the constant claims he makes to have bounded all thought and [to] have completely clipped the wing of errant apriorism."[30]

Mead's job with the Wisconsin Central Railroad lasted only until the middle of September. But before he could begin to worry seriously about the prospect of unemployment, he obtained another position—surveying a line from the Red River valley to Minneapolis for the Minneapolis and Pacific Railroad. By the end of the year, however, this second railroad job had come to an end, and so had Mead's short-lived career as a surveyor. He took up residence in Minneapolis with another of his Oberlin classmates and in January 1885 began to support himself by working as a private tutor for boys preparing for college.[31]

With his feet barely on the ground in Minneapolis, Mead began suggesting that Castle—who was growing restless in Honolulu—should join him in setting up a preparatory school. His proposal was that they could "unite in such work for four or five years and put by a reasonable amount of money, sell out [for a] comfortable sum, go to Germany, and then—I am willing to leave the future to the fates."[32] But Henry was apparently not excited by the prospect of teaching preparatory students in Minneapolis; moreover, the wealth available in his family made such employment unnecessary as a means to furthering his formal education. Instead of embracing Mead's proposal, he sailed for Europe in the late summer of 1885 and that fall began one and a half years of study in philosophy at the University of Berlin.

For several months in the fall and winter of 1885–86, Mead entertained hopes that he might yet lure Castle to Minneapolis. He had learned that a teaching position in the area of metaphysics and moral science would be opening up the following year at the University of Minnesota, and he strongly encouraged Castle to apply for the job.[33] But when nothing came of this scheme Mead went on with his tutoring, writing frequently to Henry in Berlin. "I want to know what your constructive philosophy is Henry," he wrote early in 1886. "You must not keep it from me."[34] As for himself, Mead was still searching for a philosophy that he could consider satisfactory—and he had all but given up hope of finding a basis for such a philosophy in Kant's writings: "I can never satisfy myself by finding a perfection of arrangement and hypotheses for phenomena which go not beyond me and discarding the other world of noumena as beyond my reach. Perhaps I could be satisfied if I understood Kant better or studied him under the walls and taverns of German universities. If so shed light and influence upon me Henry for I want some basis, and if you really feel that you have found it I will have confidence to look for it myself, for I esteem my mind as of much the same make as yours, though lacking much in power." [35]

The following fall found Mead "teaching ten hours a day" but looking forward more hopefully to the possibility of resuming his own schooling. His mother had recently declared her intention to teach for a number of years longer, and her immediate future consequently seemed secure. Mead thus felt free to pursue further study in the field of philosophy. "Next year I am going to cut loose for 4 years of study to be got in some way if I have to beg for it from Minneapolis to Berlin or elsewhere. . . . I shall try first for a fellowship at Johns Hopkins." [36]

Castle, on the other hand, was now thinking seriously of giving up the study of philosophy for a career in law—an idea that Mead looked upon with something akin to horror: "No, do not be a lawyer. Come Henry, let us carry out our old scheme and be together and think and write and talk and be ourselves and not push ourselves in to jackets to fit the absurd standards of men who do not think and to whom the possession of a thousand dollars is worth more than all [the] beauty in the world." [37] But Henry ignored Mead's advice, set sail from Germany late in 1886, and enrolled at the Harvard Law School in January 1887. There, not long after his arrival, he received a two-day visit from Mead, who had probably come east to visit his mother at Abbot Academy. Henry reported their reunion in a letter written to his sister Helen on January 9, 1887:

> Thursday afternoon, as I came back from the Law School just before supper, I saw a light burning in my room. I ran upstairs in a hurry—and—yes—it was just as I expected or hoped, there sat George. I will not attempt to describe the meeting, but the three years and a half rolled away in a minute. . . . The thread was taken up just where time and fate had broken it, and it seemed as if it were no longer ago than yesterday that it was broken. We fell into

our usual strain, our usual topics. . . . We feel as much for each other or more I think, than when we graduated, but we are not quite so near to each other. My feeling has passed utterly away from objects which his still glorifies, and in philosophy he has had to stand still.[38]

It was no doubt this visit, as well as the mere presence of Castle in Cambridge, that led Mead to focus upon Harvard in his subsequent deliberations concerning the possibility of further philosophical study. In April 1887 he was asking Henry about Harvard application procedures, and by late summer, after much vacillation related to problems of financing, he made up his mind to leave Minneapolis for Cambridge.[39] Castle's response was immediate and enthusiastic:

> Your letter reached me yesterday, and brought joy to my soul. It turns the prospect of a return to Harvard into a pleasant thought for me. You must on no account give it up. . . . You will surely be able to pick up some tutoring while there, and a scholarship besides, and if you will room with me it will be a good deal cheaper you know. The one important thing now, my boy, is for you to get into Royce's private course on Kant. The one imperative condition is that you shall know German enough, and you must go right to work at once. Do not neglect this, but go right to work. You must know German enough, so that you can understand a passage in a philosophic author *without translation*. . . . This course of Royce's is going to be a big chance, and you must not miss it. It will be the first chance that either you or I have had, for direct immediate contact with an important thinker.[40]

At Harvard (1887–88)

Mead finally left Minneapolis for Cambridge early in September 1887, stopping en route to visit his sister's family in Cortland, New York, and his mother in Andover, Massachusetts. He had earlier hoped to devote much of his time during these visits to the study of German in preparation for Josiah Royce's course on Kant, but by September 7 he had given up this plan. "My German is nothing at the present time," he wrote Henry from Cortland. "I have forgotten everything. I think I had better omit the class in Kant."[41] Thus when the fall term began Castle was enrolled in Royce's course, but not Mead.

Early in October, Castle wrote to Helen at Oberlin, giving her a brief report on activities at Harvard: "I am settled down here comfortably in the room at 11 Sumner Street, with George. . . . My law lectures are in full swing, but the Kant course has not begun as yet. . . . Royce is anxious to begin I know, for he told George Mead so. George has got all his courses settled, and has got to work. He takes a course in ethics with Palmer, a course on Spinoza and Spencer with Royce, and two Greek courses. The Kant course he will not take regularly, but expects to come in and listen. He also has a course with old Bowen, so you see he has work enough on his hands." [42] Subsequent letters from Castle to his family in the fall and winter of 1887–88 do not indicate that Mead followed through on his plan to sit in on sessions of Royce's course on Kant. But Henry clearly found the sessions worthwhile. "The course with Royce on the *Critique of Pure Reason* is beginning to go on very nicely," he wrote on December 6. "At first it was not very interesting; we did not get into the heart of the subject, and the Professor was disposed to do more than his share of the talking, or more than we thought was his share. But lately the work began to wax warmer, and we are having some lively discussions." [43]

Concerning his relations with Mead, Henry wrote repeatedly about how well the two roommates were getting along: "George Mead and I are having a delightful time together. We have found touch with each other perfectly. As for philosophy, he is catching up with me with giant stride, and I presume I shall soon see him disappearing in the distance. We differ, of course, and stimulate each other. But we feel together on all important points. We live in one small room without feeling cooped up, and have not had a quarrel yet." [44] But this idyllic living arrangement was not to last. Late in January, Mead's need for funds led him to accept a tutoring position that required him to move to another residence, about a ten-minute walk from 11 Sumner Street. "George Mead has left me, and I am utterly desolate," Henry reported to his parents on February 1. "He has taken charge of a youth of eleven years, and this necessitates his moving and going to live with him. It is a blow to us both, but he could not afford to let the chance go by." [45] Shortly thereafter, however, this blow was overshadowed by an event of greater importance. Henry, who had been invited to join his brother Will in the latter's Honolulu law office, decided rather abruptly to suspend his studies at Harvard to return home and apply at once for admission to the bar in Hawaii. Accordingly, he left Cambridge in late March and early in April set sail from San Francisco for the Islands. [46]

Castle's departure from Cambridge was fortunate in at least one respect: it led Mead to resume his correspondence, thus providing us with
some direct testimony concerning his Harvard experience. The eleven-
year-old boy Mead had been hired to tutor, he wrote Henry early in
May, was turning out to be "a tremendous nuisance. . . . I shall, I think,
not take him next year." [47] As for his own course work, Mead wrote
late in May that he was preparing for an honors examination and also
had seven papers to write before the end of the term. One of these
papers, an essay on Aristotle's philosophy, was for a course he had
begun with Royce but was completing with Professor George Herbert
Palmer, as nervous exhaustion had forced Royce to take a medical leave
of absence. Royce had sailed from Boston on February 27 bound for
Australia, and Mead wondered if any word of him had reached Henry
in Honolulu. "Do you hear anything of Royce? Came across a story of
him yesterday. He said that he kept feeling that he was a d——d fool
and did not think he had any ground for it and so concluded that he
must be pretty sick. Trust he will be back next year." [48]

By the middle of June, Mead had almost completed his year at Harvard, due to a superhuman effort during the early part of the month.
He wrote Henry of his future plans:

> You have no need to reproach me for not writing. I am too
> busy when I am doing the year's work in two weeks to write even
> to my own mother. It is [the] Harvard system you know. I don't
> know how I have gotten through.
>
> Prof. Palmer told Mr. Beech that I had done very well indeed
> this year. Inasmuch as I have done nothing in his course beyond
> attend the lectures and that not invariably by any means I was
> rather surprised. My examination in ethics I am very doubtful
> about, it was a thesis upon the subject, "Is it necessary to take
> anything into account in estimating the worth of an action beyond
> the pleasure produced."
>
> I did poorly in Aristotle. One reason was that I did not know
> that the final examinations came at 9:30 instead of 10 and so lost
> ½ an hour and one or two questions I could not answer. I presume
> I may have a B in that course. He gave me you remember high B
> on the midyears with the promise of A if I did well on the final. . . .
> My course in Phil. 13 which I was to carry on myself I accom-
> plished by handing in three theses on Moral Philosophy before

Aristotle, Aristotle's Ethics, and Spinoza's Ethics. They were very shabby productions I can assure you. They went to Prof. Palmer. My exam in Greek 11 was all right, it was easy. . . .

My Honor's exam in Phil. was better. It consisted of a thesis to be written in one day and an oral exam by the 5 Phil. Profs. I wrote on the subject "How large a share has the subject in the object world." Prof. Palmer told me he considered it very good. The oral went off quite well. I wrote and talked on the basis of "Green's Prolegomena" and nobody there floored me though they discovered some writings of Mansel's and Hamilton's with which I was not acquainted, especially their argument for God from the principle of non contradiction and James the next morning came round to look me up and told me that he wanted me to go out with him this summer and teach his boy. There is no money in it but it will give me a pleasant place to pass the summer without expense. . . . Prof. James told me that he had had several applications for the place but that I took care of myself so well in the examination that he wished me especially [to take the position] as he could then have someone to whom he could talk metaphysics. . . .

I should add to my inducements for going to James', that I shall need all the influence I can get next year and Palmer upon whom I have made the most impression is not to be here. If Royce should not come back, it would be a sorry place to study philosophy in. Then there would be absolutely nobody but James left of any consequence. . . . But Royce is expected back so I suppose I shall have no difficulty. I shall take his course. I suppose I shall have had enough of German to manage it. I shall take work with James in Physiological Psychology. That is absolutely all that I can get in philosophy. I shall take a year of Sanskrit and a course with Allen in Plautus and a Seminar in Alcestis in which Latin will be spoken entirely. Then I shall read in philosophy, join the Philosophical Club, and do what I can to gain the attention of the powers that be.[49]

Early in July, Mead wrote Castle from James's summer home near Chocorua, New Hampshire. He reported that he had taken his B.A. degree from Harvard magna cum laude[50] and was looking forward to a summer of "magnificent tramps and views, swims and fishing excursions" to augment his tutoring responsibilities. "I shall here have very little work to do, just see to the arithmetic and United States History of a small docile boy ['Harry' James, age 8]. Otherwise I am my own master. The family is a pleasant one consisting of Prof. and Mrs. James, four small children, Mrs. James' sister and mother. . . . Mrs. James is about 40 I should [think], pleasant and devoted to her children. The sister may be 28 or 30, pleasant, very well informed I should judge, a teacher I think, not pretty but with a good complexion and character in her face." [51]

Looking back on the preceding academic year, Mead was encouraged by the success he had enjoyed, even though he had not applied himself to his studies as industriously as he might have: "If with such slight work I can come out with flying colors as I did, I think I may get abroad next if I work. . . . I am going now to have a Ph.D. from Berlin at any cost." But before he could expect to go to Berlin, there was another year of work at Harvard. Professor Palmer, with whom Mead had done much of his work the first year, would not be in residence for the next year, and this Mead considered "a burning shame" because Palmer had "succeeded in getting up a most exaggerated idea of me and my abilities." However, Mead was thinking of taking a course with Professor Charles Carroll Everett at the Harvard Divinity School, of whom James had said that "after Royce he is the strongest man in the university, very subtle and original." And, of course, Mead was still hopeful that Royce would be teaching again in the fall. "James says that Royce broke himself down by taking no vacations and foolish eating and drinking, that he has been very proud of his strength and never took precautions, and that he has been troubled about money matters as well." [52]

One more of Mead's letters from the James summer residence has been preserved, in which he recounts James's receipt of a letter from George Santayana, who was studying in Germany on a Harvard traveling scholarship: "James read to me a letter from Santiana [sic]. He is discouraged and disheartened with philosophy, calls Wundt a survival of the Alchemist and does [not] see any prospect of getting anything more abroad and wants to use his fellowship in Harvard next year. He says he may develop out of his disgust a system if he has sufficient audacity to, and means to do this next year I believe. James thinks he lacks the virile dogged qualities which make a successful worker in this or any direction." [53] If Santayana did in fact return to Harvard the next year, Mead observed, there was a chance that his scholarship might be made available to another student. "I should apply for it and there is a dim possibility that I should get it. . . . In that case I should, of course, get abroad a year earlier." Otherwise he would hope to obtain a two-year traveling scholarship at the end of the coming school year. And if no scholarship were forthcoming, he would borrow the money he would need for study in Germany. Meanwhile, however, he would have to deal with the problem of supporting himself for another year at Harvard. In this connection he had been given some helpful moral support from James, who "is very kind to me. I have every consideration here and he told me that he could assure me $100 next year. Of course I shall not borrow through him but it was very kind and unexpected, and what made my heart burn was that he said he might possibly be able to get the *Nation* to take some review of mine or perhaps keep back the review until they had seen mine, and you know they pay well, $20 a page. He said he made a good deal of money in this way as a young man." [54]

Although no further letters written by Mead from Chocorua have been preserved, a letter he wrote to Castle two years later suggests that Mead's relationship with James underwent some strain as the summer of 1888 drew to a close. Mead reported in a letter of 1890 that he had received from James a copy of the latter's just published work, *The Principles of Psychology:* "James has sent his Psychology to me. Two large volumes—just out. . . . He didn't direct it to the man who had made an ass of himself, but did send it to Halle [where Mead's sister and brother-in-law were staying] while I was there. How he could have secured the address I don't know, may have got it from my mother. He is a fine fellow—so much genuine human nature in the man. He would have made a better hero of a Turgenieff novel than professor of philosophy." [55] What had Mead done which led him to feel in retrospect that he had "made an ass of himself" in the eyes of James? On this question the extant letters of both Mead and Castle are strangely silent; indeed, one suspects that some of the letters Mead wrote Castle during the latter part of 1888 were later destroyed precisely because they addressed this embarrassing topic. Fortunately, the solution to this minor mystery is supplied by another source—the letters James wrote to his wife in New Hampshire during his periodic visits to Cambridge in the late summer of 1888.

James's letters reveal that the cause of Mead's subsequent embarrassment was nothing more than a summer romance. Mead, it seems, was for a short time romantically involved with Margaret Gibbens—Mrs. James's sister. James's attitude toward Mead's emotional turmoil near the end of the summer was one of sympathetic understanding: "Poor wretch! Just like me a dozen years ago."[56] Mead was a "fine manly fellow and a fit object for any woman to adore," but James was not enthusiastic about having to engage in "unwelcome spectatorship" of such adoration at close range.[57] (There is, in fact, some evidence that James may have asked Mead to cut short his summer of tutoring and return to Cambridge rather than pursue his romance with Margaret at Chocorua.[58]) James's official position on the matter seems to have been one of laissez faire—"Give them their rope, & let them settle it themselves, there is no other possible way"[59]—but this did not prevent him from encouraging Mead to think seriously about going abroad to study at the end of the summer. "Mead spent an hour with me—in unchanged condition," James wrote his wife in early September when both he and Mead were back in Cambridge, "—but I think he rather warmed to the prospect of going to Germany."[60]

James must have been persuasive, for Mead did not return to Harvard in the fall of 1888 as he had previously planned. Instead, he sailed for Europe (at his own expense rather than with any Harvard scholarship assistance) and enrolled at the University of Leipzig, there to realize his dream of studying in Germany.[61]

Although Mead's stay at Harvard lasted only a single year, it nevertheless made a significant impact upon his intellectual life. During the preceding four years, as Castle had noted following their reunion early in 1887, Mead's philosophical development had been at a standstill. He had made sporadic attempts, mainly through his reading of Kant, to move beyond the orthodox Scottish philosophy he had encountered at Oberlin, but these attempts had been largely unsuccessful. At Harvard, however, he had begun to move forward. Here it was Royce, Mead subsequently recalled, who had made the greatest intellectual impression upon him. While he admired the personality of James, he had not actually studied under James, and he admitted that during his Harvard student days he had failed to appreciate James's intellectual power as a philosopher.[62] Royce's influence, on the other hand, had been immediate and profound, even though Mead was able to study with him just a little more than a single semester: "I received an impression from him of freedom of mind, and of dominance of thought in the universe, of a clear unclouded landscape of spiritual reality where we sat like gods together—but not careless of mankind—and it was a vision that followed me for many years."[63] Mead cannot have very fully understood Royce's philosophy after so slight an exposure, but that did not keep him from assuming the essential truth of Royce's idealistic metaphysical vision. No doubt a young man with an interest in Kant, but who had been longing for several years to discover a constructive philosophy that went beyond Kant, was bound to find Royce's metaphysics intoxicating and its truth a matter of course: "I was so grateful to him for the world which the magic of his presentation offered me that I was quite willing to take for granted his claim that it involved and expressed all truth, and solved all problems. What I gained from him was detachment, objectivity, and imaginative reach."[64]

Chapter 2

Early Life and Letters: Part 2

Study in Germany (1888–91)

Soon after Mead arrived in Germany in the fall of 1888, he was joined by Henry Castle, who had departed Honolulu in September, intending to resume his studies at the Harvard Law School. Upon arrival in Cambridge, however, he found that the law school would not allow this because he had left the year before without having taken the required examinations. Seeing no way to circumvent the rule governing this matter, Castle decided to join Mead in Leipzig. He sailed in November with plans to take courses in Roman law, political economy, and philosophy in the German university system.[1]

During the 1888–89 academic year, Mead and Castle roomed and studied together, first in Leipzig and then in Berlin. Mead's formal studies for the winter semester—the only semester he spent in Leipzig—consisted of three courses in philosophy taken under Professors Wilhelm Wundt (fundamentals of metaphysics), Max Heinze (history of more recent modern philosophy), and Rudolf Seydel (the relationship of German philosophy to Christianity since Kant).[2] There is reason to think, however, that Mead may not have gained much from these courses: Castle reported that the lectures at Leipzig were somewhat disappointing—a fact more significant for him than for Mead since the latter "could hardly expect anyway to do more in the first semester than get a good hold of the language, so that after all, it is of very little consequence what lectures he hears." Mead, he continued, was beginning to focus his attention more and more upon physiological psychology as a possible field of specialization:

By the rarest piece of good luck in the world, George ran across Professor G. Stanley Hall of Johns Hopkins, just the one man on

[handwritten marginalia: "Mead wanted to make a specialty of physiological ... but American was not opposed to unchristian theory yet"]

our planet whom for the moment he wanted to see. Stanley Hall is the most eminent physiological psychologist in America, and having been through the whole mill here, could advise George just what to do, and how and where to go to work to do it. Physiological Psychology is a science as yet very much in the air, which has hardly materialized yet, and poor George was utterly at a loss how to begin. Every professor whom we visited here had a different piece of advice to impart. . . . George thinks he must make a specialty of this branch, because in America, where poor, bated, unhappy Christianity, trembling for its life, claps the gag into the mouth of Free Thought, and says "Hush, hush, not a word, or nobody will believe in me any more," he thinks it would be hard for him to get a chance to utter any ultimate philosophical opinions savoring of independence. In Physiological Psychology, on the other hand, he has a harmless territory in which he can work quietly without drawing down upon himself the anathema and excommunication of all-potent Evangelicalism.[3]

Early in March 1889, Mead moved on to the University of Berlin from which he wrote several months later that he was "reading with weary regularity Anatomie and Physiologische Psychologie and attending some lectures."[4] During the summer semester of 1889 he enrolled in lecture courses given by Professors Hermann Ebbinghaus (experimental psychology), Friedrich Paulsen (history of more recent modern philosophy, with consideration of the modern development of culture in its entirety, psychology and anthropology, and philosophical exercises based on Schopenhauer's *The World as Will and Idea*), and Wilhelm Waldeyer (general anatomy).[5] Castle had meanwhile become engaged to marry nineteen-year-old Frida Stechner, daughter of the Frau Stechner at whose home Mead and Castle had taken rooms in Leipzig. Castle followed Mead to Berlin for a brief stay in the spring and early summer, but his heart was clearly elsewhere. He married Frida Stechner in September 1889 and shortly thereafter sailed with his new bride to the United States. After spending much of the fall in Cambridge, the Castles proceeded to Hawaii where Henry, instead of resuming his pursuit of a career in law, soon found work as an editor with the Honolulu Gazette Company. A daughter, Dorothy, was born to Frida and Henry Castle in June 1890.

According to the records of the Humboldt University in Berlin, Mead studied under Professor Ebbinghaus (psychology with consideration of experimental and physiological psychology) during the winter semester of 1889–90 and under Professors Wilhelm Dilthey (ethics, presented in its principles and particular explications) and Otto Pfleiderer (philosophy of religion) during the summer of 1890.[6] But, unfortunately, there exist no letters throwing additional light upon Mead's activities and studies during this academic year. None of the letters Mead wrote to Castle during the fall of 1889 have been preserved, and Mead allowed his correspondence to lapse entirely during the first half of 1890. Castle mentioned this in a letter written to his sister Helen in late June 1890 as she was preparing to go to Berlin to further her own education: "I wonder if you will see or hear anything of George Mead. I have not heard anything from him for six months."[7] Mead finally wrote Castle in August, little knowing that his letter would console a man broken in spirit by a recent disaster: Frida Castle, only four weeks a mother, had been thrown from a carriage pulled by a frightened horse and killed.[8]

Mead probably first learned of Frida Castle's death from Helen Castle, who had taken up residence in Berlin during the summer of 1890. The catastrophe, as their son was to report many years later, did much to pull the two together: "Helen Castle was none too strong, and she as well as others have said that George Mead saved her life or reason at that time."[9] In the ensuing months Mead wrote numerous letters to Castle that, in addition to expressing sympathy, gave some indications of the directions his intellectual life was taking after two years of study in Germany. Mead's letters of this period give vent to his strong desire for involvement in social and political action. Mead's mind was clearly full of the spirit of social reform, and, what is especially noteworthy, this spirit was almost wholly secular in tone; instead of framing his social ideals in terms of that Christian pietism with which he had struggled in the early 1880s, he was now prepared to find his inspiration in developmental psychology and the literature of European socialism. Extracts of the following letter, written in October 1890, are typical of what he wrote to Castle that fall.

The only inspiring work that can be found is in the practical application of morals to life—in education—of character and body especially—and in politics, and that we cannot get a foothold in society where we can work out to this end seems very improbable.

We must get into politics of course—city politics above all things, because then we can begin to work at once in whatever city we settle—because city politics need men more than any other branch—and chiefly because according to my opinion the immediate application of the principles of corporate life—of socialism in America—must start from the city. . . .

I hope to get a place in some city where you can start as a lawyer. Minneapolis would be just the place—for it has the right soil—a university, a newspaper that needs buying out—but in any case we must equip ourselves with the knowledge of the runnings of city government here—get a hold upon the socialistic literature—and the position of socialism here in Europe. We must go back full and with such a hold upon the sources that we can keep full. We will move heaven and earth to keep together and work together—it is a great inspiring work. . . .

One doesn't want too much political economy, but he wants a program for an American city that he can defend at every point and that is adaptable. . . . This in connection with a vigorous spreading of . . . methods that apply the psychology of moral development to the child—the vigorous organizing of movements of physical culture will give the breath of new ideas where the air is now so thin that it cannot come without appreciation.

I am not discouraged—but am perfectly willing to fail as far as that is concerned. I want a few years of activity that I can throw myself into and I am perfectly willing to see no success. The subjective return is enough.[10]

Mead's letters of this period also indicate that he was still directing much of his attention to problems in the area of physiological psychology. "The greatest conquest I have made in these last days," he wrote, "is the confident belief that space is a construction of our eye—that the three dimensions rest simply upon the optic nerve and the sense of touch and especially the hand." He was, in short, working out a physiological reformulation of the Kantian view that space is a form of sensibility that the human perceiver imposes upon sensible data: "It seems a small thing, but to me the distance is immeasurable between saying that space is a form of sensibility and that it is a construction of our eye and hand and ear."[11] It was just this line of inquiry, as a matter of fact, that he subsequently chose to pursue as the topic of his proposed Ph.D. dissertation. More important, one sees here an anticipation of the treatment of space that appears many years later in his mature theory of perception, although in 1890 Mead had not yet begun to locate spatial perception within the context of a functional analysis of conduct. This latter development had to await his subsequent encounter with the thought of John Dewey.

Both of the two main interests Mead expressed in his letters to Castle in the fall of 1890 are reflected in the lecture courses he attended during his last two full semesters at the University of Berlin. Thus in the winter semester of 1890–91 he studied physiology under Professor Hermann Munk and pedagogics under Professor Paulsen. And in the summer semester of 1891 he took history of philosophy under Professor Dilthey, philosophical exercises based on Kant's *Critique of Pure Reason* and anthropology and psychology under Professor Paulsen, and general or theoretical political economy under Professor Gustav Schmoller.[12] In light of the considerable emphasis Dilthey's work places upon the social dimension of human existence, it would be valuable to know what key ideas, if any, Mead acquired from the two courses he took from Dilthey at Berlin. On this subject, however, Mead's letters to Castle are wholly silent.

One further point concerning Mead's intellectual development can be gleaned from his letters to Castle during the 1890–91 academic year. In late April 1891 he wrote that he had recently "swallowed Fichte's *Die Bestimmung des Menschen* at one dose" and that he was a quarter of the way through Schelling's *Das System der Transcendentalen Idealismus*. The former, he remarked, was "easy reading and I feel I have a real hold on F. now—with a good study of a critic of him I shall be fertig [finished] with him." Schelling, he said, "reads very clearly—I am surprised—fine simple sentences, and the terminology does not offer me difficulties."[13] It would thus appear that despite his earlier enthusiasm for Royce's brand of objective idealism, Mead was just beginning his study of some of the classics of German idealism after two and a half years in Germany.

The summer and fall of 1891 brought two particularly significant changes in Mead's life. During the summer he obtained a teaching position at the University of Michigan in Ann Arbor, where he would be working under the chairmanship of John Dewey. He wrote enthusiastically to Henry in late July, reporting what he had so far been able to learn about his new teaching duties:

> [I] have heard from Dewey[a] pleasant letter, and one that promises very satisfactory work. The Phys. Psy. I have to my-self—a course in the History of Phil. and a half course in Kant—and another in Evolution. Doesn't it make your mouth water my boy—come and do likewise eventually.
>
> My head is full of schemes for the course—especially for this Hist. of Phil.—am sure I can give it a Verständlichkeit that will awaken interest and combine a system of essay writing with it which will compel comprehension and work.
>
> Kant will be a most admirable desert. The drudgery will be the Phys. Psy. for I shant have much opportunity for original work and to use it for pedagogical purposes is hard.[14]

It was no doubt the promise of this employment that led Mead and Helen Castle to finalize an engagement they had entered into in January 1991: they were married in Berlin on October 1, 1891, with Mead's sister and brother-in-law, Alice and Albert Swing, as their witnesses.[15]

Before the Meads could begin their new life in Ann Arbor, however, Mead had a good deal of work to finish in Berlin. He had earlier obtained permission from President James Burrill Angell of the University of Michigan to arrive in Ann Arbor somewhat after the beginning of the academic year so that he might remain in Berlin long enough to complete all the requirements for his degree.[16] But as the end of October approached it became apparent to Mead that he would not be able to complete his work in the time he had remaining. Thus, in his final letter to Henry from Berlin he regretfully announced his decision to leave Germany without the degree.

> I find that even now, though I calculated that I allowed myself time enough from what the Dekan told me last semester, it would carry me to the 29th of November probably or the 20th anyway to finish up, even on an application to the Minister, who in this case would not help at all. I talked with great unction with the Dekan and Professors Dilthey and Zeller, but though they were very kind and appreciative and cudgeled their brains for some way out they

could find none. . . . So I have decided to postpone, send in my
thesis by next April, go over to Berlin reaching there the first
of July and take my mündliche, and finishing the Promovierung
before the fifteenth. . . .

I am on the whole glad for I can make much more out of my
thesis than I have so far or could in the few days left. I can see now
a vast field that I haven't touched and see also how much more
effectively I can use the material.

It is now and will remain largely a criticism from a Kantian
or at least metaphysical standpoint of the sensational doctrine of
space—and finally a reconstruction of the facts from a speculative
standpoint. I have acquired a respect for the work done and the
men who have done it on the subject which is far beyond what I
had 3 months ago. A steady clearing up of the physical processes,
and unflinching determination to express the facts of sensation
with perfect simplicity are features that call for enthusiasm when
one finds them freed from all bitterness of polemicism and always
kept fresh by constant contact with Mother Nature. Such men as
Hering, Helmholst, Stumpf, one must doff his hat to. The latter
[has] real speculative depth. I shall send you his "Raumsinn."

. . . I am ashamed of course to go back without the degree but
I am really surer of it now than if I were to take my examinations
and hand in my thesis tomorrow. My year's work will grind into
me just what I shall [need] if I haven't it now, and I want to make
my thesis a worthy beginning for my Opera omnia.[17]

Mead's optimistic plans for the completion of his thesis and other
degree requirements never materialized. Upon arrival at the University
of Michigan he became immersed in his new teaching and research responsibilities. Only once in his subsequent correspondence with Castle,
and that in a letter written almost a year and a half after his move to
Ann Arbor, did he mention "beginning work on my thesis."[18] Sometime after this letter was written Mead apparently gave up the idea of
obtaining a degree from the University of Berlin. Thus the man who
had resolved in 1888 that "I am going to have a Ph.D. from Berlin at
any cost" was in the end unable to make good on this promise to himself. However, Mead's failure to complete work on his Ph.D. seems
not to have been a serious impediment to his academic career, either at
Michigan or later at the University of Chicago.

The Ann Arbor Years (1891–94)

When Mead arrived in Ann Arbor from Berlin in the fall of 1891, he brought with him a solid background in physiological psychology, a sympathy for metaphysical idealism, and a strong desire to become involved in practical endeavors that would allow him to work for the realization of moral ideals in areas such as education and municipal politics. But there is no evidence that he had worked out in his own mind a unified synthesis of these facets of his intellectual life. The beginnings of such a synthesis are evident, however, in various letters he wrote to Castle and others during the Ann Arbor period. And these beginnings reflect at almost every step the influence of John Dewey.

Shortly after his move to Michigan, Mead wrote Castle that he found the intellectual atmosphere congenial and his departmental colleagues, Dewey and fellow instructor Alfred Lloyd, much to his liking. Both Dewey and Lloyd, he reported, were Hegelians, but Hegelians of a distinctive and original sort; Mead was therefore able to report that there were "some surprising bits of American speculation springing up" around him.[19] In fact, although Mead was perhaps unaware of it at the time, his arrival at Michigan coincided almost exactly with the early stages of Dewey's well-known transition from Hegelian idealism to functionalism and experimentalism.[20] We can see this transition underway, for instance, in Dewey's "Introduction to Philosophy: Syllabus for Course 5," a document Dewey prepared for a course in February 1892, just after Mead's first term of teaching in Ann Arbor.[21] Since there is much in this syllabus that helps explain the new lines of thought evident in Mead's letters of this period, it is worthwhile to digress here to examine several of its central ideas.

Philosophy, Dewey claims in this syllabus, attempts to understand the generic features of the *whole* of life or experience. And this whole he construes in a Hegelian manner: it is a dynamic and organic unity that manifests itself in each of its parts. Only when the parts are seen as functioning aspects or partial manifestations of this whole, rather than approached in isolation from it, can their true nature and meaning be adequately grasped. As long as human thought is dominated by a piecemeal approach to the data of experience, the whole that philosophy seeks is bound to seem "remote, and capable of description only in unnatural ('metaphysical,' 'transcendental') terms." Dewey suggests that philosophy has recently acquired the conceptual means to describe the generic features of experience in a way that is concrete and natural—"thus translating philosophical truth into common terms." Two developments, in particular, have made this possible. First, psychology has succeeded in revealing, at least in outline, the fundamental structure of action at the level of the individual organism. Second, as human social or political life has become more fully developed and self-conscious ("has become freer," in Dewey's Hegelian terminology), the underlying principle of all social action has become apparent.[22] Let us follow Dewey in looking briefly at each of these developments.

Dewey links the first development to the discussion of the reflex arc model of action in such works as Herbert Spencer's *The Principles of Psychology* (1878), Eduard von Hartmann's *Philosophy of the Unconscious* (English translation, 1884), and William James's *The Principles of Psychology* (1890). James, for instance, illustrates the typical phases of a reflex arc by means of the example of a young child confronting a burning candle: (a) the candle provides stimuli initiating nerve currents that flow through the sensory nerves to the brain; (b) in the brain these nerve currents are coordinated and related to reminiscences of past experiences (e.g., an experience of having been burned) by means of ideational processes; (c) resultant nerve currents then move outward from the brain via the motor nerves to the muscles where they bring about muscular responses (e.g., a withdrawal of the hand from the vicinity of the candle). "The conception of *all* action as conforming to this type," James says, "is the fundamental conception of modern nerve-physiology."[23]

Dewey is not at all critical of this conception in his 1892 syllabus; in this respect his position here differs from the one he would take in his 1896 essay on "The Reflex Arc Concept in Psychology." By 1896 Dewey was prepared to reject the reflex arc model of action as being overly mechanical; in 1892 he was simply inclined to stretch the reflex arc concept in the direction of his later organic or functional model of action. This stretching takes the form of an attempt to view the reflex arc as exemplifying the same kind of Hegelian organic unity he professed to find in experience regarded as a whole. Every reflex arc, he claims, consists in a unified coordination of various subordinate acts or elements (e.g., sensing, nerve currents, muscular movements) that are to be understood as both *members* and *organs* of the completed psycho-physical action. They are members insofar as they are phases that perform a specific function within the action as a whole; they are organs insofar as the whole action expresses itself through them. Consider, for instance, the activity of the eye in a given reflex arc. This activity is a subordinate action that performs a specific function within the unity of the larger act of which it is a part. At the same time, the "activity of the eye is, in reality, nothing but one differentiation of the action of the entire organism. The organism resides (dynamically) in the eye."[24]

Turning next to the second development mentioned earlier, Dewey contends that the same kind of structure is present in any complete social action. Just as the parts of a reflex arc are to be understood as functional phases of an organic whole, so the human individual should be seen as both a member and an organ of the social groups of which he is a part. He is a member insofar as he is a functioning phase of a social whole; he is an organ insofar as the social whole expresses itself through his actions. Apart from his relationship to larger social wholes, the human individual would be a merely natural being having a certain bodily constitution subject to physical conditions. It is by entering into a social whole, by sharing in the actions of a social whole and allowing the social group to express itself through him, that the individual becomes something more than a merely natural being. For it is in this way that the natural individual is "spiritualized"; indeed, his functioning in this manner "is his spirit." Moreover, this process in which human social action spiritualizes (expresses itself in or becomes embodied in) the natural is not restricted to the relationship between society and the human individual. It also characterizes the relationship between society and the physical world of nature in general. The modern development of industry and commerce, Dewey claims, has helped us to see the physical world not as an end in itself but as material for human action. And when elements in the physical world are utilized by human society as materials for its action, they, too, become "spiritualized": they acquire new meanings and a fuller reality. "Iron, coal and water, for example, get their fuller reality . . . in the locomotive when that functions as part of man's action."[25]

The fundamental structures of the whole that philosophy seeks to apprehend, Dewey concludes, should be viewed as organic structures of action. By thus reading reality in terms of action, philosophy can reconcile the conflict between the material and the mental that has been one of its persistent problems in the modern period. "So read, the opposition between the internal and the external, the physical and the psychical, ceases to be ultimate and becomes instrumental." The first step toward the overcoming of this conflict has been sketched above: to construe the physical as the content or material of action. The second step is to regard mind also as a phase of action. Mind is not a thing; it is that process whereby human action experimentally works out or discovers how it can most successfully utilize and enter into its materials.[26]

It is possible that sometime during his first year at Michigan Mead read Dewey's 1892 syllabus. But even if he did not, he must have been exposed to its central ideas through conversations with Dewey, for the influence of these ideas is obvious in his letters to Castle. Consider, for example, his remarks concerning the *Thought News*, a new monthly newspaper that Dewey planned to edit and publish in cooperation with the somewhat eccentric journalist Franklin Ford.[27] In late February 1892 Mead sent twenty-five copies of an advertising circular describing *Thought News* to Castle, along with a letter urging him to subscribe and to secure additional subscribers among his acquaintances in Honolulu. The underlying assumption of *Thought News*, he told Henry, was that "the conditions are free enough now so that the organic intelligence of America can express itself articulately as it has already dynamically in the locomotive and telegraph. These latter are only bits of human Mind or Mind in any case—as truly so as the brain, not metaphorically but actually—literally. They are part of the mechanism of intelligence—and the brain cells are not more. They are the objective side of course; the subjective is the universal self, I suppose. But for the immediate purpose of News reporting, the recognition of all the outer paraphernalia of society as only the objective expression (not metaphorically) of intelligence puts a new light on everything."[28]

It might be argued that Mead was here attempting merely to report Dewey's Hegelian ideas rather than to express his own. But in a letter Mead wrote to his wife's parents at the end of his second semester in Ann Arbor he makes it quite clear that Dewey's ideas were rapidly becoming his own. Helen Mead had gone to Hawaii for the summer to visit her parents, and apparently the Castle family had offered to pay Mead's way as well, for in June he wrote thanking them for their generous offer and explaining his decision to remain in Ann Arbor to continue his work. This letter is particularly helpful in assessing Mead's intellectual development, for it contains a long summary of the directions in which his thought had been moving during the 1891–92 academic year.

I have been able in the year that I have passed here to make a synthesis of the abstract thinking that I have done, have studied and listened to ever since I became interested in philosophy, and [the] meaning of American life—have been able to follow the connection that has gradually been established between abstract philosophy and daily life.

I have learned to see that society advances, men get closer and closer to each other and the kingdom of heaven is established on the earth, so far as man becomes more and more organically connected with nature. This has generally been laid up against America as materialism—and she has been scouted as sunk in money getting and as letting go [the] spiritual side of life. But it seems to me clearer every day that the telegraph and locomotive are the great spiritualizers of society because they bind man and man so close together that the interest of the individual must be more completely the interest of all day by day. And America in pushing this spiritualizing of nature is doing more than all in bringing the day when every man will be my neighbor and all life shall be saturated with the divine life.

I have seen also that in conquering the material world we not only get new spiritual forces in society, but also that all matter—especially the human organism—becomes spiritual, when one sees in it the process of life and thought. That the body and soul are but two sides of one thing, and that the gulf between them is only the expression of the fact that our life does not yet realize the ideal of what our social life will be, when our functions and acts shall be not simply ours but the processes of the great body politic which is God as revealed in the universe.

For me in Physiological Psychology the especial problem is to recognize that our psychical life can all be read in the functions of our bodies—that it is not the brain that thinks but . . . our organs in so far as they act together in processes of life. This is quite a new standpoint for the science and has a good many important consequences—especially does it offer new methods of experiment which must be worked out. . . .

Please excuse this very abstract statement—but I wanted at least just to indicate that my work here was not simply carrying on the technical labors in my position as teacher and experimenter but that what I am at work on has all the meaning of social and religious life in it. . . . I can't do my work successfully without working out my standpoint consistently in all directions. I am unwilling to experiment as most of the physiological psychologists have done heretofore—at haphazard. I must have a consistent ground for investigation, and this must be worked out before the work itself can be done.

Helen and I are very fortunately situated here. There is no freer place for thought and investigation in the world than here, and Mr. Dewey is a man of not only great originality and profound thought but the most appreciative thinker I ever met. I have gained more from him than from any one man I ever met.[29]

Several brief comments are in order concerning the respects in which this letter reveals the impact of Dewey upon Mead's thought during the Ann Arbor period. First, and most obviously, Mead explicitly acknowledges the great influence of Dewey in its final paragraph. Second, Mead follows Dewey in viewing human social life as an organic whole that expresses itself in (and thus "spiritualizes") human individuals and also physical nature insofar as the latter is utilized as an instrument for the realization of human purposes. Indeed, Mead sees the spiritualization of nature in such instruments as the telegraph and the locomotive as itself contributing to the further spiritualization of human individuals: these instruments bring human individuals closer together, thereby helping them to participate more fully in an organic social whole. Third, Mead's conception of this advancing human social life as a manifestation or expression of "the divine life" is part and parcel of the kind of Hegelianism Dewey was espousing during this period. (Dewey's view on this matter, while not evident in his 1892 syllabus, can be seen quite clearly in his "Christianity and Democracy," an essay first presented as an address to the Students' Christian Association at Michigan in March 1892.[30]) Finally, Mead accepts Dewey's functional view of the mental and physical as two aspects of a single life process. And this view he regards as providing the basis for a new approach to his own research in the field of physiological psychology. No doubt it was this approach he had in mind when he wrote Castle in December of his second year at Michigan that "I have at last reached a position I used to dream of in Harvard—where it is possible to apply good straight phys. psy. to Hegel, and I don't know what more a mortal can want on earth." [31]

The few additional letters that survive from Mead's three years in Ann Arbor report the birth of a son, Henry Castle Albert Mead, in the fall of 1892; they indicate that Mead was promoted to the rank of assistant professor at the end of the 1892–93 academic year. [32] But they reveal only one further fact of importance about his intellectual life: he had not yet begun to focus in any systematic way upon the social psychological concerns that were to occupy center stage in his later thought. Instead, the bulk of his research during this period took the form of laboratory work in the field of physiological psychology. [33] It is important to bear in mind, however, that for Mead this laboratory work carried with it, as he pointed out in one of the 1892 letters previously quoted, "all the meaning of social and religious life." And certainly some dimensions of what he took to be the larger meaning of his work in physiological psychology appear to foreshadow concerns that would assume greater prominence in his subsequent thought. A noteworthy example of such foreshadowing can be seen in an unpublished manuscript of a Sunday morning chapel address on "The Psychology of Jesus' Use of Emotions" he delivered to a meeting of the Students' Christian Association at the University of Michigan in late February 1893. The gospel of love taught by Jesus, Mead maintained in this rambling address, was a call to a kind of life that went beyond mere conformity to traditional religious forms and rituals. But the love Jesus urged upon us was not to be confused with passive emotion or sentimentalism; rather, it required "the most complete and absolute activity our natures are capable of." Christian love, Mead held—and here he sought to make his point by means of a lengthy digression moving from James's theory of emotion to a summary of current knowledge concerning the function and physiology of the emotions—had to be of a sort leading to activity deeply rooted in our social nature. Such love "must have back of it the instinctive actions of the whole social, in other words religious, nature," and it must lead us to identify with the shared interests of all those involved with us in a common social life. It is this richer sort of social life to which we are called by the gospel of love. And it is this life that is symbolized by Jesus' notion of the kingdom of heaven. [34] Mead here anticipates, as we shall see in chapter 8, a number of ideas he was to develop more fully, but in a thoroughly secularized form, in his later discussions of ethics and moral psychology.

The End of a Friendship

During his final year in Ann Arbor, Mead was joined by Castle, who had set aside his newspaper work to engage in further study. Recently remarried, Henry brought with him his new wife, Mabel Wing Castle, and his three-year-old daughter, Dorothy. The Castles rented a house not far from the Meads, and Henry enrolled as a student at the university for the fall term of 1893. His course of study quite obviously reflected Mead's guidance: Castle elected no fewer than four courses taught by Dewey. All of Dewey's courses, he wrote home to Honolulu, were "very interesting and edifying. He is unquestionably a very fresh and original thinker, and I am getting much new light from him." [35] The Meads and the Deweys, Castle observed, were "on terms of the most delightful intimacy." He then went on to report his impressions of the Deweys and Ann Arbor:

> Mrs D. . . . is one of the most refreshing persons I have come in contact with; a mind rich and varied, with wide experience, and finding the world constantly interesting and entertaining. Mr Dewey is a tall dark, thin young man, with long black hair, and a soft, penetrating eye, and looks like a cross between a Nihilist and a poet. He is, I believe, about thirty-five, but seems much younger. . . . The Deweys live on the corner, and only one house separates them from George and Helen, who are most beautifully located with a splendid outlook, and the woods behind them coming right up to their back yard. Ann Arbor is one of the loveliest villages I have ever seen anywhere; all the streets pretty, up hill and down, fine pasture, and forest. George and Helen are fortunate to live in such a place. [36]

Given this pleasant setting and Mead's evident enjoyment of his work at the University of Michigan, the decision to leave Ann Arbor must have been difficult. But when at the conclusion of the 1893–94 academic year Dewey accepted the chairmanship of the department of philosophy at the recently established University of Chicago, Mead moved with him to accept an appointment as assistant professor in the same department.[37] Mead's long career at the University of Chicago (1894–1931), however, is a subject for later discussion. What must concern us here is the final phase of his friendship with Henry Castle.

Earlier in 1894 the Castles had returned to Honolulu because of the rapidly declining health of Henry's eighty-five-year-old father. Samuel Northrup Castle died that July, and in late summer Henry and Mabel Castle resolved to follow through on earlier plans for a European trip. When they left Honolulu in September, however, Mabel Castle was six months pregnant; she therefore elected to stay in Philadelphia with a close college friend, who was also a physician, until after the baby was born. Henry and his four-year-old daughter, Dorothy, meanwhile went ahead to visit Dorothy's maternal grandmother in Germany. Late that November Mabel Castle gave birth to a daughter named Elinor.[38] Shortly thereafter Castle wrote from Leipzig to tell his wife that he had changed his mind about the advisability of her making the trip to Europe; he now felt it best for all of them to make a "speedy return" to Honolulu. Having secured Mabel's consent to this change of plans, he and his young daughter sailed from Bremen on January 28, 1895, aboard the North German Lloyd Steamer *Elbe* bound for New York.[39]

They were never heard from again. On Wednesday morning, January 30, at approximately 6:00 A.M., when most of the passengers were still asleep, the steamship *Elbe* was struck by a small Scotch steamer, the *Craithie,* as the two ships sailed through the North Sea midway between the English and Dutch coasts. Less than twenty minutes after the collision the *Elbe* sank, taking with her all but a score of the 240 passengers and 160 crewmen abroad. Henry and Dorothy Castle were among those lost at sea.[40]

George and Helen Mead, who had been expecting the Henry Castle family to visit them in Chicago early in February, received word of the sinking of the *Elbe* on the morning of January 31, 1895. Mead learned of the disaster first and broke the news to his wife, urging her to take the first train to Philadelphia so that she could be with Mabel Castle at the earliest possible moment.[41] Mead later wrote of his friendship with Castle both in correspondence addressed to members of the Castle family and in the "Recollections of Henry in Oberlin, and After," which accompanied the collection of Henry's letters he and Helen Mead edited for the family in 1902. But nowhere did he more trenchantly summarize the significance of this friendship for his own intellectual life than in a letter written to his wife as she journeyed to

Philadelphia to comfort Mabel Castle. Henry's tragic death, he wrote, had brought so vividly to his mind their shared years at Oberlin in the early 1880s that he was now living them over "almost day by day."

That was the romantic period—the Sturm und Drang Periode of my life when the outside world and the world of thought had the purple hues of distance—and the life was inseparably connected with Henry. Between that and Ann Arbor lies a period of grappling with a feeling for the reality of the world in a scientific statement, and then when I came to know John [Dewey] I found the possibility of asserting the reality and living in it. But none of this has the rich coloring—the fullness of interest—which belongs to Henry's and my valiant attacks upon the Giants of unreason and prejudice in Oberlin days. We could get no further there, because we had no art but that of denying, but we *felt* there was a positive basis for the denial and this gave those years a real romance. Henry is a larger part of my Oberlin life than all the rest put together; his friendship was more education than what beside the place afforded.[42]

Chapter 3

From Hegelianism to Social Psychology

Considered purely as a formative influence upon Mead's philosophical development, the Mead-Castle friendship must take second place to his subsequent relationship with John Dewey. The former clearly did much to stimulate and nurture Mead's early intellectual life, but it was the latter that gave his later philosophizing a lasting direction. Indeed, it would not be too much to say that his association with Dewey, first at Michigan (1891–94) and then at the University of Chicago (1894–1904), was the single most important factor in the shaping of Mead's mature philosophical orientation. Chapter 2 traced the initial stages of this influence as it appears in letters Mead wrote to Castle and others from Ann Arbor; the present chapter shows that the same influence permeates Mead's earliest professional writings—essays and reviews published during his first decade at the University of Chicago. Mead's early years at Chicago were, however, more than an extended apprenticeship under Dewey. I shall therefore look also at some of the main respects in which Mead's intellectual efforts began to diverge from those of Dewey during this period.

Philosophy, Psychology, and Pedagogy

The academic department Dewey began to chair at Chicago in 1894 encompassed faculty in the areas of philosophy, psychology, and pedagogy. Its nucleus, in addition to Dewey himself, consisted of Mead, James H. Tufts, and James Rowland Angell—all of whom had previously been affiliated with the University of Michigan.[1] Tufts, who had taken his B.A. and M.A. degrees at Amherst and his B.D. at Yale, taught philosophy and psychology for two years in Dewey's department at Michigan before leaving in 1891 to study in Germany. (It was this vacancy that Mead filled at Michigan in the fall of 1891.) After completing his Ph.D. at Freiburg, Tufts joined the faculty of the University of Chicago as an associate professor of philosophy in 1892; a year later he took advantage of his position to recommend to President William Rainey Harper that Dewey be appointed to head the Chicago department of philosophy. Angell, son of President James Burrill Angell of the University of Michigan, was a student of both Tufts and Dewey at Ann Arbor. Following his graduation from Michigan with an M.A. degree in 1891, he had taken another M.A. at Harvard where he studied under Josiah Royce and William James. He then spent a year studying in Germany before accepting a position in the department of philosophy at the University of Minnesota in 1893. Dewey brought him to Chicago in 1894 as an assistant professor of experimental psychology and director of the psychological laboratory.[2]

Angell, it is worth noting, had more than his Harvard background in common with Mead: both men had left Germany without completing work on their Ph.D.s. Their lack of this degree was of little concern to Dewey, but it bothered President Harper—a fact Mead mentioned in a letter to his wife in the summer of 1901, when both he and Angell were overdue for promotion to the rank of associate professor: "Mr. Dewey has been at the President about Jimmie Angell's and my advancement. His [the President's] ribs stuck first at the fact that we have no Ph.D.s. Mr. Dewey spoke lightly of the honor and the President was pained at the lack of feeling for the degree. Well, said Mr. D., they might take an hour off some day and take it. And the President was shocked at Mr. D.'s levity."[3]

Mead was finally promoted to the rank of associate professor in 1902, by which time he had demonstrated his scholarly competence in a number of published essays and reviews on topics ranging from psychological theory to pedagogy and social reform. Most of these writings clearly display the influence of Dewey. Some of them cite Dewey directly; almost all of them build in some way upon ideas Dewey was developing in the years following 1892. One of Mead's earliest papers, for instance, "A Theory of Emotions from the Physiological Standpoint" (presented at the annual meeting of the American Psychological Association in 1894), was obviously written in close consultation with Dewey: the abstract of this paper, which is all that has been preserved, begins with a reference to Dewey's "A Theory of Emotion" (1894), an essay in which Dewey in turn acknowledges Mead's contribution to the subject in a footnote.[4] Similarly, Mead's essays, "Suggestions Toward a Theory of the Philosophical Disciplines" (1900) and "The Definition of the Psychical" (1903), both of which are discussed more fully in the next chapter, explicitly attempt to develop in new directions the organic and functional analysis of conduct presented by Dewey in his 1896 essay, "The Reflex Arc Concept in Psychology."

Other essays and book reviews Mead published during this period reflect the blend of Hegelianism and instrumentalism characteristic of Dewey's evolving thought at the time. A good example of this combination is Mead's 1901 review, "A New Criticism of Hegelianism: Is It Valid?" Here he argues that "with Hegel, philosophy becomes a method of thought rather than a search for fundamental entities"; the function of philosophy, "which it belongs to the genius of Hegel to have made conceivable," is not to disclose the nature of reality but to formulate "the method by which the self in its full cognitive and social content meets and solves its difficulties."[5] The Hegelian method Mead has in mind is dialectical in character; it negates or dissolves established objects of thought that have come into conflict, thereby preparing the way for a new synthesis in which the difficulties at hand are overcome. This dialectical process is possible precisely because the objects of thought and experience are "means for the purpose of conduct, not fixed presuppositions of conduct." As such they are always open to reinterpretation or reconstruction.[6] In the years following 1903, Mead seldom linked his own approach to philosophy with that of Hegel. Yet he continued to place major emphasis upon the reconstructive function of thought, and his conception of the intellectual method to be employed in the realization of this function never departed significantly from the view he had set forth in his early Hegelian period: he simply stopped speaking of this method as Hegelian or dialectical and began referring to it instead as the method of reflective, scientific, or experimental intelligence.

Dewey's continuing influence upon Mead during their shared decade at the University of Chicago is further evident in the growing interest Mead began to take in educational theory. This interest was greatly stimulated by the famous University Elementary School that Dewey founded at Chicago in 1896 and supervised until difficulties with President Harper led to Dewey's resignation in 1904.[7] Mead and his wife not only enrolled their son in the school but also prepared for publication a series of lectures Dewey gave to Elementary School parents and other interested persons in the spring of 1899; these lectures were published in 1900 as *The School and Society*.[8] In addition, Mead helped raise money for the school. And after the Elementary School had been absorbed into the University's School of Education, he served for a time as president of its parents' association. It was to this body that he delivered a 1903 address, "The Basis for a Parents' Association."[9]

That Mead fully embraced the fundamental educational ideas underlying Dewey's work at the Elementary School can be seen in his 1903 address and in two of his earliest essays, "The Relation of Play to Education" (1896) and "The Child and His Environment" (1898).[10] In these writings Mead subscribes to Dewey's desire to correct traditional educational methods so far as they fail to seize upon the motivation supplied by the natural interests and curiosity of children with respect to the world around them. Like Dewey, he wants to change the essentially passive role that traditional schooling imposes upon children and to overcome the gap between school activities and life outside the school. Most especially, he agrees with Dewey about the pedagogical value of including a practical or manual training component in the education of young children. One of the tasks of the early elementary school, Mead argues, is to present children with a social and physical environment that contains "real life processes in planting and gathering food, in cooking and making it ready, in building and decorating, in buying and selling, etc." Exposure to such "real life processes" will not only capture the interest of children and call forth spontaneous activities; it will also encourage them to coordinate and develop control of these activities by engaging them in larger patterns of conduct whose significance they already recognize and respect.[11]

Mead's Early Writings on Social Reform

Dewey's influence is also apparent in two of Mead's earliest essays on social philosophy. In "The Working Hypothesis in Social Reform" and a review of Gustav Le Bon's *The Psychology of Socialism*, both published in 1899, Mead argues for an approach to social reform that is experimental or "opportunistic" rather than utopian or "programmatic."[12] Given the complexities of the human social process, he maintains, it is wholly implausible for anyone to claim detailed knowledge concerning an ideal future society in which every significant social conflict will once and for all be resolved. Such utopian visions are little more than sweeping compensatory illusions; they are elaborate daydreams in which every felt social distress is imaginatively overcome. And any serious attempt to employ them as a basis for social reform is likely to be "not only a failure, but also pernicious."[13] Instead of expending our energies in the pursuit of grandiose utopian schemes for the creation of an ideal society, we should focus our attention on specific problems in our present society. Furthermore, we should attempt to deal with these problems in a manner that emulates the methods used in the natural sciences. This means that we should carefully examine the forces and conditions that give rise to the difficulties we wish to resolve; we should seek knowledge of laws and regularities that will make possible some measure of intelligent control over these forces and conditions. And when we move beyond analysis of social problems to propose strategies for their solution, we should treat these proposals not as fixed programs but as working hypotheses. The test of any such hypothesis is to be found in its capacity to "*work* in the complex of forces into which we introduce it" when we engage in the actual practice of social reform.[14]

Like many other reform-minded thinkers at the turn of the century, Mead was confident during his early Chicago years that social problems would prove readily tractable to a properly scientific approach. "We are getting a stronger grip on the method of social reform every year," he wrote in 1899, "and are becoming proportionately careless about our ability to predict the detailed result."[15] To the extent that Mead attempted to justify this confidence, he did so in terms of three assumptions. First, he suggested that social phenomena would be found to resemble physical phenomena in exhibiting lawlike regularities; discovery of such laws would provide a basis for control in the former sphere just as it had already done in the latter. Second, Mead thought that scientific methods of inquiry were superior to earlier intellectual methods as means for arriving at reliable knowledge of both physical and social laws. Third, he held a "belief in the essentially social character of human impulse and endeavor." By this he meant that human behavior is typically grounded in social impulses that require social solidarity for their satisfaction; human nature, in other words, contains motive forces whose fullest expression is achieved through co-operation as opposed to conflict. Intelligent social reform becomes possible, Mead maintained, just insofar as we can learn to apply reflective consciousness to the tasks of discovering and implementing social arrangements that draw upon these impulses so as to overcome social problems. "We cannot make persons social by legislative enactment, but we can allow the essentially social nature of their actions to come to expression under conditions which favor this. . . . We assume that human society is governed by laws that involve solidarity, and we seek to find these out that they may be used." [16]

All three of these assumptions underlying Mead's early confidence in a scientific approach to social reform can be plausibly viewed as extensions, if not actual ingredients, of the Hegelianism that Dewey had inspired in Mead while the two were still at the University of Michigan. The assumption that social phenomena display intelligible patterns or laws, for instance, is part and parcel of any essentially Hegelian interpretation of the human social process. Moreover, Mead's faith in the superiority of scientific methods of inquiry was clearly bolstered by his Hegelian view of the growth of knowledge. The superiority of these methods, he thought, was largely due to the fact that they treated knowledge claims as provisional hypotheses; the door was thus left open for subsequent reconstruction of such claims through a dialectical process initiated by contradictions or problems arising in the course of ongoing experience. When the scientifically oriented thinker recognizes a statement about the world as a working hypothesis, Mead pointed out in one of his 1899 essays, "he knows that further investigation will show that the former statement of his world is only provisionally true, and must be false from the standpoint of a larger knowledge, as every partial truth is necessarily taken over against the fuller knowledge which he will gain later." [17] Similarly, Mead's early Hegelianism lurks behind the fundamentally optimistic conception of human nature in the third assumption discussed above. We saw earlier that in 1892 Mead was prepared to speak of human social evolution as a movement toward greater "spiritualization," a process in which individuals become more and more organically related to each other as well as to nature. It is obviously a short step from this claim to the view that human behavior is shaped from the outset by social impulses that seek expression in just such organic relations.

The Beginnings of Mead's Interest in Social Psychology

We have so far noted several respects in which Mead's intellectual efforts during his first decade at Chicago were directed along lines of thought similar to those pursued by Dewey. But some divergence in their respective interests was to be expected, if for no other reason than that division of labor within the department required them to teach different courses. Thus, Mead seems from the outset to have had a somewhat deeper interest in the history and philosophy of the physical sciences than did Dewey—an interest obviously related to his teaching of courses in this area both at Michigan and at Chicago. In addition to courses in the philosophy of science and the history of philosophy, Mead regularly taught courses on the methodology of psychology and comparative psychology, which he had also taught at Michigan.[18] His teaching of comparative psychology no doubt accounts for the fact that his interest in animal psychology was stronger than Dewey's. John B. Watson, who received his Ph.D. from Dewey's Chicago department in 1901 and then stayed to teach psychology for seven years before moving to Johns Hopkins, later recalled Mead's early interest in animal psychology in an autobiographical statement: "I took courses and seminars with Mead. I didn't understand him in the classroom [Watson admits that he had the same difficulty with Dewey's classes], but for years Mead took a great interest in my animal experimentation, and many a Sunday he and I spent in the laboratory watching my rats and monkeys. On these comradely exhibitions and at his home I understood him. A kinder, finer man I never met."[19]

A glance at Mead's subsequent work is sufficient to show that his early interests in the history and philosophy of the physical sciences and in comparative psychology were more than passing fancies. The former interest is reflected in much of his writing, from his short 1894 paper, "Herr Lasswitz on Energy and Epistemology," to such essays as "Scientific Method and Individual Thinker" (1917) and "Scientific Method and the Moral Sciences" (1923); it can also be seen in his 1930 Carus Lectures (posthumously published in *The Philosophy of the Present*) and in many of the manuscripts posthumously published in *The Philosophy of the Act*. Moreover, Mead taught a wide variety of courses in this area over the span of his long career at Chicago.[20] The later manifestations of his interest in animal psychology are admittedly less striking. Only one of the essays published during his lifetime is explicitly devoted to this topic, his brief 1907 essay, "Concerning Animal Perception."[21] Nevertheless, Mead regularly taught a course in comparative psychology throughout the period extending from 1894 to 1911. And even after he dropped this course to devote more of his teaching time to offerings in the area of social psychology, he continued to make frequent references to animal intelligence and behavior in his writings and lectures on human social conduct.[22]

To these two respects in which Mead's intellectual interests began to diverge from those of Dewey during their decade together at Chicago must now be added a third line of inquiry that emerged in Mead's thought in the late 1890s: those reflections that led him to the formulation of his genetic and social theories of human self-consciousness, language, and reflective intelligence. This is the line of inquiry whose subsequent development constitutes his most original contribution to the pragmatic tradition in American thought.

The earliest indications that Mead's thought was beginning to move in the direction of his later social psychological theorizing take the form of brief remarks made in three book reviews he published in the years 1895, 1897, and 1901. In the first, which appears in a review of C. L. Morgan's *An Introduction to Comparative Psychology,* Mead criticizes the familiar epistemological claim that the human individual has no direct experience of the mental or psychical life of any individual other than himself. According to this view, the human individual can at best only infer conclusions about the existence and nature of another's psychical life by means of an assumed analogy between the other and himself. To this claim Mead responds with a counterargument grounded in a genetic and social understanding of how the distinction between the psychical and the physical arises in our experience: "We are as essentially social beings as physical and physiological beings. . . . The development of the distinction between the physical and the psychical in others proceeds *pari passu* with that in the child's consciousness of himself—if for no other reason because he could never form the conception of himself as psychical without the conception of others."[23] A second passage clearly anticipating Mead's later social conception of the human individual appears in his 1897 review of G. Class's *Untersuchungen zur Phaenomenologie und Ontologie des Menschlichen Geistes.* Here he suggests that the social sciences have recently been moving toward a new understanding of the individual personality, which sees human personality as an expression or outgrowth of social relationships rather than as something whose existence and nature are fundamentally independent of such relationships. According to this new view, with which Mead is obviously in agreement, "personality is an *achievement* rather than a given fact."[24] Finally, in his 1901 essay "A New Criticism of Hegelianism: Is It Valid?" (a review of Charles F. D'Arcy's *Idealism and Theology*), Mead again briefly expresses his commitment to a social and genetic view of the human self. There is no doubt, he says in defending his interpretation of Hegelian idealism against D'Arcy's criticisms, that "the immediate analysis of consciousness reveals an essentially social nature in the self. From childhood up we see that the individual recognizes and formulates the personalities of others before he does his own; that the formulation of his own personality is the result of the organization of that of others."[25]

In making these points about the social nature of personality and self-consciousness, Mead could lay no claim to originality: similar ideas had recently been more fully articulated in publications by Royce and James Mark Baldwin.[26] Mead does not explicitly acknowledge the contributions of Royce and Baldwin in any of the reviews from which the three passages cited above are taken, but the following evidence strongly suggests that one or both of these authors served as the inspiration for Mead's remarks. (1) The first and third passages cited from Mead's reviews of 1895 and 1901 correspond almost exactly with ideas Royce had presented in his 1894 essay, "The External World and the Social Consciousness."[27] (2) The second passage, from Mead's 1897 review, resembles Baldwin's claim in his *Social and Ethical Interpretation in Mental Development* (1897) that "a man is a social outcome rather than a social unity."[28] Furthermore, in a 1905 review of the work of D. Draghiscesco, Mead remarks that "Professor Baldwin in his *Mental Development* has described, perhaps, as satisfactorily as any psychologist, the process by which the child's own personality arises out of the differentiation of a general social consciousness into an ego and alii."[29]

But whatever we may conclude about the inspiration for Mead's earliest published remarks touching on social psychological topics, it is clear that these remarks would possess little significance if he had not subsequently incorporated their key ideas within a set of highly original social psychological theories. Chapter 4 traces the development of the fundamental concepts underlying these theories in a series of essays he published between 1900 and 1913. At present the stage is set for this later discussion in comments on those factors in Mead's academic and intellectual life that help explain the increasing attention he paid to social psychological ideas during his first decade at Chicago.

First, the Hegelianism that characterized Mead's philosophical orientation during this decade made him receptive to views propounded by Royce and Baldwin in their discussions of human personality. Royce, as a matter of fact, had explicitly pointed out the close connection between his own social treatment of self-consciousness and the account of self-consciousness found in Hegel's *Phenomenology*.[30] Mead implies a similar connection when he embraces a social account of self-consciousness as part of his defense of Hegelianism in his 1901 review of D'Arcy's *Idealism and Theology*. In addition, Mead's early writings on social psychology were preceded by his involvement in Dewey's Elementary School; no doubt this involvement helped to turn his attention in the direction of social psychological questions. More important, social psychology in general and the writings of Baldwin in particular were topics of considerable current interest in Mead's immediate intellectual circle at Chicago in the late 1890s. Tufts, for instance, published short reviews of current social psychological literature in several volumes of the *Psychological Review* between 1895 and 1899.[31] Further, both Dewey and Tufts published reviews of Baldwin's *Social and Ethical Interpretations in Mental Development* shortly after it appeared in 1897. And this same work by Baldwin was the subject of presentations by Dewey, Tufts, Mead, and George E. Vincent of the sociology department at a meeting of the University of Chicago sociology club during the 1898–99 academic year.[32]

While all of these factors may have contributed in varying degree to Mead's early interest in social psychology, it is doubtful whether that interest would have achieved fruition in a body of original theoretical work had he not begun to teach a course in the subject midway through his first decade at Chicago. He taught the course for the first time in the fall of 1900 and offered it regularly thereafter, in one version or another, throughout his career. From 1900 to 1905 the course was called contemporary social psychology, but in 1906 Mead simplified the title to social psychology. By the winter term of 1915 the course had begun to enjoy considerable popularity, as is indicated in one of Mead's letters to his son in January of that year: "I see Irene [Tufts] and Edith Cutting and Ed. Thomas four times a week among seventy others in Social Psychology. The course has not been properly worked [out]—

in other words I haven't worked it out. It is neither a graduate nor undergraduate course. I supposed that a prerequisite had been added this year so that such a horde would not invade the room, led I fear largely by its supposedly snap variety."[33] Beginning in the 1916–17 academic year, Mead solved this problem by listing his course as advanced social psychology and teaching it as a sequel to an introductory course on elementary social psychology. The latter course was taught for many years following 1919 by Professor Ellsworth Faris of the Chicago department of sociology. Not only did Mead's course, in its various forms, serve as a major stimulus and vehicle for the development of his social psychological theorizing, but it was also largely responsible for his widespread influence as a teacher at Chicago, an influence that reached well beyond the department of philosophy to students from such fields as education, psychology, and sociology.[34]

Chapter 4

The Development of Mead's Social Psychology

The least neglected facet of Mead's much neglected contribution to American thought has been his social psychology. Even here, however, interest has generally been restricted to certain portions of the posthumously published *Mind, Self and Society*. This volume, which is based primarily upon stenographic student notes taken in Mead's 1928 advanced social psychology course at the University of Chicago,[1] provides a readable account of the conclusions at which Mead had arrived in this field near the end of his career. But there is little in it that helps the reader trace the roots of Mead's social psychological work in the psychological functionalism of the early Chicago School or locate this work in the larger framework of his thought as a whole. For a fuller appreciation of Mead's contributions to the study of human social conduct we must look beyond *Mind, Self and Society* to selected portions of his other writings, particularly to the best of those periodical articles he wrote during the first half of his career at Chicago.

A careful examination of selected essays Mead published between 1900 and 1913, the years when he was working out his key social psychological ideas, confirms an observation John Dewey made in his prefatory remarks for the 1932 publication of Mead's *The Philosophy of the Present:* "When I first came to know Mr. Mead, well over forty years ago, the dominant problem in his mind concerned the nature of consciousness as personal and private. . . . I fancy that if one had a sufficiently consecutive knowledge of Mr. Mead's intellectual biography during the intervening years, one could discover how practically all his inquiries and problems developed out of his original haunting question."[2] Mead's struggle with this "original haunting question" led him to a growing emphasis upon the social dimensions of human conduct. And his consequent analysis of sociality as a dominant feature of conduct greatly enriched the organic model of action initially set forth by Dewey, thus providing the conceptual framework within which Mead's mature social psychology was to develop.

Mead's Early Functionalism

As Darnell Rucker has pointed out in his excellent study, *The Chicago Pragmatists,* Dewey and Mead were primarily responsible for the creation of the functionalist approach to psychology that constituted the basis for much that was distinctive in the philosophy of the Chicago School.[3] At the heart of their functionalism was a new organic concept of action, whose most celebrated articulation is to be found in Dewey's 1896 essay, "The Reflex Arc Concept in Psychology."[4] Since Mead's earliest published attempts to deal with the nature of human consciousness "as personal and private" involve extensive references to Dewey's essay, it is worthwhile to summarize its central points.

In this essay Mead's more famous colleague strongly criticized the stimulus-response model of action (the "reflex arc concept") as being based upon a serious conceptual confusion. The advocates of this model had failed to see that "stimulus and response are not distinctions of existence, but teleological distinctions, that is, distinctions of function, or part played, with reference to reaching or maintaining an end." Dewey argued persuasively that stimulus and response were to be understood as functional moments within an ongoing process of coordination, which "is more truly termed organic than reflex, because the motor response determines the stimulus just as truly as sensory stimulus determines movement." Dewey's analysis of the mutual adjustment involved in concrete action is well illustrated by the example of a child reaching for a flickering candle: in this reaching the act of vision must not only stimulate but also continue to control the movement of the child's arm. "The eye must be kept upon the candle if the arm is to do its work; let it wander and the arm takes up another task." The movement of the arm must, in turn, control the act of seeing; if it does not, the eye wanders and the reaching is without guidance. What most requires emphasis here is that the coordinated acts of seeing and reaching continually exchange functional roles within the complex act of which they are phases. What is at one moment a guided response may at the next moment become a guiding stimulus. Furthermore, not only does the stimulus guide the response, but the response shapes the quality of what is experienced. As Dewey put it, the response is not simply *to* the stimulus; it is *into* it. The response does not merely replace the sensory content of the stimulus with another sort of experience; rather it mediates, transforms, enlarges, or interprets that initial content in terms of its significance for ongoing conduct. When a child responds to the act of seeing a flickering candle, the mere seeing is transformed into, for example, a seeing-of-a-light-that-means-pain-when-contact-occurs.[5]

As long as such conduct proceeds smoothly, Dewey contended, it involves no conscious distinction of stimulus and response. But suppose that the child is torn between a tendency to grasp the candle and a tendency to avoid it as a possible source of pain. In this type of situation doubt as to the proper completion of the act gives rise to an analysis whose purpose is to resolve the inhibiting conflict. "The initiated activities of reaching, . . . inhibited by the conflict in the coordination, turn round, as it were, upon the seeing, and hold it from passing over into further act until its quality is determined. Just here the act as objective stimulus becomes transformed into sensation as possible, as conscious, stimulus. Just here also, motion as conscious response emerges." Thus we see that the reflective isolation of stimulus and response as components of action has a particular genesis and function. It is the failure to note this genesis and function, Dewey held, that lies behind the mechanical conjunction of stimulus and response characteristic of the reflex arc model of action.[6]

Dewey concluded this now classical statement of psychological functionalism with the observation that the real significance of the organic conception of action would be seen only in its application to fundamental problems of psychology and philosophy. And it was just such application that Mead undertook in two essays published in 1900 and 1903. The first of these essays, "Suggestions Toward a Theory of the Philosophical Disciplines," was an ambitious neo-Hegelian attempt to characterize the respective provinces of metaphysics, psychology, deductive and inductive logics, ethics, aesthetics, and the general theory of logic in terms of the "dialectic within the act" as organically understood. The second essay, "The Definition of the Psychical," was less ambitious in scope, although more obscure in development; here Mead narrowed his focus to the discipline of psychology, seeking to delineate more fully its distinctive subject matter as a phase of "psychical consciousness" or "subjectivity" within conduct. It is the considerable space both essays devote to this latter topic that makes them important for the present purpose.

In "Suggestions Toward a Theory of the Philosophical Disciplines," Mead presented his discussion of subjectivity as an extension of Dewey's remarks concerning the genesis and function of our awareness of sensation as a distinct element in experience: "Professor Dewey maintains in his discussion of the Reflex Arc that the sensation appears always in consciousness as a problem; that attention could not be centered upon a so-called element of consciousness unless the individual were abstracting from the former meaning of the object, and in his effort to reach a new meaning had fixed this feature of the former object as a problem to be solved" (sw 6).[7] Holding with Dewey and William James that the content or meaning of the objects we experience is derived from their roles in our conduct, Mead pointed out that as long as action with respect to objects proceeds without a hitch, their meanings typically remain unquestioned. But when an object calls out conflicting reactions, its content is to that extent ambiguous and in need of examination. In such situations "our conscious activity finds itself unable to pass into an objective world on account of the clash between different tendencies to action," and "we are thrown back upon an analysis of these spontaneous acts and therefore upon the objects which get their content from them" (sw 8). Our experience takes a subjective turn, Mead suggested, when such conflict or ambiguity cannot be adequately resolved by a simple reshuffling of already existing meanings. For in these cases the conscious solution of our problem requires an abandonment of old universals and a quest for new meanings or objects to which we can more successfully relate. During the period when this quest is underway, our attention must turn from the temporarily impoverished world of objects to the flux of immediate and personal consciousness. Subjectivity thus enters conduct as "a position midway between the old universals, whose validity is abandoned, and the new universal, which has not yet appeared" (sw 12).

Subjective or psychical consciousness takes as its starting point whatever unproblematic meanings can be abstracted from the conflicting elements of the problem to be solved. For instance, the child who hesitates when faced by the flickering candle has before him "neither the object which burned nor yet the plaything," for both of these meanings are in question. But he does have "something behind each and true of each—a bright moving object we will say" (sw 13). This latter meaning is objective (i.e., it is part of the world of unproblematic objects) but not sufficient by itself to give direction to the conduct that has been inhibited. The task of subjectivity or the psychical phase of experience is to take conduct beyond this stage of abstraction to a stage of synthesis in which the abstracted meanings find their places in a reconstructed world of objects. This is accomplished by giving free play to conflicting tendencies to respond, tendencies that must for the time being be regarded merely as elements peculiar to the immediate consciousness of the individual attempting to solve the problem at hand. It is this "constructive power proportional to the freedom with which the forces abstracted from their customary objects can be combined with each other into a new whole . . . that comes nearer answering to what we term genius than anything else" (sw 20). The problem is solved to the extent that these tendencies find a harmonious expression in terms of new objective meanings. When a solution is found, the subjective phase of conduct has done its work, and attention is once again focused on a realm of unproblematic objects.

Mead thus proposed that we construe the distinction between subjective and objective elements of experience as functional, rather than metaphysical. The marks of the subjective or psychical state are to be understood in terms of "their position in the act, the when and the how of their appearance" rather than as characteristics of an entity that exists independently of conduct (sw 16). Failure to appreciate the functional nature of subjectivity, Mead maintained, has characteristically led either to an untenable psychophysical parallelism or to a kind of idealism in which all experience is reduced to states of individual consciousness. In either case, the mistake lies in the attempt to "objectify the psychical state, and deprive it of the very elements that have rendered it psychical" (sw 16).

Mead continued his attack on traditional conceptions of subjectivity and also further articulated his own view in "The Definition of the Psychical." In the constructive portion of this essay, he again took as his point of departure a suggestion attributable to Dewey: that when an object loses its validity because of a conflict in our activity, it also loses its form and organization. According to this view, the meanings abandoned in such cases are not simply transferred intact to the subjective realm. Rather, the psychical character of the situation is due precisely to the disintegration of the problematic objects and the whole effort of the individual toward reconstructing them (SW 40–42). In what form then, Mead asked, do the meanings or objects that have become problematic enter into psychical consciousness? He found the clue to his answer in the same source that had provided Dewey with much of his inspiration, James's *The Principles of Psychology*. No better description of psychical consciousness can be found, Mead suggested, than that supplied by James in his famous chapter on "The Stream of Consciousness." For all of the characteristics James attributes to the stream of consciousness are unmistakably present in the psychical phase of problem-solving:

> The kaleidoscopic flash of suggestion, and intrusion of the inapt, the unceasing flow of odds and ends of possible objects that will not fit, together with the continuous collision with the hard, unshakable objective conditions of the problem, the transitive feelings of effort and anticipation when we feel that we are on the right track and substantive points of rest, as the idea becomes definite, the welcoming and rejecting, especially the identification of the meaning of the whole idea with the different steps in its coming to consciousness—there are none of these that are not almost oppressively present on the surface of consciousness during just the periods which Dewey describes as those of disintegration and reconstitution of the stimulus—the object. (SW 42–43)

Psychical consciousness as here described is clearly concerned with the immediate, with that which is peculiar to the individual and a moment of his existence. It is just these characteristics, Mead maintained, that enable it to perform its functional role in the reconstruction of conduct (SW 36). For the task of subjective consciousness is to introduce novelty into a situation in which the old has broken down, and this can be accomplished only by a consciousness that is not essentially tied to the world of accepted meanings and objects. Inspection of the old world can supply us with data, with conditions for the solution of the problem that has arisen, but it cannot be expected to supply us with the new meanings required for the reconstruction of that world. New meanings must arise from the reflecting individual's immediate awareness of his own activities and shifting attention as he seeks to harmonize the habitual tendencies that have come into conflict within his conduct (sw 52, 45). It is here "in the construction of the hypotheses of the new world, that the individual qua individual has his functional expression or rather is that function" (sw 52).

Introduction of "I" and "Me"

Mead argued in "The Definition of the Psychical" not only for the functional importance of personal and private consciousness as the locus of cognitive reconstruction but also for the suggestion that the human individual qua individual could be defined in terms of this reconstructive function. But herein lies a problem that Mead himself was quick to see. The human individual or self as ordinarily construed is an object, and as such it belongs to the world that it is the task of subjectivity to reconstruct. To the extent that the self as object is not infected with the problem at hand it may, of course, enter into the statement of the conditions to be met by any possible solution of that problem, but it cannot be expected to provide that solution (sw 53). How then can it be said that the task of reconstruction is performed by the human individual?

It was in his attempt to deal with this problem that Mead first employed the terms "I" and "me" to refer to the self functioning as subject and the self functioning as object, respectively. These terms had been given popular currency by James in a chapter of his *The Principles of Psychology* that dealt with "The Consciousness of Self," and Mead borrowed them for his own purposes. In speaking of an "I" and a "me" Mead sought to make the point that, according to the functionalist view, the human individual or self may enter into conduct in two distinguishable senses. On the one hand, the self may enter into conduct as a meaningful stimulus for the intelligent control of action. In this case the self functions as an object; this is what Mead had in mind when he spoke of the "me." The "me" is thus a *presentation* that performs a mediating role within an ongoing process of experience or action (sw 53–54). On the other hand, as Mead's discussion of subjectivity makes clear, the human individual may also enter into conduct as an agent of reconstruction. Here the immediate and direct experience of the individual qua individual functions as a source from which spring suggestions for new ways of ordering the process of conduct when habitual actions and meanings have become problematic. The self functioning in this latter sense is what Mead meant by the "I": it is "the self in the disintegration and reconstruction of its universe, the self functioning, the point of immediacy that must exist within a mediate process" (SW 53–54).

This distinction does not, however, appear to provide a wholly adequate solution to the problem that was its occasion. For if the objective status of the "me" renders it an unacceptable candidate for the functional role of reconstructor, then a similar reservation must apply to the qualifications of the "human individual" with whom Mead wished to link psychical consciousness. More generally, it would seem that any attempt to identify psychical consciousness as belonging to a finite self must inevitably tie that consciousness to an item in the world of experienced objects. Thus Mead's introduction of the term "I" in this context appears to be either a misleading use of the personal pronoun to refer to immediately felt action (as opposed to objects that may arise within it) or a device for bringing in through the back door an implicit reference to the same object self he has thrown out the front. The former interpretation seems most consistent with Mead's descriptions of subjectivity and with his reference to the subject self as "the act that makes use of all the data that reflection can present, but uses them merely as the conditions of a new world that cannot possibly be foretold from them" (SW 54). Unhappily, "The Definition of the Psychical" leaves much room for doubt concerning Mead's precise view on this matter. Perhaps this is one of the reasons he was to refer to this essay some years later as one in which his position had been developed "somewhat obscurely and ineffectually, I am afraid" (SW 106).

Perceptual Objects and the Social Genesis of Consciousness

While the two essays we have considered emphasize the self functioning as subject, Mead's subsequent early publications show a dominant concern with the self as object. His initial inquiries into the reconstructive role of subjectivity seem to have led to a greater interest in the functional nature of those objects to which subjectivity stands in contrast. And this latter interest came, in turn, to be focused in his social psychological work upon questions concerning the social and functional nature of the object self.

The first step in this line of development is seen in Mead's contributions to the functionalist view of perceptual objects in his 1907 essay,

"Concerning Animal Perception." Here, as in his earlier articles, he carried on the articulation of the organic model of action advocated by Dewey in 1896. But now Mead turned his constructive efforts to the task of locating human perceptual consciousness of physical objects within conduct and distinguishing it from so-called animal perception. Two of the basic ingredients of perceptual consciousness, he pointed out, are readily found in animal conduct. These are the two classes of sensory experiences involving, respectively, the "distance" sense organs (e.g., the visual, olfactory, and auditory organs) and those of "contact" (e.g., touch, taste). But although animal behavior contains a coordination of these two types of experiences, Mead was inclined to doubt that it involved any perceptual consciousness of physical things as these are encountered in human experience. The grounds for this doubt are revealed in his examination of the prerequisites for the appearance of physical objects within the act.

Physical objects are to be understood as presentations arising through a particular kind of mediation within conduct. More specifically, they take shape within conduct only insofar as the contact experience that is likely to be encountered in responding to a particular distance stimulus is presented along with that stimulus (sw 79). Mead expressed this point best when he said several years later (in the introductory paragraphs of "The Mechanism of Social Consciousness") that the physical object is "a collapsed act" in which immediate sensuous content is merged with imagery drawn from previous responses to similar stimuli (sw 134). Now the presentation of such objects can take place only if the appropriate elements within experience are consciously isolated and the relational connections between them attended to. But Mead found no convincing evidence that nonhuman animals possess the capacities required to accomplish these tasks. Consequently, he believed it likely that animal conduct proceeds without any awareness of perceptual relations: its modification presumably takes place in the unconscious manner typical of certain kinds of human learning—for instance, the development of finer sensory discrimination and related muscular adjustments involved in improving one's tennis game through practice (sw 74).

Furthermore, Mead held that if physical objects are to appear within the field of stimulation, then that field must be organized around enduring substrates with which varying sensory qualities can be associated. The experiential basis for such substrates, he suggested, had been correctly located by G. F. Stout in what the latter termed "manipulation," the actual contact experience or handling to which distance experience characteristically leads (SW 77). "Our perception of physical objects always refers color, sound, odor, to a possibly handled substrate," which is reflected in the familiar philosophical distinction between primary and secondary qualities (SW 78). Here again humans have a clear advantage over nonhuman animals in that their hands provide them with a wealth of manipulatory contents that can be isolated from the culminations of their activities. In nonhuman animals, however, "the organs of manipulation are not as well adapted in form and function for manipulation itself, and, in the second place, the contact experiences of lower animals are, to a large extent determined, not by the process of manipulation, but are so immediately a part of eating, fighting, repose, etc., that it is hard to believe that a consciousness of a 'thing' can be segregated from these instinctive activities" (SW 79).

These early suggestions outlining a functional view of perceptual objects were to be greatly elaborated in Mead's later philosophical writings. Indeed, well over 150 pages of the posthumously published *The Philosophy of the Act* and almost half of *The Philosophy of the Present* are devoted to the further working out of this view, especially with reference to the nest of epistemological and ontological problems raised by the impact upon philosophy of the twentieth-century revolution in physics. But of more immediate interest for our present purpose is Mead's extension of his earlier discussion, in a series of articles published between 1909 and 1913, to include the *social* dimension of perceptual consciousness. An examination of these articles discloses the sources of several of his most important social-psychological ideas and reveals the manner in which he employed these to greatly enrich the functionalist understanding of human conduct and consciousness.

Beginning with "Social Psychology as a Counterpart to Physiological Psychology" (1909), Mead's thought is less dependent upon Dewey's work than had previously been the case. Mead continued to maintain the functionalist orientation of Dewey's paper on the reflex arc concept, but he now came to believe that an adequate functionalism had to emphasize not only the organic nature of human conduct but also its fundamentally social character. Whereas his earlier discussions had sought to clarify the manner in which perceptual objects and subjective consciousness function in the control and reconstruction of conduct, his emphasis now fell upon the objective social conditions that make these developments within conduct possible. He moved, in short, toward a genetic and increasingly social functionalism.

Following the lead of such thinkers as William McDougall, Josiah Royce, James Mark Baldwin, and Charles Horton Cooley, he began to maintain that human conduct was shaped from the outset by social instincts—in which the term "social instinct" meant "a well defined tendency to act under the stimulation of another individual of the same species" (sw 98).[8] Mead found in this idea, first, an important suggestion bearing upon his discussion of perceptual objects. An adequate recognition of the social dimension of human action, he now realized, would allow one to enlarge that discussion by pointing out how social objects, particularly human selves, arise within the process of conduct. If objects are to be functionally understood as meaningful presentations that guide action, and if human action is characteristically social, then clearly it becomes reasonable to speak of selves as social objects. The content of such objects is implicit in those social instincts that sensitize us to social stimuli; their structure and meaning are implicit in the organized responses we make to these social stimuli. "The implication of an organized group of social instincts is the implicit presence in undeveloped human consciousness of both the matter and form of a social object" (sw 98).

But how do the social objects that are "implicit" in our organized social instincts become explicit elements of consciousness? The problem here, as Mead saw it, was to explain in terms of a functional conception of the social act how human individuals might come to analyze the relations within their social experience and thereby grasp the meaning of what they and others were doing. Baldwin and Royce had earlier suggested that the solution to this problem was to be found in instinctive human tendencies to imitate and then oppose the responses of others. Through such imitation and opposition, individuals come to differentiate between self and other, thus making it possible for them to grasp the social meaning of their own conduct. Mead, however, found this theory implausible. The idea of an imitative instinct, he pointed out, does not fit well with the observed nature of social conduct: "The important character of social organization of conduct or behavior through instincts is not that one form in a social group does what the others do, but that the conduct of one form is a stimulus to another to a certain act, and that this act again becomes a stimulus at first to a certain reaction, and so on in ceaseless interaction" (sw

101). Moreover, if we mean by "imitation" what is usually meant by that term, then this theory puts the cart before the horse. It attempts to account for the rise of human consciousness by means of a mechanism that itself presupposes such consciousness. "Imitation becomes comprehensible when there is a consciousness of other selves, and not before" (SW 100). The notion of imitation as it has been employed in social psychology, Mead concluded, must be replaced by a fully developed "theory of social stimulation and response and of the social situations which these stimulations and responses create" (SW 101). Baldwin and Royce were correct in arguing that mature human consciousness is of social origin, but they erred in giving undue emphasis to those social situations in which one individual does what others are doing. The social foundations of consciousness are rather to be found in conduct where the action of one individual calls out an appropriate (and usually dissimilar) response in another individual, and where this response becomes, in turn, a social stimulus to the first individual.

Mead's own social psychological theory concerning the genesis of consciousness was only briefly sketched in his 1909 article, but he sought to supply the needed details almost immediately in three subsequent essays: "What Social Objects Must Psychology Presuppose?" (1910), "Social Consciousness and the Consciousness of Meaning" (1910), and "The Mechanism of Social Consciousness" (1912). The central concept of the theory developed in these essays was that of "gesture," which had first been spelled out in Wilhelm Wundt's *Völkerpsychologie*. The gesture, as Mead understood it, is a preparatory stage of social response—a bracing for movement or an overflowing of nervous excitement that might reinforce the agent and indirectly prepare one for action. Examples include changes of posture and facial expression, flushing of the skin, audible changes in the rhythm of breathing, and certain vocal outbursts (SW 110, 123). These early indications of incipient conduct acquire their status as gestures through their functional role in social interaction, for they quite naturally come to serve as stimuli calling out anticipatory responses from the other individuals involved in the social act. The initial phases of these latter responses serve as gestures that may call out a modified social response from the first individual, and so on. In this manner there is set up a "conversation of gesture," a "field of palaver" consisting of "truncated acts" (SW 109, 124). Unlike the imitative conduct emphasized by Baldwin and Royce, such conversations of gesture presuppose no consciousness of

meaning or of social objects. Consider, for instance, the familiar pre-
liminaries of a dog fight. Here is a palaver of mutual bristling, growling,
pacing, and maneuvering for position. The two animals appear to com-
municate quite effectively, yet it is highly doubtful that either has any
consciousness of self or is able to assess the significance of its own
actions.

The importance Mead attributed to the conversation of gesture as
a social condition for the emergence of human consciousness derives
from his Jamesian view regarding the behavioral basis of meaning, a
view he shared with such thinkers as Royce, Dewey, and James Rowland Angell (sw 111). The contents of meanings in our consciousness of
objects, he held, are supplied by our consciousness of our own "generalized habitual responses." "These contents are the consciousness of
attitudes, of muscular tensions and the feels of readiness to act in the
presence of certain stimulations" (sw 129). But if we are to appropriate
these contents in a genuine consciousness of meaning, we must isolate
them from the stimuli that call them forth and then grasp the relation
between these two elements of experience. Only in this manner is it
possible to understand the one as meaning the other. The importance of
the conversation of gesture, Mead argued, is that apart from this type of
conduct there is no functional basis for such an analysis within the act:
"There is nothing in the economy of the act itself which tends to bring
these contents above the threshold, nor distinguishes them as separable
elements in a process of relation, such as is implied in the consciousness
of meaning" (sw 129). Only in the conversation of gesture do we find
a situation in which attention is naturally directed toward one's own
attitudes; here alone do we find conduct in which "the very attention
given to stimulation, may throw one's attention back upon the attitude he will assume toward the challenging attitude of another, since
this attitude will change the stimulation." Moreover, the conflicting
acts and consequent inhibitions inherent in the conversation of gesture
are ideally suited to bring about within the act the continual analysis
of stimuli from which consciousness of relation may eventually arise
(sw 131).

The apparent failure of the conversation of gesture to produce consciousness in nonhuman animals, Mead suggested, can be traced in
part to the relatively low level of inhibition found in their behavior.
The higher level of inhibition present in human conduct is "an essential phase of voluntary attention" and leads to an abundance of gesture

not found in other animals (sw 110). Furthermore, the nonhuman conversation of gesture lacks the diversity of *vocal* gesture to be found in even the most primitive human social interaction. Such vocal gestures, which may have originated in the sudden changes of breathing and circulation rhythms associated with preparation for violent action, have come to "elaborate and immensely complicate" the human conversation of gesture (sw 136). The vocal gesture, moreover, is of particular importance in the development of consciousness because it, more than any other kind of gesture, presents to its author the same stimulus content as it presents to the other individuals involved in the social act. It thus provides an ideal mechanism through which the individual can become conscious of his own tendencies to respond (sw 137).

It should be noted here that Mead had little to say concerning the physical basis of the consciousness whose development he sought to describe. The determination of the physiological conditions necessary for the rise of consciousness, he held, is a task for physiological psychology. As the title of an earlier essay ("Social Psychology as a Counterpart to Physiological Psychology") suggests, he viewed his own social psychological work as complementing the physiological approach by providing an account of the equally important social conditions for the genesis of consciousness. It was a cause of considerable dismay to Mead that many psychologists of his day acknowledged the physical foundation of consciousness but were apparently oblivious to its social basis. They spoke of introspective self-consciousness as if it were the source of all experience, and they maintained that one could only hypothesize concerning the existence of selves other than the one present to introspection. A proper understanding of the role played by the conversation of gesture in the genesis of consciousness, Mead argued, reveals how profoundly mistaken this kind of psychology is. For from the social psychological standpoint introspective consciousness is a relative latecomer to the field of experience. It is a subjective phase of human conduct ("subjective" in the functional sense explained previously) that is preceded and continually conditioned by experience in an objective world of social objects (sw 112).

The first steps in the child's development of introspective self-consciousness, Mead pointed out, are to be found in his instinctive social responses to the gestures of those about him. Gradually, through the conversation of gesture, the child comes to attend to his own responses and begins to merge the imagery of past responses with the stimulus content provided by the gestures of others. It is through the merging of these two components that the child "builds up the social objects that form the most important part of his environment" (sw 137). The social consciousness of other selves achieved in this manner precedes consciousness of the self that is analyzed in introspection. The self of introspective consciousness, the "me," is constituted by the merging of imagery drawn from the remembered responses of others with the gestures by which the child stimulates himself. But this merging takes place only after other selves have arisen as social objects in the child's environment. The child acquires his consciousness of himself as object by transferring the form of these earlier social objects to his inner experience (sw 139). The "me" of introspection is thus "an importation from the field of social objects into an amorphous, unorganized field of what we call inner experience. Through the organization of this object, the self, this material is itself organized and brought under the control of the individual in the form of so-called consciousness" (sw 140). The child's social consciousness of other selves antedates even his consciousness of physical objects. Or, more accurately, his experience becomes reflective—becomes perceptual in the fullest sense—in the recognition of selves, and only gradually does he arrive at a reflective experience of things that are purely physical (sw 112–13). The physical form of the "me," like its social structure, is an importation from the child's environment. The form of the physical object is given first in things other than his physical self. "When he has synthesized his various bodily parts with the organic sensations and affective experiences, it will be upon the model of objects about him" (sw 138).

The Social Self

Having thus traced the social genesis of introspective self-consciousness, Mead returned in the concluding paragraphs of "The Mechanism of Social Consciousness" and in "The Social Self" (1913) to a topic he had briefly discussed ten years earlier: his functional understanding of the sense in which the self is both subject and object. A comparison of these two discussions is worthwhile not only for what it reveals about the development of Mead's thought but also for the light it throws on his subsequent employment of the terms "I" and "me."

Recall that Mead's initial emphasis upon the distinction between a subject and object self was dictated by his functionalist treatment of psychical consciousness. In the context of that early discussion, the "me" was taken to be a meaningful object serving to guide ongoing conduct, while the "I" was identified with the immediate flow of experience as distinguished from the objects that ordinarily control it. The "I" becomes available to introspective consciousness, Mead held, only in the presence of a situation in which old objects have broken down and new ones adequate to guide conduct have not yet appeared; here the "I" takes the form of an immediately experienced interplay of conflicting suggestions, from which arise novel meanings allowing for the reconstruction of problematic elements in the world of objects.

Such, in outline, was Mead's position in 1903. In the essays of 1912 and 1913 his approach to these matters had modified in accordance with the genetic and social orientation he had increasingly adopted in the intervening years. There is no indication that he had changed his earlier view of the reconstructive function of psychical consciousness, but his emphasis now fell primarily upon its social origin and structure. Instead of involving merely an interplay of conflicting suggestions, inner consciousness is said to possess a dramatic or dialogic structure imported from the individual's social experience. The "I" and the "me" are understood in terms of their functional roles within this process.

The "me," as has been remarked previously, becomes an object of consciousness through a development of the conversation of gestures. The crucial mechanism is the individual's capacity to respond to his own gestures. In thus responding, an individual tends to bring to bear upon his conduct memory images of responses made by others to similar gestures. These images are merged with the stimulus content of the gesture to constitute the "me" as a social object (sw 140, 146). This object self remains, as in Mead's earliest essays, a presentation within conduct; but its functional role is now understood in terms of the thoroughgoing sociality of human conduct. The "I," on the other hand, is the response the individual makes to the "me." Or, better, it is the immediate act within which the "me" functions as a meaningful presentation. This identification of the "I" is the same as that somewhat dimly articulated in Mead's 1903 essay, "The Definition of the Psychical," but in his essays of 1912 and 1913 Mead avoided any suggestion that the "I" could appear in immediate awareness. Rather, he held that the "I" always remains "behind the scenes" (sw 141); it is "a presupposition, but never a presentation of conscious experience" (sw

142). The elusiveness of the "I" is to be explained by the fact that "we can be conscious of our acts only through the sensory processes set up after the act has begun" (sw 143). Our acts or responses can, of course, become presentations within a subsequent act, but they are then parts of a "me" and no longer an "I."

This last point is amplified by Mead's attempt, in "The Social Self," to do justice to the full complexity of the self as presented in introspective consciousness. Analysis of such consciousness, he pointed out, does reveal moments in which we are aware of the self as both subject and object. "To be concrete, one remembers asking how he could undertake to do this, that, or the other, chiding himself for his shortcomings or pluming himself upon his achievements" (sw 142). But the subject self thus presented is not the "I." It is rather another "me" standing alongside of, evaluating or making suggestions to, the first "me." Just as one can respond to one's own actions with respect to another self and thereby be presented with a "me" standing over against that self, so one can respond to one's action with respect to the "me" and thereby be presented with a second "me" standing over against the first. Confusion of this second "me" or reflective self with the "I" is what leads to the mistaken assumption that one can be directly conscious of oneself as acting and acted upon (sw 145).

Since we tend to respond to ourselves in the roles of others in the social environment, sometimes even assuming their characteristic intonations and facial expressions, both the structure of inner consciousness and the content of the "me's" there presented are largely importations from objective social experience. In the young child such inner consciousness is loosely organized and quite personal; it involves an obviously social interplay between the remembered "me" who acts and the response of an "accompanying chorus" of others who figure prominently in the child's social experience. Later this drama becomes more abstract, and we have in its place an inner process of symbolic thought. "The features and intonations of the *dramatis personae* fade out and the emphasis falls upon the meaning of inner speech, the imagery becomes merely the barely necessary cues" (sw 147).

We may note in this connection that Mead's view concerning the relation of this dialogic structure of inner consciousness to the "I" and "me" is easily misunderstood. Consider, for instance, the problems of interpretation posed by the following typical passage: "The self-conscious, actual self in social intercourse is the objective 'me' or 'me's' with the process of response continually going on and implying a fictitious 'I' always out of sight of himself" (sw 141).[9] Now it is natural, perhaps, to think of this as meaning that the "I" first responds to the "me," then the "me" responds to the "I," and so on. But this line of interpretation must surely be incorrect. For Mead's functional definitions of the "I" and "me" rule out this kind of interaction by placing the two on different ontological levels. We may, consistent with Mead's view, speak of the "me" as an agent in relation to other *objects;* but in relation to the "I" it can be no more than a presentation. This being the case, the correct interpretation of Mead's meaning here must be as follows: the "I" of one moment functions as a gesture calling out the "I" of the next moment, which, in turn, functions as a gesture for the "I" of a succeeding moment, and so on. Any or all of these "I's" may carry memory images of previous social responses, these images merging with the immediate stimulus content of the gesture to yield a corresponding presentation of a "me." And since the memory images involved in different acts may be as various as the social roles we play (sw 146), we may have a plurality of "me's."

Because Mead was primarily concerned with the social character of inner consciousness in his essays of 1912–13, he did not emphasize the factor of novelty as he had done in "The Definition of the Psychical." But this omission was not indicative of any loss of interest in that topic, for the claim that novel elements are continually emerging within conduct appears again and again in his later works. Moreover, in the 1928 lectures, later published as *Mind, Self and Society*, he attributes the introduction of novelty in human conduct to the "I," just as he had in 1903. This attribution is perfectly consistent with the interpretation of the "I" and "me" sketched above. To say, as Mead does in his 1928 lectures, that the "I" is responsible for the fact that "we are never fully aware of what we are, . . . we surprise ourselves by our own action"[10] is simply another way of making the point that the living act is always something more than the presentations that arise within it.[11]

Unfortunately, the lectures recorded in *Mind, Self and Society* do not provide any clear discussion of the functionalist conception of conduct that underlies the whole of Mead's thought. And, consequently, his treatment of the "I" in this context seems unduly arbitrary and mysterious. Indeed, at least one able critic has gone so far as to argue that in these lectures Mead employed the "I" primarily as a residual category for a group of "heterogeneous phenomena" that could not conveniently be explained in terms of the social structure attributed to the "me." [12] But if my reading of Mead's early essays is correct, his later use of the terms "I" and "me" is a consistent outgrowth of his early functionalism, and, viewed in this light, the phenomena he identifies with the "I" are not at all "heterogeneous."

Concluding Remarks

By the time he published "The Social Self" in 1913, Mead's struggles with that "original haunting question" of which Dewey spoke had led him to almost all the major ideas of his mature social psychology. His later essays and lectures extend and refine these ideas in important ways, but they involve no significant departure from the genetic and social functionalism developed in the essays just examined. That this continuity of Mead's social psychological work has been so often overlooked is due in part to his tendency in later years to refer to his position as a form of behaviorism. Mead's thought was indeed always concerned with conduct or behavior, but never in quite the sense now suggested by the term behaviorism. Rather, his work remained rooted in that organic model of conduct he had embraced in the early years of the Chicago School. It is their testimony to this fact that makes his publications of 1900–1913 valuable documents for any student of Mead's social psychology.

Chapter 5

Behaviorism and Mead's Mature Social Psychology

In the opening section of *Mind, Self and Society,* [1] Mead declares his intention to approach the field of social psychology "from a behaviorist point of view." He hastens to tell his audience, however, that the sort of behaviorism he wishes to espouse is by no means identical with that popularized by John B. Watson: "The behaviorism which we shall make use of is more adequate than that of which Watson makes use. Behaviorism in this wider sense is simply an approach to the study of the experience of the individual from the point of view of his conduct, particularly, but not exclusively, the conduct as it is observable by others" (MSS 2). Mead thus endorses behaviorism insofar as it emphasizes the need to study overt behavior, but he rejects Watson's claim that psychology should make no reference to consciousness, mental states, or any "inner" experience that is not publicly observable. Watson's approach to subjective or private elements in experience, Mead observes, is reminiscent of the strategy adopted by the Queen of Hearts in *Alice in Wonderland:* "Off with their heads!" (MSS 2–3). Instead of simply ignoring the existence of these elements of experience, Mead wants to understand them by locating them within the conduct of the individual and by relating their structure to the larger social process of behavior in which the individual is typically involved. His own approach, he says, "is behavioristic, but unlike Watsonian behaviorism it recognizes the parts of the act which do not come to external observation, and it emphasizes the act of the human individual in its natural social situation" (MSS 8).

Such passages make it obvious that Mead's mature social psychological approach to human conduct must be distinguished from that of classical behaviorism. Nevertheless, students of Mead's social psychology who read only *Mind, Self and Society* are likely to have a seriously inadequate conception of what he had in mind when he used the term "behaviorism" to characterize his position in the 1928 lectures upon which this volume is based. For such readers will be wholly unaware of the relationship between these lectures and the psychological functionalism Mead had endorsed during the early years of his career at the University of Chicago. An examination of this relationship reveals that when Mead used the term "behaviorism" in 1928 he was doing little more than giving a new name to a functionalist viewpoint whose foundations were laid well before Watson came upon the scene with his "behaviorist manifesto" of 1913. My aim here is thus to clarify the nature of Mead's so-called behaviorism by exhibiting those of its conceptual foundations that are assumed but not made fully explicit in his mature social psychological lectures and writings.

Mead and Psychological Functionalism at Chicago

Many of Mead's most important social psychological ideas can be found in journal articles he published in the years leading up to 1913. Hence, it can hardly be claimed that these ideas depend in any way upon the orientation that Watson introduced into the mainstream of American psychology with his 1913 essay "Psychology as the Behaviorist Views It."[2] Rather, the root ideas of Mead's social psychology should be viewed as creative elaborations of the organic conception of conduct proposed by John Dewey in his 1896 essay "The Reflex Arc Concept in Psychology."

Dewey's concerns in that essay, it is important to note, were conceptual rather than methodological. He offered no recommendations concerning what data psychology should seek or how it ought to obtain them if it were to be considered scientific; rather, he was recommending a new conceptual framework in terms of which psychological data (whether "mentalistic" or "physicalistic") were to be interpreted. There was no attempt here to restrict the scope of psychological inquiry either to consciousness or to overt behavior. Both consciousness and overt behavior were proper subject matters for psychology, but both were to be understood functionally in accordance with the organic conception of conduct. In short, the threat to psychology that Dewey sought to allay was not the specter of methodological subjectivism; it was the ghost of a body-mind dualism that lingered on and threatened to impede a truly unified understanding of psychological phenomena.

In this respect Dewey's essay was entirely representative of the functionalist school of psychology that grew up around him, Mead, and James Rowland Angell at the University of Chicago in the years following 1894. These functionalists, as Edna Heidbreder has pointed out, were always more interested in conceptual reform than in any attempt to restrict the subject matter of psychology on methodological grounds.[3] In particular, they did not expend much intellectual energy on the question of whether consciousness or overt behavior or both together constituted the legitimate subject matter of psychology. "That question did not become an issue in American psychology until the rise of classical behaviorism; and both before and after that momentous event, the main concern of the functionalists lay elsewhere. It lay in treating psychological processes as functions."[4] When Angell, for instance, criticized psychological structuralism in his 1907 essay, "The Province of Functional Psychology," it was not because he rejected the structuralists' attempt to study elements of consciousness through the method of controlled introspection. Indeed, Angell indicated that he found "extremely useful the analysis of mental life into its elementary forms" and was inclined to "regard much of the actual work of my structuralist friends with highest respect and confidence." What Angell did object to, however, was the structuralists' attempt to describe the *contents* of consciousness in isolation from any consideration of the *operations* or *functioning* of consciousness under actual life conditions.[5]

"All of us in the Chicago group," Angell said later in a statement summarizing his involvement in the development of psychological functionalism, "had been deeply influenced in coming to the view above presented [functionalism] by ideas which presently were embodied in a brilliant paper which Dewey published at about that time on the reflex arc concept."[6] Now if this statement is accurate in Angell's case, it applies with even more force to the thought of Mead. For Mead's social psychological writings are permeated with Dewey's concern about overcoming mind-body dualism and psychophysical parallelism. Moreover, all of Mead's contributions to this enterprise are grounded in the organic model of conduct outlined in Dewey's 1896 essay. This grounding, as has been shown, is obvious in some of Mead's earliest publications. In both "Suggestions Toward a Theory of the Philosophical Disciplines" (1900) and "The Definition of the Psychical" (1903), for instance, Mead explicitly acknowledges Dewey's essay as the inspiration for his own attempts to formulate a functional treatment of reflective consciousness (or "psychical experience," as he often calls it). The same grounding is present, but less explicitly so, in the 1928 lectures of *Mind, Self and Society*. Mead had by this time greatly enriched Dewey's initial model by expanding it to include the social dimensions of conduct. And it is his emphasis upon these social dimensions of the act that allows him to give a genetic and functional account of mind that far surpasses his original efforts to deal with the problem of the psychical. The definition of the social act that Mead here sets forth readily reveals the influence of Dewey. "The social act," Mead tells us, "is not explained by building it up out of stimulus plus response; it must be taken as a dynamic whole—as something going on—no part of which can be considered or understood by itself—a complex organic process implied by each individual stimulus and response involved in it" (MSS 7).

Mead's Alleged Rejection of Functionalism

Given the passages quoted so far in this chapter, one might well conclude that Mead saw no fundamental opposition between Dewey's brand of functionalism and a broadly conceived behaviorism. And this conclusion is essentially correct. But it is well to note that some commentators either claim or imply that by 1928 Mead had rejected his earlier functionalism in favor of behaviorism. Andrew J. Reck, for instance, in his introduction to Mead's *Selected Writings* views Mead's development in this way: "Outgrowing exclusively physiological psychology and also, in due time, functional psychology, Mead arrived at a position which is known as social behaviorism."[7] And David Miller claims that in the years following 1905, Mead "no longer applied the term 'functionalism' to his theory, but emphasized that it was a behavioristic theory and more specifically a social behaviorism. This he did for the reason that the earlier functional psychology did not emphasize sufficiently either the social character of behavior or the behavioral character of mind and reflective thinking."[8] Now, as a matter of fact, Mead did not himself use the term "social behaviorism" in any of his writings; nor does the term appear in any of the extant student notes based upon his course lectures on social psychology. That label was coined by Charles W. Morris, who engaged in creative editing when he put it into Mead's mouth at two points in the text of *Mind, Self and Society* (MSS 6, 91) and then employed it in the subtitle ("From the Standpoint of a Social Behaviorist") to that volume.[9] Nevertheless, Reck's and Miller's observations do contain a good bit of truth. Mead certainly began to characterize his position somewhat differently after 1905—and substantially for the reasons mentioned by Miller. Moreover, as Reck points out elsewhere in his introduction, Mead did occasionally speak in his later years as if he thought that behaviorism had made a significant advance over functionalism. Witness his capsule history of psychology: "Psychology became in turn associational, motor, functional, and finally behavioristic" (MSS 21). But the departure from functionalism suggested by these considerations is more terminological than substantive. That Mead came to speak of himself as a behaviorist does not indicate a rejection of his earlier functionalist orientation.

A careful reading of the journal articles Mead published between 1905 and 1928 reveals the following points.

First, one of Mead's infrequent criticisms of "functional psychology" appears in his 1910 essay, "What Social Objects Must Psychology Presuppose?" His objection here is that this school of psychology fails to regard consciousness as a genuine phase of conduct; the functional psychologists speak of functions instead of faculties when dealing with consciousness, but, in practice, their work harbors a vestigial mind-body dualism (SW 105). Now it is unclear just which functional psychologists Mead had in mind here. Perhaps he was thinking of William James or perhaps even of Angell. (The latter speaks of his "adoption of parallelism for practical purposes in teaching and writing."[10]) In any case, Mead's point is that the "functional psychologists" do not take their functionalism seriously enough. "Subjective self-consciousness," he argues in this essay, "must appear *within* experience, must have a function in the development of that experience, and must be studied from the point of view of that function" (SW 112). Mead furthermore claims (SW 106) that this point is simply a reassertion of a position he had attempted to articulate in an earlier essay, "The Definition of the Psychical" (1903), which is openly based upon the foundations laid in Dewey's paper on the reflex arc. Thus we can hardly construe this line of criticism as involving a significant departure from Dewey's position. I would suggest, rather, that if Mead avoided the terms "functionalism" and "functional psychology" in referring to his own position after 1905 this was because he associated these terms with psychophysical parallelism and not because he wished to reject functionalism of the Deweyan variety.

Second, the 1910 essay cited above is one of a series of six articles published between 1909 and 1913 in which Mead first committed to print the key ideas that were to provide the foundation for his mature social psychology. In these articles Mead is highly critical of earlier psychological treatments of social conduct, but there is nothing to indicate that his own approach to sociality involved an abandonment of Dewey's functionalism. On the contrary, the analysis of social action Mead develops here is an attempt to enrich the organic model of action initially set forth by Dewey (see chapter 4).

Finally, the earliest published essays in which Mead refers to his own position as one of behaviorism are "A Behavioristic Account of the Significant Symbol" (1922) and "The Genesis of Self and Social Control" (1925). The second is the more important because in it he quite explicitly states the nature of his commitment to behaviorism. His criticism of "prebehavioristic psychology" in this essay is essentially the same as that he had previously urged against "functional psychology." Prebehavioristic psychology had one foot in the realm of consciousness and one foot in the world of physiology and physics; in short, it was subject to all the well-known inconveniences of Cartesian dualism. Behavioristic psychology, on the other hand, has chosen to focus upon external conduct rather than psychical states. It deals with acts as processes and finds its subject matter wholly within the one world with which the other sciences deal (sw 267–68). But this nondualistic virtue of behaviorism, it must be noted, is one that is shared by Dewey's approach to conduct and thought. Hence, we need not think of Mead's adoption of the term "behaviorism" as signaling a movement away from Dewey's organic conception of the act. Mead's continued allegiance to the Deweyan perspective is obvious even in the words he chooses when praising behaviorism. The advantages of behaviorism, he says (in language that might have been taken directly from Dewey's 1896 paper), is that "it has been occupied with the act as a whole, not a nervous arc" (sw 370).

In spite of these points, however, it might be argued that there is at least one important respect in which Mead's conversion to behaviorism is substantive rather than terminological: his attitude toward introspection as practiced by the structuralists. "The opposition of the behaviorist to introspection is justified," he says in *Mind, Self and Society*. "It is not a fruitful undertaking from the point of view of psychological study" (MSS 105). Now certainly this sounds as if Mead had been significantly influenced in his methodology by the pronouncements of classical behaviorism. And it would be foolish to deny that this methodological conviction is one of the reasons for his choice of the behaviorist label to characterize his own approach to psychology. His social psychology, he says, "is behavioristic in the sense of starting off with an observable activity—the dynamic on-going social process, and the social acts which are its component elements—to be studied and analyzed scientifically" (MSS 7). But at the same time Mead had been critical of introspection, as practiced and interpreted by the Wundtian structuralists, since at least 1903. In his "The Definition of the Psychical," published in that year, he laments the failure of Wundt to treat psychical experience functionally, and he speaks disparagingly of "the professional gymnastics of the trained introspectionist" that distort rather than elucidate the nature of such experience (SW 41). Thus Mead was already opposed to introspectionism—at least of the Wundtian variety—in those days when he was regarding himself as a functionalist and long before behaviorism became the vogue in American psychology.

Moreover, the suggestion that Mead follows the lead of the behaviorists in his attitude toward introspection loses all plausibility once we note that he has no intention of drawing from this methodological stance the radical conclusions that Watson and other classical behaviorists wished to draw from it. Mead does not, for instance, accept Watson's claim that a scientific psychology must concern itself only with that which is publicly observable: "That which belongs (experientially) to the individual *qua* individual, and is accessible to him alone, is certainly included within the field of psychology, whatever else is or is not thus included" (MSS 5). Furthermore, Mead rejects as "misguided and unsuccessful" Watson's attempt to reduce consciousness or mental phenomena to nonmental behavior. The fundamental misconception underlying this reductionistic program, Mead contends, is Watson's assumption that one must opt either for the older conception of consciousness as involving a special mental substance or for an outright denial of the existence of consciousness. But surely there is another alternative: one may reject the older conception of consciousness and then go on to conceive of consciousness "functionally, and as a natural rather than a transcendental phenomenon" (MSS 10). This third alternative, quite obviously, is precisely the one that Mead himself pursues. He refuses to interpret private introspective data along the lines of the earlier dualism or psychophysical parallelism, yet he does not wish to deny the existence or importance of such experiences. He wants to approach these data by beginning with publicly observable conduct, and in this sense he regards his approach as behavioristic. But his behaviorism seeks to explain, rather than explain away, these so-called inner experiences. And it seeks to do this by tracing the genesis and function of such experiences within conduct organically understood.

All of these observations point in the direction of the conclusion suggested at the beginning of the present section, namely, that Mead saw no fundamental opposition between the type of behaviorism he wished to espouse and Dewey's brand of functionalism. If further evidence for this conclusion is needed, it can be found in Mead's posthumously published *Movements of Thought in the Nineteenth Century*. Here, in the course of a lecture on psychology, Mead speaks of Watson and Dewey as representing two alternative ways of developing the point of view of behaviorism. Both Watson and Dewey take the behavioristic point of view, Mead claims, insofar as they focus upon conduct, action, or behavior rather than upon states of consciousness. They differ, however, in that Watson approaches the act from an external point of view and tries to ignore consciousness; Dewey, on the other hand, seeks to interpret consciousness functionally by explicating the role it plays in the course of conduct.[11] In short, Mead construes behaviorism quite broadly as meaning any psychological orientation that takes organisms and their conduct as its primary subject matter. And in this broad sense, of course, Mead's own views had been behavioristic since at least 1900.

Mead and the Behaviorist Tradition

E. G. Boring points out in his *A History of Experimental Psychology* that "for a while in the 1920s it seemed as if all America had gone behaviorist. Everyone (except the few associated with Titchener) was a behaviorist and no behaviorist agreed with any other."[12] If this was the intellectual climate at the time in the field of psychology, then it is not surprising that from 1922 onward Mead chose the label behaviorism to characterize his own approach to social psychology. But there is at least one respect in which this choice might now be considered unfortunate: it has tended to conceal the fact that the model of conduct upon which Mead's social psychology is based differs fundamentally from that which has come to be associated with the behaviorist tradition in American psychology from Watson to the present.

Mead, as we have already noted, was well aware of the differences between his brand of behaviorism and that of Watson. He criticizes Watsonian behaviorism on a number of counts in *Mind, Self and Society:* its approach to consciousness is reductionistic rather than functional (MSS 10), it neglects the "inner" phases of conduct (MSS 6), and it does not fully appreciate the ways in which language and thought are rooted in the social dimensions of human behavior (MSS 69, 100–109). But, unhappily, none of these criticisms goes to the heart of the matter. What Mead should have done—and, indeed, what Dewey did do in his contribution to the volume entitled *Psychologies of 1930* [13]—was to call into question the mechanical stimulus-response model of conduct utilized by the classical behaviorists. For it is quite clear that this model is an attempt to conceptualize conduct in the very ways criticized by Dewey in his 1896 attack on the reflex arc concept.

While Mead does not directly attack the classical behaviorist model of conduct, we can easily demonstrate that his approach to conduct in *Mind, Self and Society* is in fundamental opposition to that model. For the classical behaviorist, conduct is an affair in which independently existing stimuli mechanically elicit unconditioned or conditioned responses from an essentially passive organism. For Mead, however, the organism is "acting and determining its environment. It is not simply a set of passive senses played upon by stimuli that come from without" (MSS 25). What the organism will respond to, and hence what will function as a stimulus for it, depends upon what it is in the process of doing. More generally, whereas the classical behaviorist attempts to conceptualize conduct by reducing it to parts (e.g., stimulus and response), Mead holds that such parts can be adequately understood only if they are viewed as functionally discriminable phases within ongoing conduct. His approach to conduct is holistic and organic: conduct is to be regarded as "a dynamic whole . . . no part of which can be considered or understood by itself" (MSS 7). When he deals with gestures in his analysis of social conduct, for instance, he points out that they "are always found to inhere in or involve a larger social act of which they are phases" (MSS 69n). And a similar concern for holism is evident in his claim that "for social psychology, the whole (society) is prior to the part (the individual), not the part to the whole; and the part is explained in terms of the whole, not the whole in terms of the part" (MSS 7).

Mead's opposition to the mechanical stimulus-response model of conduct is further evident in his conception of the role played by the response within an act. Whereas the classical behaviorist thinks of the response simply as a separate happening called out by the stimulus, Mead always emphasizes that the response mediates or interprets the stimulus. In other words, he takes seriously Dewey's insistence that conduct is a process of adjustment in which the organism does not simply respond *to* a stimulus, but *into* it. This understanding of the response as mediating the stimulus underlies Mead's whole attempt to trace the genesis of language from simpler forms of social conduct. The mechanism of meaning that makes language possible, he tells us, is found within the social act in which "the adjustive response of one organism to the gesture of another is the interpretation of that gesture by that organism—it is the meaning of that gesture" (MSS 78). Similarly, this notion of mediation within the act lies at the heart of Mead's temporal analysis of conduct, an analysis hinted at but not developed in *Mind, Self and Society*. Thus when he speaks (in *The Philosophy of the Act,* for instance) of the perceptual, manipulatory, and consummatory phases of conduct, he never construes these as mechanical stages in a sequence triggered by a stimulus. Rather, he regards the several phases of the act as ways in which an organism transforms or interprets the content of an initial stimulus in terms of its significance for ongoing conduct.[14]

Finally, and perhaps most important, Mead's emphasis upon the manner in which responses interpret stimuli provides the foundation for a functional treatment of social and physical objects. And this way of understanding objects differs radically from that characteristic of the entire behavioristic tradition in American psychology. For the behaviorist, objects are simply there in the environment: they are given to us, and we learn to respond discriminatively to their various features. But for Mead, objects are not simply given to us: we *constitute* them through a process of mediation. Our experience of both physical objects and persons, he argues, is rooted in the mediation provided by the complex patterns of response involved in human social conduct.

Our social conduct is responsible for "the existence of the whole world of common-sense objects" insofar as such conduct "determines, conditions, and makes possible their abstraction from the total structure of events, as identities which are relevant for everyday social behavior" (MSS 79–80). Thus Mead's discussion of the self in *Mind, Self and Society* is essentially an attempt to explain how individuals, by "taking the attitude or the role of the other" in responding to their own gestures, become socially meaningful objects for themselves. And the discussion of physical objects, both here and in such other posthumously published works as *The Philosophy of the Act* and *The Philosophy of the Present*, is an attempt to show how these objects are constituted through the mediation of social conduct and the manipulatory phase of the act as made possible by the human hand.[15]

Concluding Remarks

In light of these observations, it is accurate to say that those criticisms of Watsonian behaviorism that appear near the beginning of *Mind, Self and Society* are merely symptomatic of even more profound differences that separate Mead's social psychological orientation from the behaviorist tradition in American psychology. But my primary purpose in emphasizing these differences has not been one of driving home the thesis that Mead was no behaviorist in the narrow sense of this term. Rather, the contrast has been intended to elucidate certain features of Mead's approach to social conduct that are but vaguely indicated by the label behaviorism. The central claim has been that these features can be adequately understood only if Mead's behaviorism is seen as a consistent outgrowth of his earlier commitment to psychological functionalism. Indeed, this commitment provides the unifying core of all of his later social psychological and philosophical work.

Chapter 6

Taking the Attitude or the Role of the Other

The two immediately preceding chapters have traced the early development of Mead's social psychology and considered the nature of that behaviorism he embraced in the 1920s. Further discussion of his mature social psychological theorizing requires attention to one of its central concepts: the notion of "taking the attitude or the role of the other." While hints of this concept appear in Mead's published work as early as 1910, it is not until "The Mechanism of Social Consciousness" (1912) and "The Social Self" (1913) that it is explicitly formulated and applied.[1] Thereafter, Mead seldom broached a topic related to social psychology without making extensive use of it, as can be seen in "A Behavioristic Account of the Significant Symbol" (1922), "The Genesis of Self and Social Control" (1925), and all of the posthumously published volumes of his later work. Despite the prominence of this concept in his later writings and lectures, however, he nowhere offers a sustained and systematic analysis of the behavioral mechanism to which it refers. This chapter, therefore, first constructs such an analysis based upon relevant passages scattered throughout the works mentioned above. Then, the way in which Mead employs the concept of "taking the attitude or the role of the other" in the formulation of many of the most distinctive doctrines of his mature social psychology is examined.

Preliminary Terminological Considerations

The phrase "taking the role of the other," Mead comments at one point in *Mind, Self and Society,* "is a little unfortunate because it suggests an actor's attitude which is actually more sophisticated than that which is involved in our own experience. To this degree it does not correctly describe that which I have in mind" (MSS 161). Consider in this connection the case of a young child who in Mead's sense "takes the role" of a parent in responding to some portion of his own conduct. The child need not be "acting out" or "portraying" the role of a parent for the benefit of himself or some audience; he may be wholly unaware that he is incorporating some facet of the parent's conduct into his own behavior. "At the stage which we are considering, that of the young child, the role of the other which he assumes is taken without recognition. The child is aware of his response to the role, not of the role he is taking" (MSS 372). But it is not only the theatrical connotations of the terms "role" and "role-taking" that are potentially misleading here. We may be misled about Mead's understanding of these terms even if we construe them in a more strictly sociological sense. Suppose, for instance, that we think of a *role* as "a socially prescribed way of behaving in particular situations for any person occupying a given social position or status."[2] Then we will be led to expect that when Mead speaks of an individual "taking the role of the other," he means that an individual engages in a rather complex pattern of behavior ordinarily appropriate for a person occupying the other's social position or status. This interpretation, however, would be overly narrow. Certainly one can find passages in Mead's work where he does use the phrase "taking the role of the other" in this way, but there are also passages where this phrase or an equivalent is applied to cases in which an individual's conduct exhibits selected responses of the other that are by no means elaborate enough to qualify as a role in this restricted sense.

We can avoid some of the misleading connotations of the phrase "taking the role of the other" by using in its stead the alternative phrase Mead himself often employs, namely, "taking the attitude of the other." An attitude, he says, consists of a behavioral disposition, a tendency to respond in a certain manner to certain sorts of stimuli, or the beginnings of an action that seek an occasion for a full release or expression.[3] To take the attitude of the other is thus, in part, to import into one's conduct a tendency to respond as the other would respond to a given type of stimulus. More will be said about this shortly, but for now it is sufficient to note that an individual can take the attitude of the other without engaging in conduct of enough complexity to be considered taking the role of the other in the sociological sense of the term *role* mentioned above.

Perhaps the most important initial point to be made about Mead's use of these phrases is that he tends to employ both of them (and, occasionally, such equivalents as "put oneself in the place of the other" or "take the perspective of the other") more or less interchangeably in the course of explaining certain aspects of human social conduct at quite diverse stages in its development. Sometimes he uses them to help explain the genesis of language, thought, and self-consciousness in the social experience of the human species or the human individual.[4] At other times he uses them to explain the social behavior and further social development of individuals who have already acquired at least the rudiments of these capacities. In what follows, I shall be especially concerned to examine Mead's concept of taking the attitude of the other as it relates to the former context. This emphasis rests upon the conviction that the attempt to explain the human acquisition of language, thought, and self-consciousness lies at the heart of what is distinctive in Mead's social psychological theorizing. Moreover, if such a line of explanation is to avoid logical circularity, it must take as its point of departure a rudimentary or foundational variety of attitude-taking conduct that does not require for its exercise the capacities it is supposed to help explain. The primary question, then, is this: What kind of account do Mead's writings and lectures provide for that rudimentary attitude-taking behavior that his distinctive social psychological theories evidently presuppose? Let me begin my attempt to answer this question by locating the basis for such an account within the framework supplied by his functionalist approach to both animal and human social conduct.

Attitude-Taking and the Conversation of Gestures

The conduct of both human and nonhuman animals, Mead held from at least 1909 onward, is rooted in impulses or instincts—by which he meant congenital tendencies to react in certain ways to particular sorts of stimuli under certain organic conditions.[5] And it is because so many of these congenital tendencies "involve or require social situations and relations for their satisfaction," he points out, that the conduct of all living organisms is largely social in character; sociophysiological impulses "constitute the foundation of all types or forms of social behavior, however simple or complex, crude or highly organized, rudimentary or well developed" (MSS 228, 139n). Consider the sort of social interaction involved in one of Mead's favorite illustrations, a confrontation between two hostile dogs. The first dog snarls and bares its teeth; the second dog responds by bristling and crouching in a defensive posture; the first animal then backs off and begins pacing around the second. This whole process takes place, Mead maintains, because each of these animals has impulses seeking expression (presumably, in this case, impulses related to self-defense) that sensitize it to the successive acts of the other; the acts of the other thus become stimuli that release and guide the expression of the relevant impulses.

This simple variety of social conduct deserves further discussion because it figures importantly in Mead's understanding of taking the attitude of the other. Here we should recall what was said in chapter 4 about Mead's analysis of the conversation of gestures, which he began to enunciate in "Social Psychology as Counterpart to Physiological Psychology" (1909) and continued to expound throughout the remainder of his career. Where an early overt stage of an act by one individual releases a social impulse and calls forth an anticipatory adjustment in the conduct of another, he holds, the former bit of action is called a "gesture." And where an early overt stage of an anticipatory response to a gesture functions, in turn, as a gesture calling forth a readjustment on the part of the first individual, the result may be called a "conversation of gestures." A fragment of such a conversation of gestures taking place between two individuals, X and Y, can be schematized as follows:

> X begins an action, of which an early overt stage functions as a gesture, *a;*
>
> Y responds to *a* with an anticipatory adjustment of which *b* is an early overt stage;
>
> X responds to *b* with an anticipatory adjustment of which *c* is an early overt stage.

Suppose for purposes of illustration that X and Y are two dogs. Gestures *a, b,* and *c* might consist of such behavioral items as snarling, crouching, and pacing. In the context of the social act, these gestures function as cues or signals, guiding the conduct of the individuals responding to them. But we need not assume that the individuals who employ such cues have the capacity to hold gestures and responses apart in their experience, or that they can think of the other's gestures as signifying the conduct that their own responses anticipate. Hence, in

Mind, Self and Society Mead sometimes uses the phrase "unconscious conversation of gestures" in speaking of elementary cases of this form of social interaction. Individuals participating in an unconscious conversation of gestures respond to each other's gestures, but they are not reflectively aware of these gestures as signs having meanings (MSS 69n, 72n, 81).

Mead is inclined to doubt that the social conduct of nonhuman animals ever advances beyond the level of the unconscious conversation of gestures. But human social conduct, he maintains, is quite different—due largely to the human capacity to take the attitude of the other. Mead's first published reference to this capacity appears in his 1912 essay "The Mechanism of Social Consciousness," in which he notes that "the human animal can stimulate himself as he stimulates others and can respond to his stimulations as he responds to the stimulations of others" (SW 139). A year later, in "The Social Self," he explained somewhat more fully what he had in mind: "The very sounds, gestures, especially vocal gestures, which man makes in addressing others, call out or tend to call out responses from himself. He cannot hear himself speak without assuming in a measure the attitude which he would have assumed if he had been addressed in the same words by others. . . . It is also to be noted that this response . . . may be in the role of another— we present his arguments in imagination and do it with his intonations and gestures and even perhaps with his facial expression" (SW 145–46).

A good deal of initial illumination can be thrown upon the fundamental behavioral mechanism involved here by locating it within the earlier schema of a conversation of gestures. In the following example, individual Y is engaging in a rudimentary act of taking the attitude of the other, behavior indicated by the descriptive remarks placed in parentheses:

> X begins an act, of which the gesture a is an early overt stage;
>
> Y responds to a with an anticipatory adjustment of which the gesture b is an early overt stage (and the gesture b calls out in Y himself a tendency to respond in manner r);
>
> X responds to b with an adjustment of type r.

Suppose, for instance, that X is a mother and Y is a very young child. The mother has just noticed the child reaching for an object he has previously been scolded for touching: The mother shouts "no!" and begins to move toward the child (gesture *a*); the child utters a cry and begins to run away (gesture *b*), but then he stops short and, looking expectantly at the mother, begins to admonish himself by saying "no, no, no . . ." (response *r*); finally, the mother picks up the child and continues the scolding (response of type *r*).

The "tendency to respond in manner *r*" attributed to Y in the schema above may manifest itself in an overt response (as in this example), or it may take the form of a covert behavioral disposition or beginning of such a response—what Mead calls an "attitude." In either case, Y's tendency to stimulate himself with his own gesture brings to his conduct an element of anticipation it would otherwise lack. One important behavioral function of such a rudimentary act of taking the attitude of the other thus resides in the fact that it enables the attitude-taking individual to govern his action in the light of the probable social response of the other to that action (MSS 46, 69n, 254). From this point of view, rudimentary attitude-taking conduct might therefore be succinctly characterized as "anticipatory self-stimulation."

But to understand such conduct more fully we must note further that it cannot take place unless certain conditions are met. In the first place, Mead observes, an individual can stimulate himself with his own gesture only if he possesses "impulses seeking expression which this stimulation sets free" (MSS 360). Second, such self-stimulation can successfully perform an anticipatory function only to the extent that the gesture it involves calls forth a more or less similar response from both the attitude-taking individual and others for whom it acts as a social stimulus. At the least, such a gesture must release in the individual making it social impulses that are "functionally of the same sort" as those that the gesture releases in the conduct of others (MSS 364). Hence, the individuals implicated in a primitive attitude-taking situation must share essentially similar impulses, and, furthermore, the gesture that figures in the act of taking the attitude of the other must be of a type that might be expected to present a similar stimulus content both to its author and to others involved in the social act. This last consideration leads Mead to emphasize the vocal gesture as that most conducive to attitude-taking conduct: "The vocal gesture," he suggests in "A Behavioristic Account of the Significant Symbol" (1922), "is of peculiar importance because it reacts upon the individual who makes it in the same fashion that it reacts upon another, but this is also true in a less degree of those of one's gestures that he can see or feel" (SW 243).

unconscious conv of gestures becomes conscious when?

1)

2)

As a first approximation, then, Mead views taking the attitude of the other as a type of social conduct that emerges from the unconscious conversation of gestures when the behavior of at least one of the individuals engaged in that interaction satisfies two conditions: (1) the individual's own gestures release in him social impulses that would otherwise be released only by stimuli from others, and (2) the responses or attitudes thus called forth by self-stimulation are of a sort that the type of gestures involved might normally elicit from others. When two or more interacting individuals satisfy both of these conditions, Mead claims, we have a situation in which the unconscious conversation of gestures can become a "conscious conversation of gestures," i.e., a situation in which the individuals can become reflectively aware of the social meaning or significance of their own gestures and carry on their interaction in the light of this awareness (MSS 69n, 72n).

The Problem of Socialization

child

An example and several related passages from *Mind, Self and Society* will serve to introduce one further dimension in Mead's explication of the fundamental sociophysiological and behavioral components involved in rudimentary attitude-taking conduct. Mead invites us to consider the case of "a child crying and then uttering the soothing sound which belongs to the parental attitude of protection." This conduct, we are told, takes place just because certain parental impulses are already present in the child. Given the child's wealth of vocal gestures, he "inevitably must call out in himself the parental response which is so markedly ready for expression very early in the child's nature, and this response will include the parent's corresponding gesture" (MSS 364–65). This is not to say, however, that the child has an innate tendency to speak his parents' language. Nor that all the various types of social responses he will ever call out in himself lie already coiled in his congenital endowment, ready to spring forth upon the occasion of the appropriate self-stimulation! For Mead notes that the social responses a child initially makes to his own gestures will be characterized by "incompleteness and relative immaturity" and that "the life about him will indirectly determine what parental responses he produces in his conduct" (MSS 365). And to these remarks must be added the claim that the child's impulses are "subject to almost indefinite modifica-

tion" in the course of his social experience (MSS 349). It follows from
these observations that something more than the notions of social impulse and self-stimulation is required to complete Mead's explication
of taking the attitude of the other. He needs a mechanism of socialization that will account for the fact that the social responses an individual
stimulates himself to make are gradually shaped and molded until they
closely resemble the complex responses others make to his gestures.

Several of Mead's predecessors (e.g., Gabriel Tarde, James Mark
Baldwin, and Josiah Royce) had employed the notion of an imitative
instinct to account for the process of socialization involved in the development of the human individual. But this notion, Mead correctly
observes, is incompatible with the functional analysis of conduct to
which he is committed: "As soon as you recognize in the organism a
set of acts which carry out the processes which are essential to the life
of the form, and undertake to put the sensitive or sensory experiences
into that scheme, the sensitive experience . . . cannot be a stimulus
simply to reproduce what is seen and heard; it is rather a stimulus for
the carrying out of the organic process" (MSS 60). Mead's analysis of
the conversation of gestures provides a case in point. According to this
analysis, one individual responds to the gesture of another in terms
of what that gesture portends for the impulses seeking expression in
the former's ongoing conduct. An instinctive tendency to reproduce
the gesture of the other would be worse than useless in this context; it
would actually get in the way of successful social interaction.

While Mead persistently rejects the idea of an imitative instinct, he
is much less clear about the alternative mechanism of socialization he
wishes to espouse in conjunction with his concept of taking the attitude
of the other. Several different hypotheses with respect to this mechanism are hinted at in his lectures and writings, but none of them is
developed in detail. Let us look carefully at each of these hypotheses,
beginning with one that is not very promising. In an early section of
Mind, Self and Society Mead argues that we can use the idea of self-
stimulation to account for a good deal of behavior that was formerly
explained by appeal to the notion of an imitative instinct. He illustrates
an alternative line of explanation by citing the hypothetical case of a
sparrow and a canary occupying neighboring cages, in which the sparrow eventually begins to utter phonetic combinations resembling the
songs of the canary. We can account for the sparrow's imitative behavior, Mead suggests, by making two assumptions: (1) that the sparrow

has social impulses or instincts that manifest themselves in vocal behavior and that can be stimulated both by the singing of the canary and by the vocal gestures of the sparrow itself; (2) that the sparrow's initial vocal repertoire has certain phonetic elements that are also present in the singing of the canary. Given these assumptions, the problem becomes one of explaining how the process of self-stimulation "selects out" the shared phonetic elements, i.e., causes the shared elements to become more prominent and more frequent parts of the sparrow's vocal behavior. Here, then, is Mead's proposed explanation: "Where the sparrow is actually making use of a phonetic vocal gesture of the canary through a common note in the repertoire of both of them, then the sparrow would be tending to bring out in itself the same response that would be brought out by the note of the canary. That, then, would give an added weight in the experience of the sparrow to that particular response. . . . Those particular notes answering to this stimulus will be, so to speak, written in, underlined. They will become habitual" (MSS 62).[6]

Mead initially presents this explanatory hypothesis as if it were adequate as it stands. But this is not the case. For the notes that are supposed to become habitual—the notes "written in, underlined"—are the *response* to the shared phonetic element, not that element itself. And why should the sparrow's response to this shared phonetic element resemble the vocal gestures of the canary? This line of explanation can become plausible only if we add a third assumption, namely, (3) that at least a fair proportion of the phonetic elements shared by the sparrow and the canary call out the same types of vocal responses in both birds. In other words, we must assume not only that the sparrow and canary share certain notes but also that these notes will tend to call out other shared notes. That such a strong assumption is required by this hypothesis renders it suspect. And the situation becomes even worse when Mead suggests later in *Mind, Self and Society* that an explanation of this sort might be used to account for the imitative behavior of those so-called talking birds that can be taught to duplicate certain human words (MSS 360). Here the need to make an assumption of type (3) would commit us to the unlikely thesis that a bird and the person who teaches it to talk must from the outset have a tendency to respond vocally in similar ways to shared phonetic elements in their vocal repertoires.

Now either Mead's presentation of this behavioral mechanism was somewhat confused in his 1928 lectures on social psychology—or, what seems more likely, the student notes upon which *Mind, Self and Society* is based are not wholly reliable records of what he actually said. For when he comes to sum up his point, he appears to change his interpretation of the mechanism it is supposed to involve without being aware that he is doing so. Consider the following passage, which follows by a few pages the explanation quoted above: "In so far as one calls out the attitude in himself that one calls out in others, the response is picked out and strengthened. That is the only basis for what we call imitation. . . . The mechanism is that of an individual calling out in himself the response which he calls out in another, consequently giving greater weight to those responses than to the other responses, and gradually building up those sets of responses into a dominant whole. This may be done, as we say, unconsciously. The sparrow does not know it is imitating the canary" (MSS 66). The mechanism described here is quite different from that which was held to be operative in the explanatory hypothesis cited earlier. There, a given response would become habitual if it is repeatedly called out in an individual both by his own gesture and by similar gestures made by others. Here, a given response would become habitual if an individual stimulates himself to make that response with one of his gestures and also observes another individual responding in a similar way to that same gesture. This latter version of the mechanism involved in Mead's explanation of imitative behavior requires the same assumption we found reason to question above and, in addition, suffers from a further defect: it assumes without argument or evidence that a response that an individual calls out both in himself and in another will be given "greater weight" and therefore will occur more frequently in his behavior.

Neither of the mechanisms Mead presents in *Mind, Self and Society* as part of his attempt to delineate a selection process that would account for the imitative vocal behavior of certain birds seems adequate to explain even the specific phenomenon it is designed to handle. Hence, neither holds much promise as a behavioral mechanism that might supply what is needed to complete his more general conception of attitude-taking conduct. Furthermore, there is good reason to doubt that this need could be met by *any* behavioral mechanism that turns wholly upon a process of selecting out or emphasizing certain elements of an individual's initial repertoire of unlearned responses. To see this, we need only attempt to use such a device to account for some obvious cases of taking the attitude or the role of the other. Recall, for instance, the child of a previous example who is observed scolding himself after he has done something for which he has previously been scolded by a parent. Can we seriously maintain that the best way of explaining this case is to hold that the child's repertoire of impulsive or unlearned behavior contains "scolding elements" that have somehow been emphasized in the course of his previous conduct? Or if we find the child taking the specific role of a teacher or a police officer in response to his own behavior, shall we say that this role-taking behavior results from the previous reinforcement of "teaching elements" or "policing elements" in his unlearned responses? Clearly this general line of explanation requires us to assume a strange and wonderful (and, hence, wildly implausible) collection of specific response elements in the initial behavioral repertoire of the child!

A much more promising basis for a hypothesis concerning the mechanism of socialization Mead needs to complete his concept of attitude-taking behavior can be found in the earlier essay in which he first mentions this concept by name. We do not "assume the roles of others toward ourselves because we are subject to a mere imitative instinct," he says in "The Social Self" (1913), "but because in responding to ourselves we are in the nature of the case taking the attitude of another than the self that is directly acting, and into this reaction there naturally flows the memory images of the responses of those about us, the memory images of those responses of others which were in answer to like actions" (SW 146). In this passage Mead is saying that although we do not possess an imitative instinct, our congenital endowment is such that we tend to respond to ourselves in the attitude of an other whenever we engage in self-stimulation. Does this mean, then, that while we do not have an imitative instinct, we do possess an attitude-taking instinct? Apparently not, for Mead neither here nor elsewhere mentions such an instinct. Rather, his view seems to be that our social impulses or instincts sensitize and lead us to respond to stimuli presented by the conduct of others; hence, when we release these impulses through self-stimulation, we respond to our own conduct as the conduct of an other. Further, when we respond to our own conduct as the conduct of an other we are, in effect, "taking the attitude of another than the self that is directly acting"; given this situation, Mead claims, memory images derived from past responses of others to similar stimuli tend to flow into our responses to our own conduct. The "memory images" mentioned here and the sense in which they "flow into" conduct involving self-stimulation can be thought of in two ways. On the one hand, we may think of the imagery as consisting of sensuous contents derived from past experience of others' responses, which merge with and fill out the present stimulus (in this case, the gesture by which the individual stimulates himself), thereby giving that stimulus additional meaning. Alternatively, we may focus upon the response tendencies or attitudes that Mead regards as providing the behavioral basis for memory imagery and then construe these as bringing a new dimension to the individual's initial impulsive tendency to respond in a certain manner to his own gesture. On Mead's functional analysis of conduct, these two ways of thinking about the mechanism described in the preceding quotation come to the same thing. For, according to this analysis, conduct is a process in which responses mediate or interpret an initial stimulus content; the stimulus acquires new meaning in virtue of the response made to it.

Unhappily, Mead's subsequent lectures and writings offer little in the way of further articulation of this hypothesis. Worse yet, in *Mind, Self and Society* he adumbrates two versions of a different line of thought that is considerably less plausible as a way of accounting for the mechanism of socialization involved in rudimentary attitude-taking conduct. All of this is somewhat strange not only because his genetic theories of language, thought, and the self require a convincing explanation of the mechanism of socialization involved in rudimentary attitude-taking but also because his functional analysis of social conduct provides the conceptual resources in terms of which the hypothesis suggested in his 1913 essay could easily have been elaborated so as to meet this need. In what follows I indicate briefly how this elaboration might have been accomplished.

The mechanism of socialization suggested in "The Social Self" is one that might be called "indirect imitation"—although Mead himself nowhere employs this label. The term "imitation" is appropriate because this mechanism involves a process whereby individuals take into their own conduct patterns of behavior they observe in others; in other words, we are not speaking here of a process in which certain elements already present in these individuals' repertoires of impulsive behavior are simply "selected out" or "emphasized" or "given greater weight." But, at the same time, this imitation is "indirect" insofar as it does not involve a tendency on the part of individuals to replicate directly whatever they observe in others. Rather, the individuals tend to imitate the behavior of others primarily in responding to their own gestures; this imitation is essentially a shaping or modifying of their impulsive tendencies to respond in certain ways to certain social stimuli provided by their own conduct.

By allowing for an imitative component in the mechanism of socialization, this hypothesis obviates the need to make those assumptions chiefly responsible for the implausibility of the two alternative hypotheses criticized earlier. In particular, there is no need for a proponent of this hypothesis to assume that one individual can acquire patterns of behavior from another only if both individuals start out with a collection of shared gestures and response tendencies. Mead was apparently led to make such assumptions in *Mind, Self and Society* because of his rejection of the notion of an imitative instinct, a rejection that tended to encompass not only the alleged instinct but also the idea that imitation could be a fundamental mechanism in the process of socialization. I suggest, however, that Mead would have been better advised to divide the issue at this point. He was right to discard the notion of an imitative instinct: such a notion can have no place within his functional analysis of social conduct. But he went astray when he failed to recognize that imitative behavior of a noninstinctive sort is both compatible with his analysis of social conduct and required to complete his conception of attitude-taking behavior.

The crucial point to be grasped here is that what I have been calling "indirect imitation" fits quite smoothly into the general framework set forth in Mead's treatment of elementary cases of taking the attitude of the other. We can best see this by attending to one of the functional tasks he assigns to such attitude-taking, namely, that of facilitating social conduct by enabling the attitude-taking individual to regulate his behavior in the light of the social responses others are likely to make to that behavior. Now if attitude-taking responses perform an anticipatory and regulative function, then it seems reasonable to expect that such responses might gradually be modified as a consequence of the actual responses others make to the gestures that call forth these anticipatory responses in the individual who is taking the attitude or the role of the other. A revised version of the earlier schematization of a simple case of attitude-taking will help to clarify this suggestion:

X begins an act of which the gesture *a* is an early overt stage;

Y responds to *a* with an anticipatory adjustment of which the gesture *b* is an early overt state (and the gesture *b* calls out in Y himself a tendency to respond in manner *r*);

X responds to *b* with an adjustment of type *s*.

The point of this schematized example is to set forth a case in which attitude-taking conduct is unsuccessful, in which it does not adequately perform its anticipatory and regulative function. Cases of this sort are, of course, likely to be common in actual social conduct. Suppose, for instance, that Y is a very young child and that X is an adult who responds to that child's gestures with elaborate behavior involving bodily movements, words, and conceptually mediated feelings that are as yet no part of the child's experiential repertoire. In this case, the child's possession of congenital social impulses and his capacity for self-stimulation will not take him very far toward successful anticipation of the adult's behavior. It is possible to see how situations like this can be rectified, however, if we assume that the anticipatory responses called forth by self-stimulation are not simply the result of social impulses but can be modified in the course of an individual's social experience. And the simplest hypothesis with respect to the nature of this modification process would be that responses of the sort an individual's gestures call out in others are gradually imported into his own attitude-taking conduct.

The hypothesis of indirect imitation, then, makes functional sense in a way that the direct imitation envisioned by certain of Mead's predecessors does not. Furthermore, no special instinct need be postulated as a part of this hypothesis. We need only assume that experience will gradually lead individuals to adopt whatever patterns of response they find most successful, i.e., most conducive to the satisfaction of impulses, in dealing with certain types of stimuli. Such an assumption is fully consonant with Mead's general approach to conduct; it has application both to the case of a simple conversation of gestures and to the more complex kind of social interaction involved in taking the attitude of the other. In the former case we cannot always expect brute impulse or instinct to supply the correct response to a gesture made by the other; past experience of the conduct of the other may play an important part in modifying an individual's impulsive social responses so that they more accurately anticipate and more successfully adjust to the action that the other's gesture portends. Similarly, individuals engaged in taking the attitude of the other can hardly help but note the responses others make to their conduct, especially when these responses are un-anticipated. And their attitude-taking behavior will be successful, will perform one of the chief functional tasks Mead attributes to it, to the extent that they adequately mirror or imitate these actual responses of the other in the anticipatory attitudes they call out in themselves with their own gestures.

Applications of the Concept of Taking the Attitude of the Other

The concept of taking the attitude or the role of the other, as was noted at the outset of this chapter, receives extensive application in Mead's later lectures and writings. Indeed, at one point or another in these works Mead makes each of the following claims concerning the way in which attitude-taking conduct contributes to the content and organization of human social experience: (1) it underlies the acquisition of significant symbols; (2) it makes possible the inner dialogue of human thought; (3) it is the behavioral mechanism by means of which the individual achieves self-consciousness; (4) it is responsible for the development of the social structure of the human self or personality; (5) it provides the principle of distinctively human social organization; (6) it enables the human individual to participate in a world of public or shared objects; (7) it is responsible for our everyday perceptual experience of distant physical objects as entities having "insides" and as existing contemporaneously with those objects that are within our grasp; (8) it yields the capacity to occupy and compare in thought different spatio-temporal perspectives. I comment upon the last three of these applications of the attitude-taking concept in chapter 10 below; in the remainder of this chapter I focus on the first five, since these are the applications most fully explored in his social psychological works.

As a preface to this discussion, let me acknowledge that whereas my earlier remarks have stressed the *anticipatory* function of attitude-taking conduct, Mead's applications of this concept often place greater emphasis upon what might be called the *reflexive* and *appropriative* functions of such conduct. Attitude-taking may be said to serve the *reflexive* function insofar as it enables individuals to attend to themselves and to grasp the social meaning of their own conduct. Even the most simple act of taking the attitude of the other is to some degree reflexive in that it involves self-stimulation, but reflexivity is most fully realized in those cases where individuals respond to self-stimulation with complex attitudes acquired through their interaction with others. Attitude-taking may be said to serve the *appropriative* function insofar as it provides a mechanism by which individuals appropriate or import into their own conduct certain features of the conduct of others. (The mechanism of socialization discussed in the preceding section obviously has to do with this function.) Every act of attitude-taking is appropriative to the extent that an individual's responses to self-stimulation are shaped by interaction with others, but such appropriation is most fully realized when taking the attitude of the other leads to the acquisition of those organized and relatively stable response tendencies that provide the social structure of an individual's self or personality. It is important to note that Mead does not himself explicitly distinguish these several functional dimensions of attitude-taking behavior.[7] Nevertheless, as we see below, each plays a significant part in one or more of his main theoretical applications of the concept of taking the attitude of the other.

  1. *The acquisition of significant symbols.* The behavioral basis of the significant symbol, Mead holds in such works as "A Behavioristic Account of the Significant Symbol" (1922) and *Mind, Self and Society,* is found in the structure of the social act. "Just as in fencing the parry is an interpretation of the thrust, so, in the social act, the adjustive response of one organism to the gesture of another is the interpretation of that gesture by that organism—it is the meaning of that gesture" (MSS 78). But individuals engaging in elementary social interaction, in an "unconscious conversation of gestures," are not aware of their own gestures and hence do not become conscious of the relation between these gestures and the responses they elicit from others. In order for consciousness of meaning to arise, such individuals must take the attitude of the other, i.e., they must respond to their own gestures as others respond to them, thus bringing both sides of the conversation of gestures into their field of stimulation (MSS 46–47). Individuals who in this manner achieve awareness of the social import of one or more of their gestures have begun to acquire language or significant symbols. These symbols undergo further development through a process of generalization in which the individuals who employ them take the attitudes not merely of specific others but of a "generalized other" in responding to their own gestures. In this way significant symbols come to take their place in a "universe of discourse," a system of shared social meanings

constituted by a community of individuals engaged in a common social process (MSS 89–90; SW 244–45).

This brief summary of Mead's treatment of the acquisition of significant symbols illustrates all three of the previously mentioned functions of attitude-taking conduct. According to this account, an individual's gestures begin to take on meaning for that individual to the degree that they call out in his own conduct attitudes that anticipate the responses of others. And these attitudes can perform their anticipatory function because they have been appropriated from the actual responses of others to similar gestures in the past. Finally, it is the tendency to take the attitude of the other that leads individuals to focus their attention upon their own gestures in a reflexive manner. The tendency to take the attitude of the other sensitizes individuals to their own gestures; the gestures, in turn, call out in the conduct of their authors socially acquired attitudes or responses that mediate or interpret these social stimuli.

2. *The inner dialogue of human thought.* Mead understands thought, mentality, or reflective intelligence in terms of its function within conduct. And this function is to bring about a resolution of those situations in which conduct is inhibited by conflicting response tendencies: "The most important activity of mind that can be identified in behavior is that of so adjusting conflicting impulses that they can express themselves harmoniously." Such resolution or adjustment "is not accomplished through a direct reorganization of motor processes" but rather by a process of analysis directed toward the field of stimulation. "Control of impulse lies only in the shift of attention which brings other objects into the field of stimulation, setting free other impulses, or in such a resetting of the objects that the impulses express themselves on a different time schedule or with additions and subtractions" (MSS 367). Now this process of analysis and reconstruction, Mead contends, is social to the core and is dependent for its very essence upon taking the attitude of the other (MSS 141n). In the first place, it makes use of significant symbols: "Mentality is that relationship of the organism to the situation which is mediated by sets of symbols" (MSS 125). And the development of such symbols, as we have seen, is made possible by attitude-taking conduct. Their importance for reflective intelligence is found in the fact that they provide tools of analysis. "When we get into conduct these symbols which indicate certain characters and their relationship to things and to responses, they enable us to pick out these

characters and hold them in so far as they determine our conduct" (MSS 122). Second, this process of analysis characteristically involves an internalized conversation of gestures. Here "the sympathetic assumption of the attitude of the other brings into play varying impulses which direct the attention to features of the object which are ignored in the attitude of direct response. And the very diverse attitudes assumed furnish the material for a reconstruction of the objective field" (MSS 375–76).

The exercise of reflective intelligence, according to this view, requires an antecedent acquisition of significant symbols: "the early stages of the development of language must have been prior to the development of mind or thought" (MSS 192). Hence, mind or thought is dependent upon the anticipatory, reflexive, and appropriative functions of attitude-taking that underlie the genesis of significant symbols. The appropriative function of attitude-taking is further evident here in that Mead utilizes it to account for the dialogic social structure of human thought. Reflective intelligence arises "through the internalization by the individual of social processes of experience and behavior . . . as made possible by the individual's taking the attitudes of other individuals toward himself and toward what is being thought about" (MSS 191–92). And these internalized social processes, he points out in "The Genesis of Self and Social Control" (1925), give to thought its social structure: "Our thinking is an inner conversation in which we may be taking the roles of specific acquaintances over against ourselves, but usually it is with what I have termed the 'generalized other' that we converse, and so attain to the levels of abstract thinking, and that impersonality, that so-called objectivity that we cherish" (SW 288).

3. *The genesis of self-consciousness.* The reflexive function of taking the attitude of the other appears most explicitly in Mead's theory of self-consciousness. The human individual, according to this theory, "enters his own experience as a self or individual, not directly or immediately, not by becoming a subject to himself, but only in so far as he first becomes an object to himself just as other individuals are objects to him or in his experience; and he becomes an object to himself only by taking the attitudes of other individuals toward himself within a social environment or context of experience and behavior in which both he and they are involved" (MSS 138). We can best understand what Mead is saying here if we recall his general analysis of the manner in which we come to experience physical and social objects. This analysis,

like his treatment of significant symbols, is grounded in his functionalist view of conduct as a process in which responses mediate or interpret
a stimulus. It is the response to the gesture, as we have already seen,
that gives meaning or significance to that gesture. Similarly, Mead regards habitual patterns of response or response tendencies as providing
the content and structure of the physical and social objects that figure
in our experience. Now to become self-conscious, we must become an
object in our own experience; this involves stimulating ourselves with
our own gestures and responding to these gestures as we have previously observed others responding to similar gestures. In short, we must
take the attitude of the other with respect to our own conduct. Attitude-
taking functions reflexively by sensitizing us to our own gestures and by
supplying the interpretive responses that provide the meaningful social
content and structure of that self that is the object of self-consciousness.

  4. *The development of the social structure of the self.* It follows from
what has been said above that if we are to attain self-consciousness of a
sophisticated sort, we must learn to respond to (mediate, interpret) our
own gestures in elaborate and complex ways. In *Mind, Self and Society* and "The Genesis of the Self and Social Control," Mead delineates
two basic stages in the child's development of a socially structured self.
In the first, a stage Mead calls "play," the child "plays that he is, for
instance, offering himself something, and he buys it; he gives a letter
to himself and takes it away; he addresses himself as a parent, as a
teacher; he arrests himself as a policeman" (MSS 150–51). In this stage
the child is "acquiring the roles of those who belong to his society.
This takes place because the child is continually exciting in himself the
responses to his own social acts" (SW 285). But these various roles are
not as yet related to one another so as to form an organized whole; the
element of organization lacking here is supplied in the subsequent stage
of development represented by the organized "game." In this second
stage, the child "must not only take the role of the other, as he does
in the play, but he must assume the various roles of all the participants
in the game, and govern his action accordingly. . . . Their organized
reactions to him he has embedded in his own playing . . . and this organized reaction becomes what I have called the 'generalized other' in his
experience which provides him with a self" (SW 285).

  Several observations are in order concerning these passages. First,
it should be clear that Mead is stressing the appropriative function
of taking the attitude of the other: the child acquires the basic social

structure of his self or personality by importing into his conduct the organized roles displayed in the conduct of others. Second, the kind of attitude-taking behavior to which Mead is referring is more complex than any we have previously discussed. For he speaks here of the individual importing not just individual attitudes but a whole system of roles—each of which presumably involves an organized set of attitudes or response tendencies. And, third, these passages deal with a type of role-taking that presupposes a good deal of prior social development on the part of the role-taking individual. The child could hardly "address himself as a teacher" or "arrest himself as a policeman," for instance, if he did not already possess the beginnings of language, thought, and self-consciousness. It is thus unfortunate that Mead does not distinguish and separately discuss at least two different levels of attitude-taking behavior: (a) a rudimentary level that does not presuppose language, thought, and self-consciousness but that plays a significant part in the genesis of these social phenomena, and (b) a more advanced level of attitude-taking that becomes possible once these capacities have arisen in the experience of the individual and that helps to account for the continued social development of that individual. Such a distinction would have done much to forestall possible confusion about the various ways in which the concept of taking the attitude of the other enters into Mead's social psychological theorizing.

5. *The principle of human social organization.* The same line of development responsible for our acquisition of self-consciousness and a socially structured self, Mead holds in his later social psychological works, also makes possible a form of social organization unique to the human species. Social organization as it is found in nonhuman vertebrate species, he notes, is generally quite limited in character and appears to be based upon relatively fixed instinctive tendencies. The societies of certain insects such as termites, ants, and bees, on the other hand, display organization of considerable complexity, which rests almost wholly upon a principle of physiological differentiation: differing physiological types of individuals (e.g., queens, fighters, workers) have evolved in these insect species, and these physiological differences largely determine how the individuals interact to form a functioning social whole. In the human species, by contrast, we find complex social organization with little or no physiological differentiation, apart from differences of a sexual or reproductive nature. Human social organization, instead of being a consequence of either fixed instinctive tenden-

cies or physiological differentiation, results primarily from our capacity to control our conduct in the light of consciously recognized social objects and meanings. Self-consciousness is one important dimension of this capacity, but so is an awareness of socially shared goals or values and of such meanings as property, rights, and obligations. Mead's central point in this connection is that these social objects and meanings are in large part constituted by the social responses of all those with whom we carry on social interaction; hence, our conduct can employ the kind of social control made possible by such objects and meanings only if we take the attitude of generalized others. In short, taking the attitude of the other is the principle of distinctively human social organization, and only those individuals who have exercised the appropriative function of attitude-taking conduct so as to acquire a self with the requisite social structure can participate fully in human society.[8]

Concluding Remarks

Enough has now been said to demonstrate the central place that the concept of taking the attitude of the other occupies in Mead's mature social psychological thought. The preceding applications also serve to indicate the considerable explanatory power of this important concept, a power that stems largely from that fact that attitude-taking behavior encompasses the several functions discussed above. Mead emphasizes now one and now another of these functions, depending upon the demands of the explanatory task at hand. Perhaps the chief deficiency in his treatment of attitude-taking, a deficiency I have sought in some measure to remedy, lies in his failure to provide an adequate explication of the mechanism of socialization required for the appropriative functioning of such conduct. We might add, too, that he tells us nothing about the relation of attitude-taking to the affective dimensions of experience, and he does not explore in any detailed way the structure of nonrudimentary sorts of attitude-taking. In spite of these deficiencies, however, this concept looms large among his original contributions to the study of humans as social beings. And his treatment of this concept is sufficiently promising to merit further elaboration and refinement by those who share his conviction that taking the attitude of the other is a fundamental mechanism of human social conduct.

Chapter 7

Mead and the City of Chicago: Social and Educational Reform

We saw in chapter 3 that Mead began to espouse a piecemeal and experimental approach to social reconstruction in his 1899 essay on "The Working Hypothesis in Social Reform"; moreover, at about the same time he began to sketch proposals for educational reform in such essays as "The Relation of Play to Education" (1896) and "The Child and His Environment" (1898). These early expressions of interest in social and educational reform were a prelude to a period of intensive engagement in organized reform activities. During what might be called the "middle period" of his Chicago career—roughly the timespan stretching from John Dewey's resignation and departure from the University of Chicago in 1904 until the years immediately following World War I—he became heavily involved in a number of voluntary organizations that sought to provide social services, study social problems, and promote social and educational reforms in Chicago. The present chapter examines the record of Mead's participation in such reform organizations and relates this participation to relevant essays he published during the same period. Its aim is to present a well-documented account of his reform activities and to note some connections between these activities and the development of his social and educational philosophy.

The University of Chicago Settlement and the Immigrants

When Mead arrived in the rapidly growing city of Chicago in the early fall of 1894, it already had a population in excess of 1.2 million persons, more than one-third of whom were foreign-born. Many of the early immigrants had taken up residence in the stockyards district a few miles to the west of the university where the men sought employment in the large meat-packing houses established by Gustavus F. Swift and Philip Danforth Armour. It was to minister to the needs of the largely immigrant population in this district that the University of Chicago Settlement House was founded in January 1894. Inspired by the social settlement movement that had begun in England in the 1870s and, in particular, by the local example of Jane Addams's social settlement at Hull-House (founded in 1889), the University of Chicago Settlement enjoyed the enthusiastic support of President Harper, who served on its first board of directors. Under the able leadership of head resident Mary E. McDowell, it soon became a thriving center of social services for the families in its neighborhood.[1]

It is not clear from historical documents just when Mead began to take an interest in the University Settlement and to donate financial support for its work. Very likely this took place shortly after his arrival at the university. Certainly he must have been fully apprised of the nature of settlement work at an early date: Dewey served as a member of the board of trustees at Hull-House from 1897 to 1903, and Mead himself gave several lectures under Hull-House auspices in 1897.[2] In any case, Mead had become closely enough associated with the University Settlement by 1907 to join McDowell in the fall of that year as a principal speaker at a Sunday morning chapel service held in the university's Mandel Hall on the occasion of what was called Settlement Sunday. His remarks on this occasion, subsequently published as "The Social Settlement: Its Basis and Function" (1908), provide a succinct characterization of those features of the settlement movement that he found especially congenial to his own views on social reform.[3]

Even though he was speaking at a chapel service, Mead could not resist the temptation to contrast the sort of moral consciousness cultivated by settlement work with that commonly found in the Christian pulpit. And his view of the latter was anything but favorable:

> The pulpit is called upon to inspire to right conduct, not to find out what is the right—unless the right is so plain that he who runs may read. While its dogma has been abstruse its morality has been uniformly simple. When, then, new problems arise, such as the question of the right of the employer to use his property rights to control and exploit the labor of children and women, the

justice of the union in its effort to advance the wage, and a hundred more such problems which have been crowding upon us, the pulpit is unable to solve them, because it has not the apparatus, and the scientific technique which the solution of such problems demands. In the meantime it holds its peace, for it must give no uncertain sound to battle. The only overt social issues with which the pulpit in recent time has identified itself have been temperance and chastity.[4]

Such a pulpit mentality, Mead argued, was quite foreign to the moral orientation of recent settlement work. Instead of attempting to bring an external set of standards to bear upon social problems, settlement workers saw that they must first take advantage of their residence in a settlement house to make themselves at home in the neighborhood they wished to serve. Having done this, their understanding of social problems, their moral judgments, and their attempts at amelioration would flow from a context of immediate human relationships—from what might be called "neighborhood consciousness." Furthermore, instead of falling back upon preformed moral judgments, settlement workers embraced a strategy of open-minded inquiry to arrive at new moral judgments capable of intelligently guiding conduct in the face of the new social problems confronting them. In this respect their moral consciousness was at one with "modern scientific consciousness." They immersed themselves in the life of their community and then sought "to approach its conditions with no preconceptions, to be the exponents of no dogma or fixed rules of conduct," in order that they might correctly identify the problems of that community and as a part of it work toward their solution.[5]

It is not difficult to detect in "The Social Settlement: Its Basis and Function" just that combination of Hegelian ideas with a commitment to scientific method that, as we saw in chapter 3, gave shape to Mead's early conception of social reform. The social settlement, he held, carried out its activities at those points in the social whole "where the most intensely interesting problems in modern industrial and social life are centered." And one of the central tasks of the settlement was to become the vehicle through which the social conflicts underlying these problems were brought to the level of reflective consciousness, i.e., were explicitly formulated and intelligently addressed. The settlement met this challenge by cultivating a species of moral consciousness that was "inquiring and scientific in method" and at the same time based upon an organic involvement in the concrete life of the surrounding community. If the settlement accomplished nothing else, Mead concluded, it illustrated in a concrete fashion "how the community ought to form a new moral judgment."[6]

Mead, of course, was not a settlement worker; he did not live in the settlement house or participate directly in its daily round of service activities. But he did for many years play a prominent role as a policy-maker and fund-raiser for the University Settlement. For fourteen years, beginning in January 1908, he served as a member of its Board of Directors, along with such University of Chicago colleagues as Charles R. Henderson, Floyd R. Mechem, William Scott Bond, Robert A. Millikan, and Nathan C. Plimpton. During most of this period he held the position of treasurer for the organization and was a leading member of its Finance Committee, chairing it from 1909 to 1913. In addition, he was a member of the Committee on Functions and Activities and for a number of years, beginning in 1911, chaired its Committee on Studies and Publications. From 1919 until his retirement from the board in 1922, he served as its president.[7]

Perhaps the most significant aspect of Mead's work on the University Settlement's Board of Directors was his leadership in the area of social research. Stimulated in large part by the example of the well-publicized Pittsburgh Survey of 1906, the board in April 1909 formally requested that Mead "investigate and report back to the Directors on the cost, possibility and advisability of a 'survey' of the settlement district"— this survey to include a careful study of such matters as the physical, economic, and industrial conditions in the Chicago stockyards neighborhood. Thus began Mead's involvement in the social survey movement promoted by social reformers in several American cities during the early years of this century. At the May meeting of the board, Mead presented a report containing detailed suggestions as to the character and extent of the proposed survey, together with estimates of its probable cost. Following a lengthy discussion, the board voted at the same meeting to approve Mead's proposals "provided such an investigation could be carried out in a scientific way."[8]

While the details of the discussion preceding this vote are not recorded in the minutes of the board, the intent of the proviso that the survey be pursued in a scientific manner is made clear by letters the board later sent to packing industry executives.[9] Certainly the board did not have in mind any sophisticated methodological canons to which it wanted the study to conform, nor did it intend for the survey to be an exercise in social research for its own sake. Rather, like the Pittsburgh Survey after which it was modeled, the Chicago stockyards survey was to be undertaken as a means to social reform. Its purpose was the acquisition of accurate and systematic knowledge of social conditions, which could then be employed as a basis for the diagnosis and amelioration of social problems in the settlement neighborhood. In calling for a "scientific" survey the board was primarily expressing its desire for a study that would be factual rather than inflammatory or sensationalistic in tone; the board did not want to antagonize the packinghouse officials whose cooperation it regarded as necessary for the achievement of needed social reform.

In the months following the board's approval of plans for the survey, Mead served as chief fund-raiser for the project, using his personal influence to secure generous gifts of financial support from such wealthy friends of reform as Mrs. Ethel Dummer, Mrs. M. D. Hull, and Mrs. Anita McCormick Blaine. In addition, he sought out and arranged for the hiring of competent social researchers to plan, supervise, and write up the results of survey interviews and investigations. Once the survey got under way in 1910, Mead—along with fellow board member and sociologist Charles R. Henderson—assumed responsibility for the overall coordination of the survey and gave regular progress reports to the Board of Directors. Finally, as chairman of the board's Committee on Studies and Publications, Mead oversaw the publication of the survey's findings in three volumes during the years 1912–14.[10]

Although the Chicago stockyards survey seems not to have resulted in any concrete social reforms, it did much to whet Mead's enthusiasm for social survey research. In 1912 he convinced Blaine to fund an exploration of the feasibility of a social research bureau that would promote and coordinate social surveys throughout Chicago. The following year Mead's idea for a social research bureau achieved at least limited realization through the efforts of University of Chicago professor of political science and city alderman Charles R. Merriam, who successfully promoted the passage of an ordinance establishing a city Department of Public Welfare, one of whose functions was to carry out just the kind of coordinated research Mead had envisioned. This department proved to be relatively ineffectual, however, until the appointment of McDowell as its commissioner in 1923.[11]

Although the University of Chicago Settlement was a focal point for much of Mead's reform activity throughout the middle years of his career at Chicago, it was by no means the only reform organization to which he devoted his time and energies during this period. In 1908, for instance, the same year in which he was elected to the settlement's Board of Directors, Mead helped to found the Immigrants' Protective League, and from 1909 to 1919 he served along with Addams as a vice-president for this private philanthropic agency. Under the directorship of Grace Abbott, the league annually assisted thousands of immigrants arriving at the Dearborn Street Station in Chicago. League workers, operating from a central office across the street from the train station, welcomed and protected the immigrants from unscrupulous cabdrivers by seeing them and their baggage safely to their destinations. In addition, the league sought to promote the welfare of immigrants by helping them secure employment, putting them in touch with educational and social service organizations, and doing what it could to protect young immigrant women from the white slave trade and prostitution. Finally, the league promoted various studies of immigrant populations in Chicago, lobbied successfully for the establishment of a federal immigration bureau in the city, pushed for revisions in state laws governing employment agencies, and succeeded in bringing about the short-lived existence of an Illinois Immigration Commission during the years 1918–21.[12]

A further illustration of Mead's participation in reform organizations can be seen in his active role on an ad hoc Citizens' Committee established in response to a strike by many of the city's garment workers in the fall of 1910. Organized on October 30, 1910, the Citizens' Committee of twenty-three persons included in its membership such prominent Chicago reformers as Addams, Abbott, Sophinisba P. Breckinridge, Ernst Freund, Julian W. Mack, Allen B. Pond, and Graham Taylor. In the judgment of the committee, a prompt resolution of the garment workers' strike was important for the welfare of both the city and the approximately 25,000 clothing employees who had left their jobs. Most of these workers, the committee noted, were immigrants, "and many of them but newly arrived." At its initial meeting the committee appointed a subcommittee consisting of Breckinridge, Anna E. Nicholes, Henderson, A. A. McCormick, and Mead as chairman to investigate the nature and validity of the grievances alleged by the striking garment workers. During the next few days Mead and his subcommittee interviewed a number of striking workers as well as officials of Hart, Schaffner & Marx, the Wholesale Clothiers' Association, and the National Wholesale Tailors' Association. On the basis of these interviews Mead drafted and submitted to the larger Citizens' Committee a report that was largely supportive of the striking workers' complaints. After some condensation and revision, the report was released by the Citizens' Committee for publication on November 5, 1910.[13] As it turned out, Mead's efforts had little impact on the outcome of the strike. On the morning of November 5, just prior to the release of the Citizens' Committee report, the International Garment Workers' Union reached an agreement with Hart, Schaffner & Marx through negotiations carried on under the auspices of the Chicago City Council. According to this agreement, all future grievances and disputes would be submitted to a committee of arbitration for resolution. The officials of the Wholesale Clothiers' Association and the National Wholesale Tailors' Association, however, refused to follow the example of Hart, Schaffner & Marx—whereupon Mead drafted on behalf of the Citizens' Committee a strongly worded statement of "Grievances against the Association Houses." In this document he argued that "it is not too much to say that at the present time the community demands that industrial struggles should be ended by arbitration, and that either party that refuses to submit its case to arbitration must meet the just condemnation of the community."[14] Again, Mead's efforts and those of the Citizens' Committee were of no avail. The Association Houses ignored the "just condemnation of the community," and the strike was eventually broken.[15]

The City Club of Chicago

Those of Mead's reform activities that did not stem more or less directly from his affiliation with the University of Chicago Settlement were often tied to his long membership in the City Club of Chicago. Founded in 1903 as a nonpartisan group "having as its object the investigation and improvement of municipal conditions and public affairs in the City of Chicago," the City Club soon became a large and influential organization: by 1920 it had more than 2,400 dues-paying members.[16] Mead joined the club in 1906 and one year later addressed its members on "The Educational Situation in the Chicago Public Schools." From

1908 until 1914 he served as chairman of the club's standing Committee on Public Education.[17]

As chairman of the Committee on Public Education, Mead chaired three different subcommittees between 1908 and 1912, each of which undertook a study and prepared a written report including proposals for reform. One, a subcommittee on libraries, issued a 1909 report severely critical of Chicago's public library service on the grounds that it was economically inefficient, utilized ineffective methods for the circulation of books, and failed to meet adequately the needs of Chicago's children, public schools, and large foreign population. The report of this subcommittee was submitted to the board of directors of the Chicago Public Library and had considerable impact upon the subsequent reorganization of the city's public library system.[18] A second subcommittee chaired by Mead carried out extensive research related to the need for vocational training in the Chicago public school system, while yet a third subcommittee formulated a legislative proposal for the funding and administration of vocational education in the public schools of the state of Illinois.[19]

As a result of his active service in chairing the Committee on Public Education, Mead was elected to the City Club's Board of Directors in 1912. In December 1915, he—along with Pond and O. C. Doering—spoke on behalf of the club at a meeting of the School Management Committee of the Chicago Board of Education. Ella Flagg Young had recently announced her intention to step down as Chicago's superintendent of schools, and the City Club, together with the Union League Club and the Woman's City Club, wished to propose the appointment of a committee of nationally prominent educators to suggest names of individuals who might be available and competent to fill this important position. Despite the combined advocacy of these three groups, however, the School Management Committee rejected the proposal. A week later the full Board of Education elected John D. Shoop as superintendent by a vote of 19 to 0.[20]

Mead served as chairman of the City Club's Board of Directors in 1917–18, and from 1916 to 1918 he also chaired the Public Affairs Committee, which was responsible for news releases and public relations.[21] In early June 1916 he drafted a letter from the Public Affairs Committee to the Chicago Board of Education objecting to a proposal to change the rules governing teacher tenure in a way that would make it possible "to drop teachers at the end of the school year without notice, assignment of cause, or opportunity of hearing." Mead attended a meeting of the school board on June 14, 1916, to present the position of his committee, but a request that he be allowed to do so was ruled out of order by the president of the board. The board then passed the proposed rule change with little discussion.[22] This action, together with the school board's ongoing attempts to exclude from the Chicago public schools any teacher actively involved in the Chicago Federation of Teachers, led to the formation shortly thereafter of the Public Education Association of Chicago, a group of concerned citizens dedicated to the promotion of legislation providing for teacher tenure and a reorganization of the governance of the Chicago school system. Mead was elected one of the vice-presidents of this association.[23]

Although no longer chairman of the Committee on Public Education after 1914, Mead continued to play a prominent role in the City Club's deliberations and actions pertaining to public education. In addition to the activities already mentioned, he served during the year 1916–17 on a subcommittee of the Committee on Public Education, which successfully carried out its appointed task of convincing Superintendent Shoop and the Chicago Board of Education to set up a Bureau of Educational Survey and School Standards. Established in late 1917, the bureau had as its purpose the systematic collection, compilation, and interpretation of statistical data concerning such matters as truancy, scores on standardized tests, ages of students at each grade level, rates of student promotion and failure, and teachers' salaries.[24] Mead also saw that current issues of public education were thoroughly aired before the membership of the City Club. At a meeting in late June 1916, for instance, he introduced a discussion by Aldermen Merriam and John S. Miller on the topic of tenure for public school teachers.[25] And in March 1917 he was one of two speakers to address the club on matters related to the reorganization of the Chicago school system. On this latter occasion Mead argued strongly that members of the Chicago Board of Education should be elected rather than appointed by the mayor.[26]

Mead's participation in the City Club culminated in his election to the presidency for two one-year terms from 1918 to 1920.[27] During his time as president he carried on a brief public correspondence with Senator Medill McCormick of Illinois concerning the latter's opposition to the proposed constitution for the League of Nations. And in March 1919 he was one of more than a hundred members of the City

Club who signed a resolution endorsing the league.[28] Following his two terms as president, Mead served for two more years on the Board of Directors. He remained a member of the City Club until his death in 1931, but played a much less active role in its activities after 1922.[29]

Educational Theory and Reform

Mead's participation in reform organizations and activities seems to have had little direct connection with the development of his central social psychological ideas, but it had an obvious relationship to his educational theorizing. Most of his contributions to investigations and reform proposals sponsored by the City Club had to do with public education. Moreover, the years of his tenure as chairman of the City Club's Committee on Public Education (1908–14) corresponded almost exactly with the period during which he devoted the greatest attention to educational issues in his teaching and writing. Between 1907 and 1911, for instance, he several times taught courses titled philosophy of education and the teaching of science in the secondary school at the University of Chicago. And from 1907 to 1909 he served on the editorial board of the Chicago-based journal, the *Elementary School Teacher*.[30] It was during this period also that Mead wrote most of his published articles dealing with educational topics. A brief chronological list of the most important of these indicates the range of his interest: "Science in the High School" (1906), "The Teaching of Science in College" (1906), "Editorial Note on the School System of Chicago" (1907), "The Educational Situation in the Chicago Public Schools" (1907), "Educational Aspects of Trade Schools" (1908), "Industrial Education, the Working-Man, and the School" (1909), "The Psychology of Social Consciousness Implied in Instruction" (1910), and "The Larger Bearings of Vocational Guidance" (1913).

Several of these essays reveal the persistence of Dewey's influence upon Mead's educational thought. The articles on the teaching of science, for example, allege that introductory courses in the natural sciences characteristically exhibit pedagogical defects of the sort repeatedly attacked by Dewey in other contexts: they approach the several sciences (and mathematics) in isolation from one another, and they fail to link scientific abstractions adequately to the concrete experience and natural interests of the student.[31] Moreover, one of the chief remedies

Mead proposes for these shortcomings—high school science courses that emphasize field and laboratory work related to the study of natural processes found in the student's immediate environment—closely resembles the strategy employed at an elementary level in science classes carried on at the University Elementary School.[32] Similarly, while "The Psychology of Social Consciousness Implied in Instruction" contains a few brief references to Mead's own social psychological ideas, its central thesis is that educators should give careful consideration to social relations in the classroom as these relate to the development of the child's personality; in this respect the essay echoes Dewey's plea for a more community-centered approach to the educational process.[33]

But the fact of Dewey's continued influence does not tell the whole story about the course of Mead's educational thought in the years after 1904: that story also involves Mead's growing interest in local educational reform. Following the demise of Dewey's elementary school, Mead increasingly turned his attention to problems of public education in Chicago. Some of these problems were administrative or procedural in character; others had to do with curriculum. The former kind of problem occupied him in two closely related publications of 1907, "The Educational Situation in the Chicago Public Schools" (originally an address delivered to the City Club) and an editorial note written for the *School Review* on "The School System of Chicago."

In these essays Mead dealt with a controversy that had been brewing within the school system during the preceding five years. At the heart of the controversy were issues concerning teacher evaluation, how best to encourage professional development among teachers, and the role of teachers in the formulation of educational policies. The focal point of dispute with respect to the first two issues was a system of promotional examinations, established by Superintendent Edwin G. Cooley in 1902, under which teachers were to take a promotional examination at the end of seven years of service in the Chicago schools. The examination focused mainly on outside academic work, and the results were to determine the teacher's eligibility for further advances in salary. Members of the Chicago Federation of Teachers protested strongly against this arrangement, arguing that evaluation and salary increases should not be based upon academic work that was extraneous to their effectiveness in the classroom. Furthermore, they took the system of promotional examinations to be a somewhat devious device for holding down salaries. Mead's view was that the promotional examinations might have been well intended, but in practice they were a conspicuous failure. They neither measured the effectiveness of teachers in the classroom nor succeeded in inducing teachers to pursue professional development outside the classroom.[34] In place of such examinations he suggested that the school system employ an adequate number of assistant superintendents or other competent specialists to monitor teacher performance through regular classroom visitation and to provide not only evaluation but helpful suggestions to promote teacher effectiveness. In addition, teachers should be encouraged—by constructive means, rather than by examinations tied to salary increases—to pursue supplementary academic work leading to professional development; this work, however, should be directly related to needs experienced by teachers in the course of their classroom teaching.[35]

As for the third issue in the controversy—the teachers' role in the formulation of educational policy—Mead argued for "democratization of the schools." By this he meant, among other things, that devices such as teachers' councils should be employed to give the teachers a voice in policymaking decisions within the school system. "It is immoral to demand that our teachers throw themselves heart and soul into the social activity of educating our children and then deny them any voice in criticizing, interpreting, fashioning the ways and means that they are to use."[36] In this connection he urged his readers to reject the mistaken notion that the practice of school administration should take as its model administration as it is found in the world of business: the business model is inappropriate here because the practice of school administration has as its ultimate end "neither the making nor the spending of money, but the development of the personalities of children by means of the personalities of the teachers." The central task of the school administrator is one of making the process of education less mechanical, of creating conditions in which the personalities of students and teachers can interact most fully and effectively. "It is just this recognition of the personalities of teachers and children, with all that it implies, which is meant by the democratization of the schools."[37]

In addition to such administrative controversies, Mead also gave a good deal of thought to the character of the curriculum in the Chicago public school system. Nowhere is this interest more evident than in his attempt to establish for Chicago's schools the significance of the vocational education movement that began to gather national momentum about 1908. Mead repeatedly addressed this topic in "Educational Aspects of Trade Schools" (1908), "Industrial Education, the

Working-Man, and the School" (1909), and in a series of editorial notes written for the *Elementary School Teacher* during 1907–9.[38] It is clear from these essays that he welcomed the vocational education movement largely on pedagogical grounds supplied by his Deweyan educational philosophy. That is, he saw vocational training as a natural extension of Dewey's emphasis upon the pedagogical value of manual training and the general desirability of bridging the gap between life within and outside the classroom. "We have suffered from a discipline which applies simply to the school room and is not the discipline of life; and the educator, especially the reform—the modern—educator, has been looking for some way of tapping the real life interest from the outside and carrying it into the schoolroom."[39] He thus found it a good omen that educators who had been trying to reach out from the school toward the realities of life should now find "industrial society knocking at the doors of the schoolhouse seeking admittance."[40]

Mead also set forth in these essays definite views concerning the auspices under which vocational education should be offered and the form it should take. He held, first, that "it should be made a part of our public school system, part of that system which we can reach by votes," rather than something pursued in separate trade schools set up by industrial manufacturers. Vocational education promised too much for the lives of future workers, for the vitality of the public schools, and for the well-being of the entire community to be "left in the hands of manufacturers who are only immediately interested in the training of skilled men."[41] Mead further argued that such education ought to be liberal rather than narrowly technical. It should not, for instance, simply teach young people to operate certain sorts of machinery. Instead, it should equip prospective workers with an ability to evaluate their tools and devise ways of improving them; it should promote skills accompanied by a kind of intelligence that would make possible flexibility and adaptation to changing circumstances, so that workers would not be doomed to obsolescence along with their machines. And it should be liberal in the additional sense of acquainting workers with the historical and social significance of their vocations, giving them an understanding of their place in a democratic society. If vocational education in America did less than this, if it neglected the "broader intellectual and spiritual interests" of the worker, then it would become an inferior education for second-class citizens; it would introduce into the school system a class distinction antithetical to the spirit of American democracy.[42]

While Mead addressed the topic of vocational education from a

Mead - he mind
use he mind
productively

national perspective in essays published between 1907 and 1909, he turned his attention more specifically to the situation in Chicago beginning in 1910. Early that year he accepted the chairmanship of a City Club subcommittee that undertook an extensive two-year study of vocational education needs in the Chicago public school system. In this capacity Mead raised funds for the research project, hired researchers, and oversaw the final publication of the research findings and recommendations—all in the same years when he was in charge of the previously discussed survey of the stockyards district sponsored by the University of Chicago Settlement. In 1912 the City Club subcommittee published a three-hundred-page document titled *A Report on Vocational Training in Chicago and in Other Cities.*[43]

In his introduction to this report Mead noted that nearly half of the children in the Chicago public schools did not complete eight years of elementary schooling. The state required children to attend school until the age of fourteen, but once they reached this age many children dropped out of the Chicago schools and sought to enter the work force. Mead and his subcommittee found that such children were not only ill prepared for American citizenship, but also that they were poorly equipped for any meaningful employment: "We find that the boys who leave school to go to work between the ages of fourteen and sixteen are idle half of the time, and earn during these two years not more than an average of $2 a week. We find that they are not needed in the industries of Chicago and that the return which they bring in to their homes is negligible. We find further . . . that they gain no training that is of value for them in later years. On the contrary their idleness during at least half the time, their frequent passing from one job to another, their lack of responsibility, necessarily leads to moral, mental, and frequently physical degeneration. During two of the most valuable years of preparation for life they are going backward instead of forward."[44]

Not content merely to report statistical findings and make general observations about the need for vocational education in Chicago, Mead and his subcommittee offered a battery of detailed recommendations for vocational education in the public school system.[45] Furthermore, once the work of this subcommittee was completed in 1912, Mead immediately took on the chairmanship of another City Club subcommittee, which drafted proposed legislation to deal with the funding and administration of vocational education in the state of Illinois.[46] In this context Mead continued his earlier opposition to the establishment of vocational schools outside the purview of the existing public school system. Such separate schools, he again argued, would inevitably acquire the "stigma of being schools solely for the laboring classes." This stigma could be avoided and existing public schools could be strengthened by the infusion into their curricula of programs enabling them to benefit from "the great popular interest which is now impelling the vocational education movement." "The public school system is good in proportion as it holds the respect and interest of all classes of people. Without the regenerating influence of the struggle to keep the school close to the needs of the people, it must inevitably become even more than its critics deem it to be today, a dispenser of a leisure class, formal, and 'academic' education. Instead of shunting this popular interest into the narrow channels of a separate vocational system, it should be utilized to keep vigorous the whole institution of public instruction, and enable it progressively to adjust itself to the changes needed." [47]

Finally, beginning at least as early as 1913 when he presented a paper entitled "The Larger Educational Bearings of Vocational Guidance" at the annual meeting of the National Conference on Vocational Guidance, Mead urged the importance not only of vocational training in the public schools but also of a concerted effort to provide young people with informed guidance as they prepared for their entrance into the world of work.[48] The value of such guidance for the future of the individual child, he noted, was too obvious to require argument. What was perhaps not so obvious was the benefit that would accrue to the schools from programs of vocational guidance. A school committed to intelligent vocational guidance would be forced to give up self-contained insularity in favor of frequent communication with other agencies affecting the life of the child, e.g., the home, social workers, employment agencies, and employers. Furthermore, it would have to engage in continual reexamination of its own subject matter and methods in the light of how its students fared once they left the school. An "acquaintance with intensive studies of the schooling and occupations of children in a poverty-stricken industrial section of Chicago," Mead testified, "has convinced me that the task of following up the boys and girls who, with incomplete schooling, search after wretched jobs, brings out with terrible force the necessity of regarding and judging our whole process of child training from the standpoint of the vocations into which we are unconsciously driving them." [49] It was for these reasons that Mead became an enthusiastic supporter of the Bureau of Vocational Guidance established under the auspices of the Chicago public school system in 1916. And it was in this spirit that he served for a number of years after that date as president of the Vocational Supervision League, a voluntary association that helped provide social workers for the bureau and also raised scholarship funds to aid older students who might otherwise drop out of school to seek employment.[50]

Concluding Remarks

Mead's middle years at the University of Chicago were anything but years of scholarly disengagement from the problems of his immediate society. Indeed, so great was his involvement with the social and educational problems of Chicago that one wonders how he ever found time to do any scholarly work! Mead's attitude toward these problems was primarily that of a social reformer rather than a disinterested scientific observer. Whether he was serving as a fund-raiser or a member of a board of directors, supervising a social survey, or chairing a civic committee, his aim was always the achievement of social improvement. In keeping with his earlier writings on social philosophy, his pursuit of this melioristic aim was consistently "opportunistic" rather than "programmatic" in character: both his participation in reform organizations and his writing on topics related to this participation were devoted to the intelligent resolution of specific social conflicts and problems instead of to the realization of any elaborately worked out utopian vision. His success in this endeavor was modest at best, but he never abandoned his confidence in the use of human intelligence as the best means to achieve needed social reform. When he finally curtailed his reform activities in the early 1920s, he did so not because of any pessimism about the prospects for meaningful social reform but apparently because he wanted to devote a greater proportion of his remaining years to scholarly research and writing.[51]

Chapter 8

Moral Reconstruction and the Social Self

While Mead was still inclined to identify his moral and social concerns with those of the Christian religion as late as 1893 when he spoke to the Students' Christian Association at the University of Michigan on the topic of Christian love, soon after moving to the University of Chicago he adopted a wholly secular orientation toward moral and social questions. It is difficult to date this conversion exactly, but, judging from the clearly secular tone of his 1899 essay on "The Working Hypothesis in Social Reform," it seems to have taken place within his first five years at Chicago. Although Mead continued to make occasional use of biblical phrases as rhetorical devices in his teaching and writing throughout the remainder of his life, his mature attitude toward Christianity fell somewhere between indifference and outright rejection. This attitude is perhaps most blatantly expressed in two letters he wrote midway through his Chicago career. In the first, he records a rare Sunday morning of church attendance with the remark that it gave him "the feeling of being plastered all over with vaseline." [1] In the second he reports his thoughts after attending a memorial service for George Burman Foster, professor of the philosophy of religion at the university: "Like all theologians Foster was bogged down in the attempt to connect some wording of the old creeds with present day problems. . . . The problems, however, of the day are not those of the inner life of individuals but of social reconstruction, and here religion has shown no leadership, nor a method that could be followed, or even avowed in social undertakings." [2]

In this chapter I examine the development of the secular understanding of morality that Mead worked out in his teaching and writing in the years after 1899. His most important contributions to this field have to do with what might be called moral psychology and moral methodology. Beginning in 1900, he espoused a functionalist moral psychology that construed moral problems, moral consciousness, and moral decision-making as functional phases of a reconstructive process taking place within human conduct. Somewhat later, once he had worked out the key ideas of his social psychology, he brought his social theories of mind and self to bear upon his analysis of the moral life. Throughout all of his essays and lectures on ethical topics, Mead consistently held that moral progress or growth takes place through reconstruction in the face of moral problems. And the central thesis of his moral methodology was that the recurring need for such reconstruction could best be met by a method of experimental inquiry analogous to that practiced in the empirical sciences.

Early Functionalist Moral Psychology

That Mead's moral philosophy was from the outset closely linked to his functionalist approach to psychology can be seen by looking at two essays he published early in his career at Chicago, "Suggestions Toward a Theory of the Philosophical Disciplines" (1900) and "The Philosophical Basis of Ethics" (1908). In the first he touches upon ethics in the context of an attempt to characterize all of the main branches of philosophy in terms of his Deweyan understanding of human conduct; in the second he builds upon the same foundation to construct the most complete published statement of his early views on moral psychology.

Environmental objects, Mead holds in the former essay, take on meanings as a result of our responses to them or our uses of them. Now, so long as conduct with respect to these objects proceeds smoothly, their meanings are not questioned, and they do not become the focus of reflective thought. But from time to time problems arise within our conduct: we are confronted with situations whose ambiguous or indeterminate character calls forth conflicting tendencies to respond. On these occasions, reflective thought is called into play to analyze and reinterpret the problematic situation so that conduct can once again be resumed (SW 8). Reflective thought thus performs a reconstructive task within human conduct, and this task can be carried out in two different ways. It can either proceed deductively by reaffirming old meanings as they apply to the problem at hand, or it can proceed inductively by searching for new meanings—thereby guiding conduct in a new direction with respect to the problematic situation. "The application of either of these methods to conduct as a whole, in their relation to the ideal or to the larger self to be obtained, fulfills the function of ethics" (sw 7).

Ethics, in other words, concerns the use of reflective thought to solve moral problems. And moral problems resemble other sorts of problems in that they involve competing environmental meanings that call forth conflicting responses from the individual confronting them. The kind of moral problem that especially interests Mead is one in which the self is torn between opposing valuations or moral interpretations of a given situation. One of these opposing lines of valuation, he suggests, is likely to be traditional and have the weight of conventional moral sentiment on its side; the other may have arisen because of some felt inadequacy in the conventional moral interpretation. When faced with a problem of this sort, moral reflection often takes what has previously been labeled the deductive approach: it simply reaffirms the old valuation while attempting to ignore or suppress any opposing tendencies. "For example, the right to the use of what is termed property being once fixed, the expenditure of it in luxuries while others may be starving arouses, when the problem is felt, first of all the idea of property itself as it is represented in all the business transactions of life. This may be affirmed in spite of the contradiction between it and the tendencies to demand assistance for the suffering" (sw 9). The chief shortcoming of this approach, as Mead sees the matter, is that its very one-sidedness may leave the self harboring a "continuous conflict which thus becomes chronic and destructive instead of being a moment in a process of natural development" (sw 22).

The idea suggested here, that a moral conflict should be treated as "a moment in a process of natural development," is arguably part of the legacy of Mead's earlier Hegelianism. And it explains why he favors what he calls an inductive approach to the resolution of moral problems. On this latter approach, moral reflection abandons old moral meanings or values that have been found to be inadequate and seeks a moral reinterpretation that will, so far as possible, do justice to all of the competing tendencies found in the morally problematic situation. Here the reflecting self treats moral problems as occasions for moral growth, whose successful resolution leads to a fuller and more coherent expression of the impulses contained within the self. It does this by adopting a method of moral reconstruction that emulates "the ideal of

deductive vs inductive approaches to morality

the scientist . . . found in the complete statement of the various conditions that must be recognized and met in any possible hypothesis" (sw 21).

Mead further elaborates these views concerning moral problems and the reconstructive function of moral reflection in "The Philosophical Basis of Ethics" (1908). Here he begins by emphasizing that conduct is a process involving a relationship of mutual determination between an organism and its environment. This point, it should be recalled, is part and parcel of the organic model of conduct that both Mead and Dewey had advocated since at least 1896. According to that model, the organism is not a passive entity from which environmental stimuli mechanically elicit responses. Rather, the organism actively selects, organizes, and interprets the stimuli to which it responds. Thus, the sensitivities and doings of the organism play a vital role in constituting the structure and content of the environment that the organism experiences.

If we combine the organic understanding of the organism-environment relationship with an evolutionary point of view, Mead remarks, we are led to the philosophically significant conclusion that the environment experienced by an organism must evolve hand in hand with the conduct and sensitivities of that organism. And applying this conclusion to the case of human experience, "we find ourselves with a consciousness which we conceive of as evolved; the contents and the forms of these contents can be looked upon as products of development. Among these contents and forms are found the temporal and spatial structures of things, of the world" (sw 82). It is precisely this last suggestion that underlies Mead's subsequent attempts to develop a constitutive account of the spatial and temporal structures of human experience. In "The Philosophical Basis of Ethics," however, his attention lies elsewhere: he wants to show that the naturalistic and evolutionary standpoint just adumbrated can shed light upon the moral dimension of human experience.

To understand properly the moral dimension of human experience, Mead contends, we must look upon moral meanings as experienced qualities that arise within the ongoing relationship of mutual determination between individuals and their environments. They are meanings accruing to certain stimuli in virtue of the significance these stimuli possess for the expression of the interests and patterns of conduct that relate the self to others. Moral consciousness, on this view, is a type of consciousness in which we become explicitly aware of these meanings;

it is a phase of conduct in which we reflectively take stock of the competing meanings involved in a morally problematic situation (sw 90). Moreover, since there is almost no aspect of a person's experience not implicated to some extent in a moral problem, moral consciousness tends to be "the most concrete consciousness—the most inclusive statement which can be given of immediate experience" (sw 84). At the outset, however, moral consciousness merely makes us aware of what is at stake in a moral problem; it does not immediately furnish a solution for that problem. Hence, there is need for a further stage of moral reflection, in which the self carries out a reinterpretation of the situation as it initially appears to moral consciousness. "If we were willing to recognize that the environment which surrounds the moral self is but the statement of the conditions under which his different conflicting impulses may get their expression, we would perceive that the reorganization must come from a new point of view which comes to consciousness through the conflict" (sw 90). At this point Mead once again distinguishes, as he did in his essay of 1900, between two methods that might be employed to achieve the needed reorganization. But whereas earlier he had distinguished between a deductive and an inductive approach to moral decision-making, he now speaks of "abstract external valuation" and "concrete valuation."

Abstract external valuation attempts to resolve moral problems by appeal to a fixed moral order "which transcends either metaphysically or temporally the moral situation" (sw 90). But, despite the superior status often attributed to the standards and meanings supplied by such an external moral order, they are "always the precipitations of earlier conduct" and hence are "pretty uniformly inadequate" to deal with new moral problems resulting from changed social circumstances. Such an approach to moral problems, Mead argues, robs the individual and the community of a vital form of intelligence that might be used to guide conduct in morally problematic situations (sw 93).

To avoid this loss of intelligence, we must reject the traditional identification of morality with conformity to a fixed moral order thought to rest upon some basis external to conduct. In its place we should substitute a view in which the moral life is seen as an evolving transaction between the self and the moral environment presented to it in moral consciousness. "The growth of moral consciousness must be coterminous with that of the moral situation. The moral life lies in the interaction of these two; the situation rises up in accusation of the moral personality which is unequal to it, and the personality rises to the situation only by a process which reconstructs the situation as profoundly as it reconstructs the self" (sw 83). On this view, in other words, moral advance does not consist in a closer and closer approximation to a fixed ideal of conduct; rather, it involves a dialectical process in which creative selves repeatedly devise new moral syntheses in the face of recurring moral conflicts.

The intellectual method best suited to bring about such moral advance, Mead claims, is that which has been most explicitly worked out in the pure and applied empirical sciences. In support of this contention he invites us to consider the case of an engineer confronted with a practical scientific problem arising from the need to design a bridge for a certain location. Here reflection begins with a consciousness of environmental characters that call for a design somewhat different from any that has been used in the past. The engineer attends to these and other data present in the environment and attempts to formulate a working hypothesis that will deal satisfactorily with all the factors in the situation. Analogously, individuals applying the method of concrete valuation begin with moral consciousness of a situation in which old meanings and patterns of behavior are felt to be inadequate. They attend carefully to the competing values resident in the situation and attempt to formulate a moral interpretation or working hypothesis that will enable them to deal successfully with the total situation. Here, as in the case of the engineer, the problem is not to be solved by appeal to any criterion or standard external to the self and its environment. Rather, the moral judgment must arise from a creative intellectual process in which old interpretations of the moral data at hand are experimentally modified until conduct can proceed in a way that realizes the fullest possible integration between the self and the moral situation (sw 91).

Morality and the Social Self

Mead does not broaden his discussion of the moral life to include insights from social psychology in either of the two essays we have just considered. In fact, it is not until his 1913 essay "The Social Self" that his published work begins to show an attempt to bring his social psychology to bear upon his understanding of the moral dimensions of human conduct. Here, after emphasizing the social basis of self-consciousness, he announces near the end of his essay that there is one further implication of the social nature of the self to which he would like to call attention: "It is the manner of its reconstruction. I wish to refer to it, because the point is of importance in the psychology of ethics" (sw 147).

In the discussion following this announcement we find him beginning to reformulate his earlier ideas about moral reconstruction in the light of his social conception of the self. Once again he regards moral values as meanings arising within conduct, where conduct is construed as a relationship of mutual determination between an individual and his environment. Further, he continues to treat moral problems as conflicts of meanings or interests that from time to time appear within this relationship. What is new here, however, is his emphasis on the social character of these problems and of the process by which they are resolved. Moral problems, he says, involve competing tendencies in the social organization of the self, and moral consciousness takes the dynamic form of an internalized conversation within the social forum of reflective thought. "Assuming as I do the essentially social character of the ethical end, we find in moral reflection a conflict in which certain values find a spokesman in the old self or a dominant part of the old self, while other values answering to other tendencies and impulses arise in opposition and find other spokesmen to present their cases. To leave the field to the values represented by the old self is exactly what we term selfishness" (sw 148).

What Mead here criticizes as "selfishness" is obviously the same mentality to which he had earlier attached the labels "deductive" and "abstract external valuation." And once again he advocates in its stead an inductive and concrete approach to moral problems, which attempts to do justice to all the competing social interests present in the morally problematic situation. This approach makes use of the social forum of reflection mentioned above, but it does so in a way that allows both the old self and the other selves, whose roles are assumed in such reflection, to enter the dialogue on equal terms. Rather than attempting to preserve the old self intact, it aims at a reconstruction of the situation that allows a new "enlarged and more adequate" personality to emerge (sw 148). Thus, the satisfactory resolution of a moral problem or conflict typically calls forth the development of a self more inclusive in its social concerns and interests than was the self for whom the problem initially arose. "The growth of the self arises out of a partial disintegration,—

the appearance of the different interests in the forum of reflection, the reconstruction of the social world, and the consequent appearance of the new self that answers to the new object" (sw 149).

Finally, in "The Social Self" Mead notes an important similarity between the reconstructive process underlying moral growth and that involved when a scientist devises a new hypothesis to replace an older theory that has broken down. He admits that there is a significant social psychological difference between scientific and moral problems: the former have to do with conflicts whose solution does not call for any fundamental reorganization of the self, whereas the latter involve "concrete personal interests, in which the whole self is reconstructed in its relation to the other selves whose relations are essential to its personality" (sw 149). Nevertheless, he claims, the process of moral reconstruction has a logic very much like that found in the growth of scientific knowledge. In both cases growth takes place by reconstruction in the face of problems or conflicts. And in both cases intelligent reconstruction requires a form of inquiry that creatively seeks new interpretive hypotheses while remaining sensitive to all the conflicting meanings, values, or observations involved in the problematic situation. The successful scientific hypothesis reunifies a problematic situation and yields a more inclusive understanding of that situation. The successful moral hypothesis reconciles conflicting values in a morally problematic situation and yields a more inclusive self.

War, Democracy, and International-Mindedness

I now want to examine Mead's response to an important historical crisis that exercised considerable influence upon his social and moral philosophizing in the years following 1913: World War I and American engagement in that conflict from April 1917 until the armistice of November 1918. The war led Mead to extend his earlier reflections on moral psychology and methods of resolving moral problems to encompass conflicts arising at the international level of social organization. We can trace this new strand in his thought by looking at "The Psychological Bases of Internationalism" (1915), a series of newspaper essays he published in the Chicago *Herald* during 1917, and his 1929 essay "National-Mindedness and International-Mindedness."

In the first of these publications Mead is mainly concerned to criticize the militaristic and narrowly nationalistic mentality evident on both sides of the conflict. Although he grants a certain kind of value in the heightened sense of national unity promoted by militarism, he sees militarism and warfare as hideously expensive methods of inspiring national self-consciousness. They lead to the wholesale destruction of lives and institutions and are antithetical to those interests of commerce, industry, the labor movement, science, and social reform that are international in character. What is needed is an alternative means by which nations might achieve a sense of unity and self-respect that does not require so great a sacrifice of competing values (ESP 151–52, 158–59).

While Mead does little more than hint at the nature of such an alternative in his 1915 essay, the hints he does supply are clearly drawn from the resources of his social psychology. The genesis of national self-consciousness, he suggests, is analogous in important respects to the genesis of individual self-consciousness: "Nations, like individuals, can become objects to themselves only as they see themselves through the eyes of others" (ESP 153). Furthermore, like individuals, nations can grow in self-understanding and more fully realize themselves only by participating in a larger social order or social process: "The function of social organization is to build up and enlarge the personality of nations as truly as that of individuals" (ESP 154). Nations can thus best move toward a wider and ultimately more fruitful kind of national self-consciousness by developing those activities with international dimensions. Citizens of all nations should strive to overcome attitudes of narrow nationalism and embrace instead a "willingness to accept the whole international fabric of society, and to regard the states and the communities of which they are the instruments, as subject to and controlled by the life of the whole" (ESP 161).

The Great War then engulfing Europe, Mead held in "The Psychological Bases of Internationalism," was being fought neither for ideas nor for a better order of society (ESP 158). But two years later, in a series of short essays published in the Chicago *Herald,* he expressed a quite different view. He was now firmly convinced that a better order of society was at stake in the battle, and he agreed with President Woodrow Wilson's justification for U.S. entry into the conflict. The preceding three years of the war, he claimed, had transformed the struggle into a contest between democracy and autocracy. Moreover, Germany's declaration of unrestricted submarine warfare had forced the United States to choose between two options: either actively intervene in the war or withdraw from the high seas and cease her role as a supplier to the Allies, thereby bringing about their collapse and a victory for the Central Powers. He therefore urged American workers to throw their energies enthusiastically into the war effort so that the battle might be brought to a conclusion favorable to democracy.[3]

It is this alteration in Mead's attitude toward the Great War during the period 1915–17 that Hans Joas has recently described as "the fall of the internationalist Mead into the sin of nationalism."[4] But Joas's characterization of Mead's change of heart is perhaps unduly harsh. For while Mead did strongly support U.S. involvement in the war, it is by no means clear that this support stemmed from any nationalistic fervor or myopia. On the contrary, Mead continued throughout this period to deplore warfare as a means of resolving international disputes. And his continuing internationalism is evident when he argues in his Chicago *Herald* essays that only the establishment of an international order ending once and for all the use of war as an arbiter of international life would justify the enormous sacrifices incurred in the ongoing struggle.[5]

But what kind of international order did he regard as holding out the greatest promise for the prevention of future wars? Mead addresses this issue by contrasting his own internationalist vision with that of Marxist socialism. European socialism, he says, has traditionally been a movement pitting the laboring classes against governments in the hands of the privileged classes. Precisely for that reason, "it has never represented the democratic attitude of the whole community and its internationalism has stood only for the solidarity of the laborers in the different countries in their opposition to the privileged groups." What Mead finds lacking in this movement is the ideal of a democratic community functioning at both the national and international levels to resolve conflicts of interest. Whereas European socialists assume the existence of irreconcilable conflicts of interest between classes, Mead holds the more optimistic view that persistent and open discussion can uncover shared interests capable of providing the basis for the solution of any social conflict. This, he suggests, is the fundamental assumption underlying the practice of democracy; democratic advance has "always been in the direction of breaking down social barriers and vested interests which have kept men from finding the common denominators of conflicting interests." Mead is thus led to hope, along with Wilson, for the establishment of a democratic international order in which will be found "rights of nationalities, government by the consent of the governed, the opportunity for the full discussion of international disputes under conditions which open the discussion to the public opinion of the world before war may be declared, and such a league of nations as will enforce this appeal to the democratic principle."[6]

Mead was still mulling over some of these same topics more than a decade after the war in the essay "National-Mindedness and International-Mindedness" (1929), in which he sought to extend his moral psychology to encompass the internationalism that had become a major theme in his thought during the war years. The human self, he here suggests, consists of two basic components—its matter and its form: "The one is the stuff of social impulses, and the other is the power which language has conferred upon us, of not only seeing ourselves as others see us but also of addressing ourselves in terms of the common ideas and functions which an organized society makes possible" (sw 358). Now among the fundamental social impulses or tendencies constituting the matter of the self is one that might be called the "hostile impulse." This impulsive tendency, above all others, is peculiarly conducive to social cohesion—as we can see from the familiar fact that nothing so easily unites a group as antipathy toward a common enemy. It is the expression of just this primal social impulse that is largely responsible for the spiritually exhilarating sense of national unity one feels during wartime (sw 356–57).[7]

But the Great War taught us, Mead contends, that war is a completely unacceptable means of achieving national unity and of adjudicating international differences. We are thus led to wonder whether human selves contain any psychological resources upon which we might call to achieve these ends without recourse to the hostile impulse. Is there, to rephrase the question once posed by William James, any psychological or moral equivalent of war? In answer to this question, Mead holds that none of the other fundamental social impulses found in the human self exhibits a unifying force capable of functioning as a psychological substitute for the hostile impulse. There is such a substitute, but it derives from the socially acquired form, rather than from the original impulsive matter, of the self. We must use the power of language and thought with which our society has endowed us to "*think* ourselves in terms of the great community to which we belong," instead of relying upon the immediate visceral responses set in operation by a fight as the source of our national pride and unity. To do this is to become "nationally minded": it is to achieve national self-consciousness by employing one's social capacity for reflective thought to discover shared values and interests lying behind the conflicting individual and class interests that normally occupy the foreground of one's everyday experience (sw 361–64).

Merely using reason to become nationally minded, however, is not enough; in addition, we must undertake the difficult task of making the shared values identified in national-mindedness genuinely operative in our lives. "Civilization is not an affair of reasonableness; it is an affair of social organization. The selfhood of the community depends upon such an organization that common goods do become the ends of the individuals of the community" (sw 369). To the extent that national-mindedness is realized in this manner, Mead holds, it will pave the way for "international-mindedness." For a nation that does not rely upon hostility toward an enemy to gain its sense of national selfhood will be more amenable to the use of intelligence to search out the interests it shares with other nations with whom it finds itself in conflict (sw 367–69). The moral equivalent of war is thus to be found "in the intelligence and the will both to discover these common interests between contending nations and to make them the basis for the solution of the existing differences and for the common life which they will make possible" (sw 366).

Scientific Method and Moral Reconstruction

While the outcome of World War I no doubt impressed upon Mead's mind the great obstacles standing in the way of the establishment of a satisfactory international order, it did nothing to dim his earlier enthusiasm for the exercise of scientific intelligence as the best approach to moral and social reconstruction. The most fully worked out presentation of his position on this matter appears in his 1923 essay "Scientific Method and the Moral Sciences," which also provides a clear expression of his mature secular humanism.

The familiar world view of traditional Christian theology, he here notes, regards the physical world as an arena in which human beings "are but pilgrims and strangers, seeking an abiding city not made with hands, eternal in the heavens" (sw 265). His own opposing view is that we are participants, not in a pilgrimage whose significance derives from some supernatural source, but in "a great secular adventure," an ongoing natural process in which human animals become social selves and in which these selves repeatedly reinterpret and reconstruct experiential meanings in an attempt to overcome problems arising in the course of their organic interactions with the rest of nature. One obvious aspect of this natural process can be seen in our interactions with our physical environment: "The scientific attitude contemplates our physical habitat as primarily the environment of man who is the first cousin once removed of the arboreal anthropoid ape, but it views it as being transformed first through unreflective intelligence and then by reflective intelligence into the environment of a human society, the latest species to appear on the earth. This human society, made up of social individuals that are selves, has been intermittently and slowly digging itself in, burrowing into matter to get to the immediate environment of our cellular structure, and contracting distances and collapsing times to acquire the environment that a self-conscious society of men needs for its distinctive conduct" (sw 265).

Another important dimension of the same process is found in the evolving transactions between selves and their social environments. And it is here that the problems of our moral and social life arise. Mead's central thesis in this essay is simply that these latter problems are as much a part of nature as are the problems encountered in our relationship with our physical environment; consequently, the scientific method of inquiry, which has proven so successful in facilitating our transactions with the physical world, should be equally applicable to problems arising in our transactions with other selves.

In actual practice, of course, we often approach our moral and social problems with intellectual methods quite different from those used in the natural sciences. In particular, when confronted with moral and social problems we tend to slip all too readily into various forms of dogmatism and partiality that have long been rejected in the sciences. Moreover, we attempt to justify this methodological disparity by arguing that methods suitable for dealing with questions of fact are inappropriate in dealing with questions of value. Or we claim that patterns of inquiry useful for ascertaining effective means are not applicable to the determination of ends. But Mead will have nothing to do with any of these dualisms. "It would be a mistake to assume that scientific method is applicable only in the fashioning and selection of means, and may not be used where the problem involves conflicting social ends or values"

(SW 254). From Mead's point of view, judgments of fact and judgments of value, judgments about means and judgments about ends, are all hypotheses arising within the "great secular adventure" of human experience. None of these judgments is infallible or absolute; all are open to reformulation or reconstruction. Thus, when conflicts or problems call for a modification of any of these judgments, we should not hesitate to use the most effective intellectual method available for this purpose. And this, Mead believes, is the method of scientific intelligence.

The adoption of this method does not, of course, guarantee a satisfactory solution to a moral or social problem—any more than it ensures an adequate solution to a research problem in one of the natural sciences. But it does encourage us to consider new hypotheses when old ones are found wanting, and it helps us to evaluate proposed solutions rigorously by relating them to a careful formulation of the conditions that any adequate solution must satisfy. The application of scientific method to moral and social problems thus requires flexibility and imagination; it also requires an impartial assessment of all the conflicting ends or values involved in the problematic situation. "Its one insistent demand is that all the ends, all the valuable objects, institutions, and practices which are involved, must be taken into account. In other words, its attitude toward conflicting ends is the same as its attitude toward conflicting facts and theories in the field of research. It does not state what hypothesis must be adopted. It does insist that any acceptable hypothesis must take into account all the facts involved" (SW 256).

Mead admits that the application of scientific intelligence to problems of social and moral conduct is not without difficulty. In particular, this intellectual approach is hindered by the presence in our moral and social experience of what might be called "incommensurable values" that resist definition or estimation in terms of the other values involved in the situation. These incommensurable values, Mead suggests, are often ideals that have repeatedly failed to effect needed social reconstruction in the past. In spite of their limitations, however, they are the objects of a profound emotional appreciation; we remain uncompromisingly committed to them because we cherish the hope that our devotion may yet help toward the realization of some more perfect way of life (SW 257–62). The difficulty that any such incommensurable value raises for a scientific approach to moral and social problems is obvious: so long as an incommensurable value occupies center stage in our reflective consciousness, there will be little possibility of our acting upon any hypothesis that adequately acknowledges competing values in a morally problematic situation.

The agent of moral or social reconstruction, Mead points out, should not brashly ignore these incommensurable values or treat them as mere idols of inferior intellects, for they and what they represent are a precious part of our social heritage. Nevertheless, their importance does not reside in their supposed absolute or uncompromisable character: we can, therefore, abandon the unconditional estimate of their worth while seeking to do justice to whatever functional significance they may possess when weighed against other values calling for realization in concrete social situations. The scientific approach to moral and social problems must thus render allegedly incommensurable values commensurable or comparable with other values present in a problematic situation. "There are no absolute values. There are only values which, on account of incomplete social organization, we cannot as yet estimate, and in face of these the first enterprise should be to complete the organization if only in thought so that some rough sort of estimate in terms of the other values involved becomes conceivable" (sw 262). Mead admits that this task may often be challenging and difficult, but he sees no reason why it should be, in principle, impossible to accomplish.

In spite of our experience of so-called incommensurable values, then, Mead holds that the method of scientific intelligence is as pertinent for the resolution of moral and social conflicts as it is for the solution of research problems in the physical sciences. In both cases problems arise not because our ideas or actions fail to conform to some perfect or eternal standard, but because our meanings, ends, or values fail to give coherent and sustainable direction to our interaction with the rest of nature. Scientific inquiry helps us reconstruct experiential meanings that have broken down; it does not give us some final vision of an ultimate reality, an absolute moral order, or a utopian society. Its task is simply to bring as much intelligence as possible to bear upon the recurring need for reconstruction in our transactions with our physical and social environments.

Scientific inquiry should thus be regarded as a highly developed intellectual tool for carrying on the great secular adventure of human experience, not as a device for either transcending that adventure or bringing it to a final consummation. And it is an important feature of this adventure that "society gets ahead, not by fastening its vision upon

Mead is
still pragmatic

a clearly outlined distant goal, but by bringing about the immediate adjustment of itself to its surroundings, which the immediate problem demands. It is the only way in which it can proceed, for with every adjustment the environment has changed, and the society and its individuals have changed in like degree. By its own struggles with its insistent difficulties, the human mind is constantly emerging from one chrysalis after another into constantly new worlds which it could not possibly previse" (SW 266). Here we see Mead espousing again the piecemeal or opportunistic approach to reconstructive thought that he had first expressed as early as 1899. Moreover, it is clear that the intervening years had done nothing to diminish his confidence that moral and social problems would prove tractable to the application of a properly scientific method. "We are getting a stronger grip on the method of social reform every year," he had written in 1899, "and we are becoming proportionately careless about our ability to predict the detailed result." [8] As if to echo this remark, he writes near the end of "Scientific Method and the Moral Sciences" that the individual who approaches a moral or social problem with the resources of scientific intelligence "does not know what the solution will be, but he does know the method of the solution. We, none of us, know where we are going, but we do know that we are on the way" (SW 266).

But how can we know that "we are on the way" if we have no detailed knowledge of where we are going? In chapter 3 I noted several respects in which Mead's early confidence in scientific intelligence as a method of social reconstruction was an outgrowth of the Hegelianism that he had imbibed during his philosophical apprenticeship under John Dewey. To these can now be added a closely related basis for optimism grounded in Mead's mature evolutionary naturalism. The use of scientific method as a tool for moral and social reconstruction, he argues in his 1923 essay, is simply a more deliberate and sophisticated manifestation of the process by which human life has been advancing from the outset: "There is a heartening feature of this social or moral intelligence. It is entirely the same as the intelligence evident in the whole upward struggle of life on earth, with this difference, that the human social animal has acquired a mind, and can bring to bear upon the problem his own past experiences and that of others, and can test the solution that arises in his conduct" (SW 266). In this sense, Mead concludes on a Hegelian note: the moral order we partly discover and partly invent as we apply scientific intelligence to our moral and social problems is part and parcel of the natural world. "The order of the universe that we live in is the moral order. It has become the moral order by becoming the self-conscious method of the members of a human society" (sw 266).

Later Works on Ethics and Social Psychology

Having looked briefly at Mead's advocacy of scientific intelligence as an approach to moral and social reconstruction, I return now to the subsequent development of that social psychological analysis of the moral life he began to articulate in his 1913 essay titled "The Social Self." Somewhat surprisingly, Mead did relatively little to work out this analysis more fully in his later lectures and writings. He did devote at least some attention to this project, however, in his regular teaching of a course on elementary ethics, as we can see from a detailed set of student notes based upon his offering of this course in the autumn quarter of 1927.[9] (It was this dimension of these student notes that led Charles W. Morris to use selections from them to create the section titled "Fragments on Ethics" that he included among the supplementary essays at the end of *Mind, Self and Society*.) Furthermore, as the main body of *Mind, Self and Society* reveals, Mead also made passing references to the analysis of morality in his lectures on social psychology during the late 1920s. More important, *Mind, Self and Society* contains numerous remarks about the process of social reconstruction, and—since Mead regards intelligent moral reconstruction as simply a form of social reconstruction—such remarks can be used to shed additional light upon his mature understanding of moral experience. An examination of relevant passages in these two sources and in his 1930 essay "Philanthropy from the Point of View of Ethics" enables us to arrive at a reasonably accurate estimate of just how far he had managed to carry his social psychological treatment of morality before the end of his career at Chicago.[10]

Mead's 1927 course lectures on ethics, so far as one can judge on the basis of student notes, were not marked by any great philosophical originality. For the most part they merely sought to elucidate and amplify materials presented in the assigned text for the course, the first edition of Dewey and Tufts's *Ethics* (1908). Nevertheless, it is easy to see the influence of his own ethical and social psychological ideas in

much that Mead says here. Consider, for instance, the following examples of such influence. (1) He criticizes both Immanuel Kant and
John Stuart Mill for holding that inclinations or desires are directed
toward subjective experiences of pleasure. Mead contends, on the basis
of his own organic view of conduct, that our impulses or desires are
typically directed toward objects or ends in our physical and social environment. "I think it is a fair test of what the object is to see that
toward which the attention must be directed to get it. If you give your
attention to the pleasure, you cut the nerve of action" (LE 128). (2) He
grants the legitimacy of Kant's ethical categorical imperative (act only
on that maxim that you could will to be a universal law), but maintains
that this principle has limited application. It is of no help in morally
problematic situations whose resolution requires a creative reinterpretation or reconstruction (LE 204; MSS 281). (3) He again compares the
predicament of a moral agent facing a problem of conflicting values
with that of a scientist confronting a research problem. Just as the
scientist must take into account every fact involved in a problem, so
the moral agent must take into account all of the conflicting interests
involved (LE 226; MSS 287). (4) He points out that moral problem solving often requires an initial stage of self-denial. "The first step is one
that involves sacrifice of the old self. You have to take other people
into account." But the result of this sacrifice is moral growth: one sacrifices a narrower self to acquire a larger or more inclusive self that
identifies as its own various interests previously seen only as belonging
to others. "The difficulty is to make ourselves realize the interests we
haven't realized before. When we do not recognize them we are self-
ish, a narrow self" (LE 222, 235; MSS 389, 388–89). (5) He holds that
"it is as social beings that we are moral beings" and "those ends are
good which lead to the realization of the self as a social being" (LE
231; MSS 385). But how do we go about becoming more fully social
beings? Mead's answer is that "our conduct ought to have the form
which would make a universal society possible. We should take into account every individual who could possibly enter into social relations."
Thus he finds, in his own social psychological view of the self, grounds
for endorsing Kant's emphasis upon universality as a key dimension of
ethical conduct (LE 228).

Mead's 1927 course lectures on ethics also display the same focus
upon moral reconstruction that we observed in his earlier essays.
Throughout these lectures Mead makes much of the distinction be-

tween customary or conventional moral thought (involving an uncritical application of societal moral standards) and critical-reflective moral thought (in which the moral agent reflectively questions and examines customary moral standards). And, as might be expected, his attention is directed primarily toward the latter kind of moral thinking. While he is willing to admit that many everyday moral judgments take place at the level of customary morality, he is especially interested in those situations in which a conflict between "authorized customs" leads the individual to employ critical reflection to revise conventional moral standards. In such situations, he claims, the morally reflective individual becomes "the instrument by which custom itself may be changed." Here customary moral values come into conflict with one another in the experience of the individual, and it is the function of the individual "to give expression to the different values and help to formulate more satisfactory standards than have existed" (LE 42; MSS 387).

The influence of Mead's distinctive social psychological ideas is most prominent in these lectures at those moments when he is attempting to explain the conditions that give rise to the capacity for critical moral reflection and make possible its reconstructive task. For it is on these occasions that he alludes to his social and genetic theory of reflective intelligence. Critical moral thought, he argues, involves rationality, and the human individual achieves the capacity for rational judgment only through social intercourse. "It is because we . . . speak to ourselves with the voice of the entire community that we are able to make such rational judgments" (LE 213). The inner dialogue of rational thought is thus a social process and "man is a rational being only because he is a social being" (LE 212–13; MSS 379). This same social conception of rational and reflective thought appears throughout *Mind, Self and Society*. There Mead claims that rational thought is "a type of conduct in which the individual puts himself in the attitude of the whole group to which he belongs" and uses this attitude of the "generalized other" to guide his actions (MSS 334, 162–63). Or, as he puts the matter in other passages, rational conduct is self-critical conduct, and self-criticism is essentially an internalized form of social criticism; it is made possible by the individual's use of significant symbols to import the attitudes of others into the social forum of his thought (MSS 255, 334–35).

But at this point Mead's attempt to provide a social psychological account of critical moral reflection encounters an obvious difficulty. How can a rational capacity, which is said to reflect generalized social attitudes, turn around and take a critical stance with respect to some of those same attitudes? How can a reflective intelligence, which is held to embody the attitudes of a society, transcend the customary morality of that society in a way that will allow intelligence to perform the reconstructive task that Mead regards as a prerequisite for moral growth? This problem, it is important to note, is not restricted to Mead's analysis of morality; it lies at the heart of the social conception of the self he presents in *Mind, Self and Society*. Much of that volume is devoted to a discussion of the ways in which societal patterns are imported into the conduct of the human individual to give rise to the phenomena of language, self-consciousness, and reflective intelligence. But this line of thought represents only one side of Mead's treatment of the self. He stresses at the same time that the self is more than a mere product or reflection of the social process of which it is a part; it is also an agent of reconstruction and a potential source of intelligent reform within that process. It is thus essential for both Mead's analysis of morality and his theory of the self that he offer an explanation of the social psychological mechanism that makes it possible for human individuals to think critically about the customs and moral standards of their own society.

While Mead fails to provide a fully developed solution to this problem in any of his lectures or writings, one can find at least the rudiments of such a solution in passages scattered throughout some of his later works. Individuals engaging in critical and creative moral reflection, he suggests in his 1927 lectures on ethics and in *Mind, Self and Society*, must have a critical vantage point from which to judge the limitations of their society's customary morality: they must conceive of themselves as representatives of a moral order differing in certain respects from that found in the prevailing moral standards of their community. And they achieve this critical vantage point not by imaginatively constructing a new moral or social order out of whole cloth, but by envisioning an order based upon principles "implied but not adequately expressed" in the society that has given rise to the social structure of their selves or personalities (MSS 217, 386; LE 237). "Take the religious genius, such as Jesus or Buddha, or the reflective type, such as Socrates. What has given them their unique importance is that they have taken the attitude of living with reference to a larger society. That larger state was one which was already more or less implied in the institutions of the community in which they lived. Such an individual is divergent from the point of view of what we would call the prejudices of the community; but in another sense he expresses the principles of the community more completely than any other" (MSS 217). Similarly, Mead claims in "Philanthropy from the Point of View of Ethics" (1930) that it is the morally reflective individual's "feel for a social structure that is implicit in what is present" that gives him "a sense of obligation which transcends any claim that his actual social order fastens upon him." In the face of a moral problem, this sense of an implied social structure often suggests a "hypothetically different order" in terms of which the conflict of values at hand might be reinterpreted and resolved. "It is an ideal world that lays the claim upon him, but it is an ideal world which grows out of this world and its undeniable implications" (SW 404).

The behavioral capacity that enables morally reflective individuals to sense such an implied social structure and give it explicit expression in a moral hypothesis, Mead further suggests, is their ability to import into their conduct the attitude or standpoint of a "generalized other." Just as individuals can advance from taking the roles of specific others to taking the generalized attitudes of their social group, so they can advance to yet more generalized social attitudes; in particular, they can employ significant symbols to identify and abstract from morally problematic values, thereby arriving at a highly generalized social attitude that provides them with "a universe of discourse" in terms of which they can address a moral problem in an impartial manner (MSS 89–90, 269n, 273n; SW 404). Such a universe of discourse "abstracts in varying degrees from the actual structure of society," but it can fulfill its reconstructive function within social and moral conduct only if it does not abstract wholly from that structure; it must contain a social order grounded in "commonly recognized conditions of conduct and common ends" (SW 404). The use of abstract thought informed by such a universe of discourse to analyze a moral problem and formulate hypotheses of an alternative moral order that would resolve the problem is what Mead understands by the term "reason" in the context of critical moral reflection. "Reason is then a medium within which values may be brought into comparisons with each other, in abstraction from the situations within which they have come into conflict with each other; and within this impartial medium it becomes possible to reconstruct values and our conduct growing out of them" (SW 406).

The task of reason in this view of critical moral reflection is obviously not one of establishing an absolute and unchanging blueprint for an ideal moral order; it is rather one of bringing the resources of a socially structured intelligence to bear upon the resolution of concrete moral and social problems. All such problems, Mead claims in "Philanthropy from the Point of View of Ethics," are specific or limited in character. They involve a conflict between specific habits, customs, or values, but this conflict always occurs within a wider social context in which many other values remain unproblematic. Surrounding any such problem there "lies the ordered community with its other standards and customs unimpaired, and the duties it prescribes unquestioned" (sw 405). It is precisely this ordered community and those of its standards that are unimpaired by the moral difficulty at hand that make possible that universe of discourse in terms of which the specific moral problem can be rationally addressed.

Mead thus remains as firmly attached to the idea of piecemeal or opportunistic reconstruction in his final works on ethics as he had been in his 1899 essay on social reform. And both early and late in his career he thought it unnecessary to worry about formulating any ultimate goal for this process. He does at one point in *Mind, Self and Society,* however, depart from his usual position by offering a suggestion as to where such piecemeal reconstruction is, or ought to be, taking us: "The human social ideal—the ideal or ultimate goal of human social progress—is the attainment of a universal human society in which all human individuals would possess a perfected social intelligence, . . . such that the meanings of any one individual's acts or gestures (as realized by him and expressed in the structure of his self, through his ability to take the social attitudes of other individuals toward himself and toward their common social ends or purposes) would be the same for any other individual whatever who responded to them" (mss 310). This ideal, which elsewhere in *Mind, Self and Society* Mead characterizes as "the formal ideal of communication" and the ideal of "universal discourse" (mss 327), appears to be an elaboration of the point he had in mind when he said in his 1927 course lectures on ethics that our conduct ought to have a form that would make a universal society possible. Clearly he is here on the verge of deriving a quasi-Kantian ethical principle from his social psychology. But nowhere in *Mind, Self and Society,* or in any of his other works, does he attempt to use this ideal as a normative criterion for resolving moral conflicts or for judging specific instances of moral reconstruction. It remains, in short, an interesting suggestion whose possible ethical implications Mead did little to develop.[11]

Concluding Remarks

Mead's lectures and writings on ethics sound a number of recurring themes closely linked to the development of his social psychology and his perennial commitment to social reform. Chief among these are his functionalist understanding of critical moral reflection, his attempt to explain how the method of scientific intelligence can be applied to the task of piecemeal moral and social reconstruction, and his social psychological analysis of the self as an agent of such reconstruction. Although Mead's works on ethics are relatively few in number and modest in scope, their original and suggestive articulation of these themes makes them worthy of continued attention by anyone interested in moral psychology and methodology.[12] They also reveal, with considerable clarity, how Mead proposed to locate moral values and moral reasoning within his naturalistic view of human social experience as part of a great secular adventure.

Chapter 9

Whitehead's Influence on Mead's Later Thought

On the morning of September 14, 1926, both G. H. Mead and Alfred North Whitehead presented papers at a session of the Sixth International Congress of Philosophy meeting at Harvard University.[1] Later that day Mead reported in a letter to his daughter-in-law that his paper, which dealt in part with the work of Whitehead, "went better than I expected. I had a good hand afterwards and—what I was especially pleased with—Whitehead said he wanted to chat with me, that he thought we could get together. There are metaphysical abysms between us but what are they between gentlemen."[2] There is no evidence that the "chat" Whitehead proposed actually took place or, indeed, that Mead ever had any other personal contact or communication with Whitehead. But numerous fragmentary discussions of Whitehead in Mead's journal articles and posthumously published writings testify that Mead had a deep and abiding interest in Whitehead's philosophy. In spite of the "metaphysical abysms" he saw looming between his position and that of Whitehead, he made repeated attempts to assimilate Whiteheadian concerns and concepts into his own evolving thought. My aim in the present chapter is to show how these concerns and concepts influenced the character of Mead's intellectual efforts during the last decade of his life.

The Beginning of Mead's Interest in Whitehead

It is clear from letters Mead wrote in the years 1920–25 that his initial reading of Whitehead was preceded by a study of Henri Bergson, and that he was interested in both of these thinkers primarily because he shared with them a desire to relate the structure of the world as known by physical science to the flow of concrete or immediate experience. More specifically, it is evident from these documents that Mead undertook his reading of Bergson and Whitehead in search of insights that would help him to bring his own social and functional view of human experience more fully to bear upon metaphysical problems related to science and its objects. Letters he wrote during the summer of 1920, for instance, show him attempting to employ a functional analysis of perceptual experience as the basis for a reinterpretation of the traditional dichotomy between primary and secondary qualities. And in this connection he was studying Bergson's *Matter and Memory* and *Creative Evolution*.[3] "I want to be sure that I have quite exhausted what I can get from Bergson," he says at one point, "before I return to the problem of perception from my own way of approach."[4] Similarly, his letters of the following summer indicate that he first began his study of Whitehead while seeking an understanding of the theory of relativity.[5] A letter written in late July 1921 reveals both the difficulty he was having with that theory and his desire to approach it in terms of his own analysis of the "distance" and "contact" dimensions of concrete perceptual experience: "I have recovered somewhat from a discouraged feeling I brought away from the Einstein dinner—that I had not grasped the import of Relativity. I think I have it. I am sorry now that I did not try out visual and contact space on the dinner party—the voila in a Universe of Discourse."[6]

His letters of succeeding days record his pursuit of further enlightenment with respect to the subject of relativity. He reports reading on this topic Albert Einstein, Arthur Eddington, and—apparently for the first time—a book by Whitehead: "It is interesting turning from Eddington to Whitehead. The latter is very deliberately undertaking to take the reality of nature in terms of actual experience, also to conceive of space and time as abstractions from spatial and temporal relations of things or rather events. He deliberately abandons the points and moments. He accepts change as involving experienced duration. But he keeps the permanent elements in objects as timeless and spaceless. It seems to be a partial surrender of the realist to pragmatism—but I am unsure of my grasp."[7] Mead further remarks that he would be "interested to see what John Dewey may say of Whitehead's book, which he took to read on the steamer,"[8] but he does not indicate the title of the book in question. Presumably it was either *The Concept of Nature* (1920) or *An Enquiry Concerning the Principles of Natural Knowledge* (1919). In any case, almost all of his subsequently published discussions of Whitehead deal either with these works or with the additional two volumes in which Whitehead set forth his early philosophy of nature: *The Principle of Relativity* (1922) and *Science and the Modern World* (1925). Mead's only references to other works by Whitehead are a brief mention of *Principia Mathematica*[9] and an indication, in an essay published in 1929, that he was awaiting the publication of Whitehead's Gifford Lectures.[10] These lectures appeared during that same year under the title *Process and Reality,* but there is no further mention of them in Mead's writings.[11]

While Mead's letters of 1920–25 enable us to date his initial study of Whitehead, they do not tell us much about the kind of influence this study had upon the development of his own ideas. We can best begin to determine the nature of this influence by looking closely at the references to Whitehead in four essays Mead published during the years 1925–29. None of these essays contains any very lengthy discussion of Whitehead, but together they encompass every remark about Whitehead that Mead published during his own lifetime. These remarks, sketchy as they are, deserve careful consideration because they help us to understand not only why Mead was drawn to Whitehead's philosophy of nature but also why he could not embrace that philosophy without reservation.

Objective Relativism and the Place of Mind in Nature

The first reference to Whitehead in Mead's journal articles appears in his 1925 essay "The Genesis of Self and Social Control."[12] The context of the reference is a discussion in which Mead emphasizes the contribution made by recent psychology and philosophy to the revolt against traditional forms of psychophysical dualism. Behavioristic psychology, he notes, has turned away from the study of psychical states and toward the study of acts as publicly observable processes; it has thereby located the subject matter of psychology within nature rather than in a separate realm of consciousness. Meanwhile, recent philosophical thought has been "transferring contents that had been the subject-matter of earlier psychology from the field of states of consciousness to the objective world" (SW 267). To illustrate this second point, Mead cites ideas found in the writings of Whitehead, Bergson, and Samuel Alexander.

He mentions, for instance, Bergson's view that "a percept is an object of possible action for an organism, and it is the active relationship of the organism to the distant object that constitutes it an object" (sw 272). Moreover, he notes with approval the doctrine of emergence "as this has been defined by Alexander in *Space, Time and Deity,* and accepted by Lloyd Morgan, in *Emergent Evolution*"—a doctrine that advances the thesis that as new organisms with new sensitivities evolve in nature there also arise new environments and new qualities of experience (sw 273). Finally, and most important for our purposes, Mead touches upon Whitehead's view of nature and suggests the possibility of generalizing Whitehead's "conception of the existence in nature of consentient sets determined by their relations to percipient events . . . so that it will cover the environment in relation to the living form, and the experienced world with reference to the experiencing individual" (sw 275).

This suggestion concerning a possible extension of Whitehead's ideas obviously requires clarification; we must digress briefly to look at what Whitehead had in mind when he spoke of "percipient events" and "consentient sets" in his early works on the philosophy of nature. According to these works, nature presents itself to immediate sense awareness as a passage of overlapping durations, each of which extends over many finite events.[13] In particular, each experienced duration extends over a "percipient event" (roughly, Whitehead says, the event that is the perceiver's bodily life) that is temporally present throughout that duration. The relation between a percipient event and its associated duration, a relation Whitehead calls "cogredience," yields unequivocal meanings to *here* and *now* within that duration.[14] Furthermore, this relation constitutes the basis for the selection of a "consentient set" of objects at rest with respect to the perspective of the percipient event. And this set of objects provides a space within which motion can take place.[15] In this manner the continuum of events in nature is differentiated or "stratified" into spatio-temporal systems relative to percipient events.[16] The relativity of these perspectives or stratifications, Whitehead holds, does not render them subjective: "they are in truth characters of nature and not illusions of consciousness."[17]

It is this Whiteheadian notion of perspectival stratifications as objective ingredients of nature that Mead wishes to generalize in his 1925 essay. He wants to suggest that the overall relationship between the experienced world and the experiencing individual is analogous to those perspectives emphasized by Whitehead. Each individual, Mead points out, experiences a world that is to some extent different from that experienced by any other member of the community; each individual "slices the events of the community life that are common to all" from the perspective of his own conduct (SW 276). How are we then to interpret these individual perspectives? One possibility is to regard them as subjective distortions of an absolute physical reality. But this line of thought leads in the direction of that psychophysical dualism that Mead, along with John Dewey, was especially concerned to avoid. In opposition to this approach, Mead advocates an interpretation of the Whiteheadian sort: let us say that "each individual stratifies the common life in a different manner, and the life of the community is the sum of all these stratifications, and all of these stratifications exist in nature" (SW 276). If we view the experience of the individual in this manner, Mead notes, then a psychology that studies that experience becomes a science of nature rather than a science directed toward a separate realm of consciousness or mind. Hence, we can take psychology out of its isolation from the other sciences and regard it as "a science of the objective world" (SW 276–77).

Thus Mead's initial endorsement of Whitehead's philosophy of nature grows out of a desire to enlist Whiteheadian concepts in support of that "revolt against dualism" that had been an important part of his own thought for many years.[18] But this is not the only thrust of Mead's discussion of Whitehead in his 1925 essay. He also sees in Whitehead's work something that had been lacking in his own earlier treatment of perceptual experience: an attempt to ground the spatial and temporal structures of the perceptual world in our concrete experience of passage. Consequently, he begins to expand his earlier account of perceptual objects along the lines suggested to him by his reading of Whitehead. The world we encounter in immediate experience, Mead claims, is a world of passage. Perceptual objects are implicated in a process of conduct that is continually passing into the future and, hence, temporality or passage is at the core of their being. In our reflective conduct, however, we tend to prescind from the element of passage in objects by an act of abstraction. The behavioral mechanism of this abstraction is a hypothetical extension of the range of our contact experience: we bring distant objects into simultaneity with our bodily life by perceiving them as they would be "if we were there and had our hands upon them" (SW 277). We thereby "introduce a fictitious instantaneousness into a passing universe" and arrive at a "seemingly timeless" spatial world of permanent objects, a useful abstraction in terms of which we assess the conditions that will confront our future conduct. The "instantaneous" or "seemingly timeless" character of this world "is due to the consentient set which each one of us selects" (sw 277).

Mead's preliminary observations concerning the compatibility of Whitehead's philosophy of nature and his own approach to experience are given little more elaboration in "The Genesis of Self and Social Control." Rather, the bulk of that essay is devoted to a presentation of the social psychological ideas that Mead had been developing in articles and lectures during the preceding fifteen years. But he does not long postpone further consideration of Whitehead's work. Near the beginning of his paper for the 1926 International Congress of Philosophy—a paper published in 1927 under the title "The Objective Reality of Perspectives"—he once again takes up the thread of his previous discussion by calling attention to "two unconnected movements which seem to be approaching a strategic position of great importance—which may be called the objectivity of perspectives." The two movements involved here are Whitehead's philosophy and "that phase of behavioristic psychology which is planting communication, thinking, and substantive meanings . . . within nature" (sw 307). And the great importance Mead attributes to their alleged convergence is due to the bearing of this convergence upon what he takes to be a crucial twofold task confronting philosophy: the task of (a) restoring to nature many of those qualities that dualistic thinkers relegate to consciousness, and (b) developing a tenable naturalistic account of mind.

Mead is convinced that the key to fulfilling the first part of this task is to be found in the sort of objective relativism suggested by Whitehead's philosophy of nature. According to Whitehead, he observes, the structures of space, time, and motion with which exact physical science is concerned exist in nature only insofar as that nature is stratified by its relation to percipient events or organisms. Yet such relativity to organisms does not make these structures any the less objective, for the stratifications or perspectives involved "are not only there in nature but they are the only forms of nature that are there." Why not, then, extend this idea of objective relativism to other sensible qualities (e.g., color, sound, odor, taste, and tactile qualities) that exist in nature as it is related to percipient organisms? And why not further apply the same notion to the other values "which have been regarded as dependent upon appetence, appreciation, and affection"? In this manner, Mead suggests, we can use Whitehead's doctrine of the objectivity of perspectives to "restore to nature all that a dualistic doctrine has relegated to consciousness" (SW 315).

He cannot contend, however, that Whitehead's philosophy of nature speaks directly to the second half of the dual task mentioned above— that of setting forth a tenable naturalistic account of human mentality. For it is part and parcel of Whitehead's epistemological realism in his early works to treat mind as something external to nature; these works construe mind as belonging to the subject matter of metaphysics, not the subject matter of the philosophy of nature. Recourse to mind and metaphysics when attempting to delineate the general notions that apply to nature, Whitehead holds, "is like throwing a match into the powder magazine. It blows up the whole arena."[19] Thus Whitehead speaks of nature as a field of phenomena "closed to mind"—i.e., "a complex of entities whose mutual relations to each other are expressible in thought without reference to mind, that is, without reference to either sense awareness or to thought."[20] This view, quite obviously, is incompatible with a central thrust of Mead's thought. Mead wants to locate the entire subject matter of psychology (including not only overt behavior but also thought and sense awareness) *within* the same nature that provides the subject matter of the physical sciences. Indeed, this concern is perhaps the primary motivation for the elaborate genetic account of mind he had by this time developed in his social psychological writings and lectures. Mind is for Mead a natural and social phenomenon; hence he can hardly accept Whitehead's intention to restrict the concept of nature to a field of phenomena closed to mind.

Despite this fundamental opposition between his naturalistic approach to mind and Whitehead's realist orientation, Mead continues to move in his 1927 essay and also in "A Pragmatic Theory of Truth" (1929) toward a partial synthesis of his social psychological ideas and the Whiteheadian view of nature. One way in which he does this is by focusing upon Whitehead's claim in *Science and the Modern World* that each event in nature "mirrors" or "prehends" in its unity aspects of all other events from its own perspective: "I do not wish to consider Professor Whitehead's Bergsonian edition of Spinoza's underlying substance that individualizes itself in the structure of the events, nor his Platonic heaven of eternal objects where lie the hierarchies of patterns, that are there envisaged as possibilities and have ingression into events, but rather his Leibnitzian filiation, as it appears in his conception of the perspective as the mirroring in the event of all other events" (sw 308–9). What particularly interests Mead about this notion is its resemblance to his own conception of role-taking as an important feature of human social experience. The human individual, he maintains, covertly calls out in his conduct the anticipated responses of others to his actions and words, thus bringing the social import of his actions into his own experience; he thereby acts "not only in his own perspective but also in the perspective of others, especially in the common perspective of a group" (sw 310). An understanding of such conduct, Mead suggests, supplies a needed corrective to a weakness in the Whiteheadian scheme of ideas. For Whitehead's view threatens to leave each individual forever locked into his own limited perspective. Whitehead needs to account for the manner in which individual human perspectives give rise to an experience of a common world, but we find only "dark hints of a theory of this common world in Professor Whitehead's publications, in exiguous phrases and appended notes" (sw 340).[21] The remedy for this weakness, as Mead sees it, consists in pointing out that the human individual puts himself "in the place of others and in their common undertakings in the world and observes things spatiotemporally and meaningfully as they observe them. Answering to these common experiences there lies before them a common world, the world of the group" (sw 341).

Mead holds that such role-taking lies at the heart of human mentality. Hence in suggesting that Whitehead's philosophy can handle the problem of the common world only by opening its doors to individuals who can take the role of the other, he is taking a large step in the direction of locating mind within a modified Whiteheadian view of nature. A nature that includes individuals of this sort, he remarks in an obvious reference to Whitehead, is "no nature that can be closed to mind" (sw 310). But Mead also believes that human mentality must be understood pragmatically in terms of its *reconstructive function* within ongoing conduct. Thus, if he wishes to tie his own conception of mind more firmly to the Whiteheadian view of nature, he must relate this reconstructive activity to the notion of nature as a system of perspectives. This he proceeds to do by calling attention to the exercise of mind in the growth of scientific knowledge. A dominant feature of this growth, Mead argues, is a process of reconstruction in which some aspect of an accepted or common world is called into question by data that cannot

 # 146-149
essence

be accounted for in terms of that world. Such recalcitrant data are initially referred to the perspectives of individuals, but science does not rest until they are successfully integrated into a reconstructed common perspective. What Mead wants most to emphasize here is that the recalcitrant data that arise within experience and call for a reconstruction of the common world "do not arise in minds which regard nature from without": rather, they arise "within nature itself" (sw 340). The whole reconstructive process "in which new common minds and new common perspectives arise" is a part of nature. And this claim "amounts to the affirmation that mind as it appears in the mechanism of social conduct is the organization of perspectives in nature and at least a phase of the creative advance of nature" (sw 316).

Passage, Emergence, and Temporality

As the preceding discussion suggests, the influence of Whitehead encouraged Mead to move toward the formulation of a philosophy of nature that would encompass his own social psychological insights as well as certain facets of nature to which Whitehead's interpretation of physical relativity drew attention. In addition, Whitehead's influence is evident in the study Mead devoted to the nature of passage and temporality in the years following 1925. One aspect of this study, which deserves discussion here because it became a focal point of Mead's thought during the last years of his life, concerns the manner in which our everyday temporal distinctions among past, present, and future are related to immediately experienced passage.

Although Mead touches upon this matter in each of the essays cited above, it is not until his 1929 essay "The Nature of the Past" that he deals with it in detail. His description of experienced passage in this essay is in essential agreement with Whitehead's account of overlapping durations: "Passage as it takes place in experience is an overlapping of one specious present by another. There is continuity of experience, which is a continuity of presents. In this continuity of experience there is distinction of happening. There is direction. There is dependence or conditioning. . . . Not only does succession take place, but there is a succession of contents. What is going on would be otherwise if the earlier stage of the occurrence had been of a different character" (sw 346). But the Whiteheadian tenor of this description should not lead us to overlook the important respects in which Mead diverges from Whitehead. First, Mead's remarks throughout the essay exhibit a *psychological* orientation. Rather than speaking primarily of passage in nature, as Whitehead characteristically does, Mead emphasizes the imagery, felt qualities, and mental processes involved in our experiencing of passage. More important, Mead clearly intends to reinterpret the Whiteheadian treatment of passage in terms of his own functional conception of experience. In so doing, he brings to fruition a number of suggestions contained in his earlier publications[22] and at the same time formulates the analysis of temporality that provides the framework for much of his discussion in the Carus Lectures of 1930.

The key to Mead's analysis of temporality in "The Nature of the Past" is found in his emphasis upon the continual emergence of novel elements in experience. No doubt Whitehead's references to the "creative advance" of nature encouraged this emphasis, as did Mead's encounter with related notions in the works of Alexander, Morgan, and Bergson. But we should also note that Mead had been stressing the importance of novel elements in experience, especially in connection with his discussion of the reconstructive function of thought, since early in his career.[23] What is significant about his treatment of this subject in the present context is that the emergence of novelty in experience is here seen for the first time not merely as a necessary condition for the reconstruction of old meanings or objects, but as a necessary condition as well for any awareness of passage.

There must, of course, be continuity as well as novelty in experience if we are to have an awareness of passage. If there were no continuity, if one aspect of the present were not encountered as conditioning a subsequent aspect, then there would be "bare replacement of one experience by another," and we would not experience passage (SW 349). On the other hand, bare continuity could not be experienced; we need the "tang of novelty in each moment of experience" if we are to have an awareness of passage. The break in continuity provided by the emergence of novelty reveals the continuity, just as the continuity provides the background against which the novel can emerge (SW 350). Experience, then, is a process in which novelty is always being introduced in the midst of continuity. And it is in terms of this ongoing process that Mead seeks to explain the differences among present, past, and future. He agrees with Whitehead in rejecting the notion of a "knife-edge" present in favor of the view that attributes temporal thickness to the experienced present: the present is something that is going on and there is passage within it. Moreover, Mead follows Whitehead in viewing experienced reality as a passage of one present or duration into another. But he goes on to argue that a present that has passed into another present does not become part of the past simply by virtue of such passage. The past is *representational* in character, a span of experience that becomes a part of the past only insofar as it is represented in the present in a certain manner. The "pasts which we carry around with us . . . are in great part thought constructs of what the present by its nature involves, into which very slight material of memory imagery is fitted. This memory in a manner tests and verifies the structure" (sw 348). Functionally understood, the past is an attempt to extend backward those conditions that bring continuity to the present. "The past is an overflow of the present. It is oriented from the present." And its decisive character is found in "the pushing back of the conditioning continuities of the present" (sw 348–49).[24]

Mead here offers only a few brief remarks about the nature of the future, but it is clear that he intends to apply to it the same kind of analysis he applies to the past. Just as the past is constructed by a "pushing back" of the conditioning continuities of the present, so the future is projected by a "pushing forward" of such continuities. We seek out reliable uniformities supplied by the present and the past, and we project these into the future, thereby extending the element of anticipation contained in the experienced present (sw 351). We thus "build out at both limits" of the present (sw 345). And the functional value of this twofold extension derives from the fact that the objects and projects that concern us in conduct typically have a temporal span greater than that of our specious presents (sw 348). We can make sense of our immediate present only by fitting it into the larger context of where we have been and where we are going, of what we have done and what we are trying to do. We can intelligently direct present conduct only if we can relate it to what has happened in the past and to what is likely to happen in the future.

Now however important Whitehead's work may have been as a stimulus to Mead at this juncture, that work clearly did not provide the functionalist orientation in which Mead's analysis of temporality is grounded. Whitehead's influence seems to have drawn Mead's attention to certain aspects of the phenomena discussed here, but the discussion itself is rooted in concerns evident in Mead's thought long before he began to read Whitehead. For example, we may note the way in which Mead's analysis of temporality in "The Nature of the Past" carries forward his longstanding emphasis upon emergence and reconstruction as fundamental dimensions of human experience. Not only are the past and future representational in character and oriented from the present, Mead holds, they are both hypothetical and subject to reconstruction. Novelty is constantly emerging in the passage of one present into another, and this novelty may call forth a revision of the future we anticipate or of the past we represent to ourselves in our attempts to extend the conditioning continuities of the present. There is thus no predetermined future and no irrevocable past independent of all human experience: "the only pasts and futures of which we are cognizant arise in human experience" and participate in the "extreme variability which attaches to human undertakings" (sw 351). If there is a real emergence of novel elements in nature and human experience, then we must give up once and for all the notion of a fixed past from which an inevitable present and future are supposed to flow. Once novelty has emerged in experience, we can, of course, establish continuity between the novel elements and earlier events by a suitable reinterpretation of the past. Indeed, this is what characteristically happens: we reconstruct the past so as to transform the unexpected emergent into something that should have been expected. "The character of the past is that it connects what is unconnected in the merging of one present into another" (sw 351). The past is itself, therefore, an emergent affair; it consists of relations between an emergent and a conditioning world—relations that are established only after the novel elements involved have made their appearance within the arena of experience (sw 354).

The Whiteheadian Influence in Mead's Posthumously Published Works

We have so far observed a number of respects in which Whitehead's influence is evident in four pivotal essays Mead published in the period 1925–29. These can be summarized, in an order slightly altered from that in which they were discussed above, as follows. (1) Mead seeks to adapt Whitehead's objective relativism to the service of his own attempts to overcome that psychophysical dualism that isolates the traditional subject matter of psychology from the realm of nature studied by other empirical sciences. (2) He attempts, under the influence of

Whitehead, to extend his own earlier discussions of perception so as to relate the spatial and temporal structures of the perceptual world to the passage of immediate experience. (3) He turns his attention to the distinctions among past, present, and future as these relate to emergence and experienced passage. (4) He brings his own notion of role-taking to bear upon the Whiteheadian conception of a system of intertwined perspectives to account for the presence of a shared or common world in the diverse perspectives of human individuals. (5) He locates his conception of mind, as social in character and reconstructive in function, within the larger conceptual framework provided by a modified Whiteheadian view of nature. These lines of influence, I shall now show, are of considerable significance in shaping the direction Mead's thought takes in those lectures and essays published following his death in 1931.

In this connection we need only mention briefly *Mind, Self and Society* and *Movements of Thought in the Nineteenth Century*, for these volumes do not contain any great wealth of material dealing with Whiteheadian themes. The former volume, which is based primarily upon lectures Mead gave for a 1928 course on social psychology at the University of Chicago, contains no explicit mention of Whitehead. But Mead does make occasional use of the notion of "perspectives" in discussing the relation between the individual and the social group. And in several places he employs Whiteheadian language in claiming that human individuals "prehend" in their own experience and, from their own unique perspectives, the structure of the larger social process of which they are a part.[25] Perhaps Mead did not make greater use of Whiteheadian terms and ideas in *Mind, Self and Society* because he had developed the main content of his lectures on social psychology well before his serious study of Whitehead began. More important, he probably did not consider his Whiteheadian concerns appropriate material for discussion in a course on social psychology.

An analogous consideration may also explain the relative dearth of references to Whitehead in *Movements of Thought in the Nineteenth Century*. The bulk of this volume is based upon lectures Mead gave in an undergraduate course by that title in the spring quarter of 1928, and, though some lectures do deal with recent philosophical developments, Mead may well have considered such a course an inappropriate forum for any extended discussion of Whiteheadian ideas. The only material in the book not based upon this course is a segment of about twenty pages taken from student notes on a course on the philosophy of

Bergson, which Mead taught in the summer of 1927 (MT 304–25). Not surprisingly, this segment contains the most fully developed references to Whitehead found in the book. In any case, this volume tells us little about Mead's interest in Whitehead that we have not already learned from our examination of the essays Mead published between 1925 and 1929. He again endorses Whitehead's treatment of relativity in terms of the notion of a system of objective perspectives (MT 315, 415), and he again relates this to his own understanding of human social conduct and the reconstructive activities of human intelligence (MT 412–17). The scattered references to Whitehead in this volume do, nevertheless, further dramatize the favorable reception Mead was giving to Whitehead's work during this period. He speaks, for instance, of the early chapters of Whitehead's *Science and the Modern World* as providing a "very adequate and admirable presentation" of the historical development of the scientific faith in the uniformity and orderliness of nature (MT 7). And he sees in Whitehead's use of the method of extensive abstraction [26] an important correction to the treatment of passage in the philosophy of Bergson. As Mead views the matter, Bergson is quite correct in his description of inner experience as a passage of temporally extended and qualitatively interpenetrating durations. But Bergson "fails to see that the flow, the freedom, the novelty, the interpenetration, the creativity, upon which he sets such store, are not necessarily limited to the interpenetration of experiences in the inner flow of consciousness" (MT 325). Whitehead enables us to overcome this Bergsonian limitation by showing us that such scientific notions as instants and point particles are ideal limits derivable, by means of extensive abstraction, from the concrete passage of nature (MT 312–15). Thus, the door is opened to our finding in the objects of experience, in the nature studied by the empirical sciences, "the same type of interpenetration, the same essential spread, as that which Bergson discovers in our inner experience" (MT 325).

When we turn to the other two volumes of Mead's writings published soon after his death, *The Philosophy of the Act* (1938) and *The Philosophy of the Present* (1932), we encounter a large number of unfinished manuscripts and fragments, only a small portion of which can be assigned any definite date. The four chapters that constitute the first half of *The Philosophy of the Present* are based upon the Carus Lectures presented at a meeting of the American Philosophical Association held in Berkeley, California, during December 1930. Of the five supplementary essays that make up the remainder of the volume, we can determine dates only for those two that are reprints of the 1925 and 1927 essays discussed above. The remaining three supplementary essays are undated, as are all of the materials in *The Philosophy of the Act*. Nevertheless, that Mead began his serious study of the theory of relativity and the philosophy of Whitehead during the summer of 1921 enables us to assign at least an approximate date to most of these undated manuscripts. For almost all of the main items included in *The Philosophy of the Act* contain references to relativity and/or Whitehead, as do two of the three undated supplementary essays included in *The Philosophy of the Present*. All of the materials containing such references, it is reasonable to assume, date from the last decade of Mead's career at Chicago.

So numerous and diverse are the references to Whiteheadian concepts in these two volumes that I cannot pretend to offer detailed analyses of them all. Fortunately, a more modest endeavor is sufficient to satisfy the aim of the present chapter. In what follows I summarize and elucidate the dominant ways in which the impact of Whitehead is evident in these materials by showing how they extend the five lines of Whiteheadian influence noted in our examination of Mead's 1925–29 essays. And to clarify the limits of his commitment to Whitehead's ideas, I also indicate the main respects in which Mead here diverges from or is explicitly critical of Whitehead.

1. *Objective Relativism*. In both *The Philosophy of the Act* and *The Philosophy of the Present* Mead maintains his allegiance to the Whiteheadian thesis that perspectives are objective ingredients of nature.[27] Moreover, he continues to apply the notion of a perspective, as we saw him do first in his essay of 1925, to the relationship between the individual and the world of his experience: "The perspective is the world in its relationship to the individual and the individual in his relationship to the world. The most unambiguous instance of the perspective is the biological form and its environment or habitat" (PA 115). But whereas Mead's earlier interest in Whitehead's treatment of perspectives had focused upon its significance for a proper understanding of the subject matter of the social sciences, his attention to this doctrine in these volumes has a much more general thrust. Here we find him elaborating his own view of experiential perspectives and applying this view to a broad range of questions stimulated in a large part by his study of Whitehead's attempt to relate the objects and spatio-temporal concep-

tions of exact physical science to our concrete experience of passage in nature.

2. *Passage and Spatio-Temporal Structures.* We have already witnessed the beginnings of the broader line of inquiry just mentioned in those portions of Mead's 1925 essay that discuss the process whereby we abstract from the passage of immediate experience to obtain a world of permanent objects existing in a "seemingly timeless" space. But these beginnings offer only a hint of the much more fully developed treatment of this and related matters in *The Philosophy of the Act* and *The Philosophy of the Present.* In these volumes Mead not only elaborates upon his earlier suggestions in great detail, he also extends his discussion to include the entities and spatio-temporal structures that figure in both Newtonian and post-Newtonian physics.

Mead's approach here turns upon a contrast between the character of our everyday perceptual world and that of a more primitive or more immediate form of experience in which there is no separation of space from time. If we could place ourselves within the experience of lower animals, he suggests, we would find that they live in a "Minkowski space-time world" in which everything at a distance is also infected with futurity (PA 147, 326–35). Similarly, to the extent that we can capture those of our own immediate experiences in which we act without thinking, we encounter a world in which distant objects lie ahead of us in time as well as in space: "In the anguished grasping at the stem of a sapling as one catches one's self in slipping on a cliff the reality of the sapling is entirely ahead." But we can capture this world of passage only with great difficulty because "we live so constantly in the world of our reflective moments" (PA 179). And this latter world, the world of our everyday perceptual experience, is one of enduring objects existing in a space from which passage has been abstracted; it is a world in which distant objects are not infected with futurity but are contemporaneous with our perceptual present.

Many of the essays and fragments in *The Philosophy of the Act,* together with significant portions of the first three supplementary essays in *The Philosophy of the Present,* are devoted to an exploration of the ways in which such mechanisms of human conduct as manipulation and role-taking lift us out of the space-time world of immediate passage.[28] And these explorations, I believe, can be viewed as the Meadian counterpart to a related line of inquiry in Whitehead's writings on the philosophy of nature. Both Mead and Whitehead seek to derive the

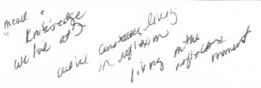

structures of the perceptual and scientific world from the passage of immediate experience, but whereas Whitehead's approach to such derivation is formal and mathematical, Mead's is grounded in that functional and genetic orientation to experience that provides the foundation for his earlier philosophical and social psychological work.

A brief comparison of Mead's approach and Whitehead's use of the "method of extensive abstraction" may help to clarify this point. Consider, for instance, the following simplified summary of the way in which Whitehead utilizes his method to derive the notion of a *moment* from the structural properties of passage presented to immediate sense awareness. A moment, he tells us, is an ideal of exact thought never actually encountered in concrete sense awareness. But we can relate this ideal to concrete experience via a route of approximation. The route involved here is an infinite series of durations, each duration extending over the next in the manner of a set of Chinese boxes. The ideal limit toward which this "abstractive set" of durations converges is a moment—the ideal of all nature at an instant.[29] Now the point of Whitehead's method is to show us that the fundamental conceptions of physical science are idealizations corresponding to patterns that a suitable analysis can extract from the concrete passage of nature presented to sense awareness. And, if I read Mead correctly, he is in total agreement with this thesis: Science, he maintains, seeks out "the enduring factors in experience to which passage is irrelevant because of the rhythmic recurrence of their patterns" (PA 175). The technique of science "seeks to render exact the enduring patterns and to find definable boundaries for a minimal passage of any required degree of temporal thinness. The ideal limit of this technique is the distribution of mass or energy particles in the universe at an instant" (PA 176).[30] But in Mead's work such pronouncements are only a prelude to a kind of inquiry of which we find no hint in Whitehead's philosophy of nature. For Mead is mainly concerned to relate the previously mentioned "enduring patterns" and the process of their extraction from passage to an analysis of *conduct*. Thus we find him asking: what are the mechanisms of behavior that give rise in experience to such items as moments, consentient sets, timeless space, and abstract time? And what functions do these perform in the economy of action?[31] Clearly Whitehead's formal analyses are relevant to such questions, but hardly sufficient to answer them.[32]

3. *Emergence and Temporality*. The scientific object, Mead holds,

"is an abstraction of that within experience which is subject to exact measurement" (PP 141). And, like Whitehead, he is concerned to keep a clear eye upon the concrete experience from which such objects are abstracted. In particular, he reminds us frequently that the emergence of novel elements is a pervasive feature of nature and that we must not lose sight of this fact simply because there is no place for emergence in a network of scientific abstractions that treats every happening as an inevitable consequence of causal antecedents. "It is the task of philosophy today," he proclaims near the beginning of *The Philosophy of the Present*, "to bring into congruence with each other this universality of determination which is the text of modern science, and the emergence of the novel which belongs not only to the experience of human social organisms, but is found also in a nature which science and the philosophy that has followed it have separated from human nature" (PP 14).

Mead's own approach to this task in *The Philosophy of the Present* involves a further elaboration of that treatment of the past and of experienced passage set forth in his 1929 essay "The Nature of the Past." We must bear in mind, he points out, that the meaningful structure of the past is as hypothetical as is the future (PP 12). Certainly there is a kind of finality or irrevocability about the past: when an event has passed it is over and done with; it cannot be changed. But this does not preclude subsequent changes in the *meaning* that we attribute to such past events. Emergence can thus be reflected into the pasts we construct, for we can change our conception of "what it was" that has happened in the light of new problems and new elements of experience arising in the present. The "empty title of irrevocability" then attaches to whatever meaning the present leads us to attribute to the past (PP 3). Now, as Mead sees the matter in *The Philosophy of the Present*, the construction of such pasts is an important part of what the scientist does in his attempt to understand nature. Indeed, it is by interpreting the past in such a way as to make the future predictable that the scientist is able at least to approximate the goal of presenting the universe as a wholly determined system. To reconcile such a presentation with the emergence of novelty in nature we need only remember the larger context in which a scientific account of the universe is located. For however successful the scientist may be in his attempt to explain and predict natural occurrences, he "will still look forward to the appearance of new problems that will emerge in new presents to be rationalized again with another past which will take up the old past harmoniously into itself" (PP 11).

It is important to note further that Mead's emphasis upon emergence in *The Philosophy of the Present* leads him to express serious reservations about Whitehead's account of the passage of nature. For although Whitehead avoids the Einsteinian conception of a noumenal space-time world in his interpretation of relativity, his ultimate description of nature nevertheless makes use of what Mead labels "a fixed geometry of space-time." And the latter professes himself unable to see how the fixed order of events thus postulated can be reconciled with emergence, even granting Whitehead's notion that the qualitative characters of these events depend upon the "eternal objects" that are said to "ingress" into them as a result of the activity of God. "Whitehead's philosophy is a valiant attempt to harmonize this sort of geometric necessity with emergence and the differences of varying perspectives. I do not believe that this can be accomplished" (PP 10–11).

If we relate this criticism to what Mead says elsewhere in *The Philosophy of the Present* and also in various passages of *The Philosophy of the Act,* it becomes clear that the root of the issue that separates Mead and Whitehead lies in their respective analyses of experienced passage. Whitehead goes astray, Mead contends, when he uses the method of extensive abstraction as a method of metaphysical abstraction and finds in mere happenings or events "the substance of that which becomes." "He transfers the content of what becomes to a world of 'eternal objects' having ingression into events under the control of a principle lying outside of their occurrence. While, then, the existence of what occurs is found in the present, the 'what it is' that occurs does not arise out of happening, it happens to the event through the metaphysical process of ingression" (PP 20).

On Mead's view, this move is an instance of what Whitehead himself baptizes "the fallacy of misplaced concreteness." For the events and the contents here torn asunder and given independent ontological status are both abstractions from the experienced passage of nature. The qualitative characters that Whitehead interprets as eternal objects are actually implicated in both the passage and the perspectival character of experience: "the so-called eternal objects must be recognized as eternal only in the sense of being irrelevant to passage, and they must be found in the organization of perspectives" (PA 539). Moreover, Whitehead's events and "event-particles" are nothing more than the result of abstracting the bare factor of passage from concrete becoming: "an event-particle should have the same relationship to something that becomes that the differential of a change such as an accelerating velocity has to the whole process" (PP 20). Finally, the space-time geometry of events and intervals that Whitehead employs in describing such passage should be regarded as a mathematical apparatus useful in achieving exactitude of measurement and calculation in dealing with certain aspects of actual becoming. It provides us neither with a concrete description of the experienced process of nature nor with a description of a noumenal reality lying beyond experience. Rather, the events and intervals to which such a geometry refers "are the constants that shake out of the elaborate mathematics which the realization of the social character of the universe has shown to be necessary" (PP 49).

4. *Sociality and the Common World.* I shall have more to say shortly about what Mead has in mind here when he speaks of "the social character of the universe." But first it is helpful to look at the manner in which he continues to emphasize the sociality of human conduct in his approach to the problem of the common world as this problem relates to the theory of relativity. In his essays of 1925–29 he stressed the mechanism of role-taking in his attempt to account for the public or shared character of perceptual objects: human individuals experience a world of public objects by bringing the perspectives of others into their own conduct and attending to features that are common to all these perspectives. This same idea, but with a new twist, occupies a prominent place in Mead's discussions of Einsteinian relativity in *The Philosophy of the Act* and *The Philosophy of the Present*. In the context of physical relativity, he points out, the problem of the common world takes on a new form. Whereas the fundamental entities of both ordinary perceptual experience and Newtonian mechanics are essentially timeless in character, a relativistic analysis yields entities whose quantifiable dimensions are inextricably tied to temporal perspectives. In this latter context, then, there is no possibility of ignoring the temporal differences of various perspectives to obtain a common world existing at an instant. One strategy that presents itself at this point is that of locating the common world outside of experience in a noumenal reality, "a reality lying behind the different perspectives, to which the reality of experience under different frames of reference belongs—a Minkowski space-time with its events and intervals" (PP 78). But this tack, which represents the view of Einstein and Eddington, involves

a bifurcation of nature that both Mead and Whitehead oppose. The need for such bifurcation disappears, Mead argues, if we allow room in nature for individuals who can bring a plurality of perspectives into their own experience through the social mechanism of role-taking. "Whitehead for example refers to a double consciousness of cogredience, in which the observer identifies himself both with the space-time of a train and with that of the landscape through which the train is moving. Evidently relativity as a doctrine would have been impossible but for this type of consciousness" (PP 78).[33] By construing such consciousness as itself part of nature (a step Whitehead does not take in his early writings), we can make room in nature for what would otherwise be incompatible meanings. On this view, the mutually exclusive spatio-temporal structures of two different perspectives are both present in nature, and "there is a form of sociality within which we can go from one to the other by means of a system of transformations, and so occupy both systems, identifying the same objects in each" (PP 79–80; cp. PA 608–9). Individuals who can participate in this form of sociality "are living in a common world" and, hence, "reference to a Minkowski world is unnecessary" (PP 82).

5. *The Place of Mind in Nature.* The preceding line of thought leads Mead to suggest, in those portions of *The Philosophy of the Present* that are based upon the Carus Lectures of 1930, that sociality is a dimension not just of human conduct and intelligence but of nature as a whole. This hypothesis turns upon an extension of his earlier notion of sociality to include any situation in which an object is what it is because it participates in a plurality of perspectives or spatio-temporal systems. By thus generalizing the conception of sociality, Mead arrives at a cosmological principle that he regards as a significant key for the understanding of both emergence and relativity. In all emergence, he holds, we find a process of readjustment in which "the emergent object belongs to different systems in its passage from the old to the new . . . and possesses the characters it has because of its membership in these different systems" (PP 65). Similarly, the experimental proofs of Einsteinian relativity oblige the experimenter to approach an object in terms of at least two alternative perspectives (Whitehead's "double consciousness of cogredience"); the experimenter then compares the spatio-temporal structures of such perspectives by means of transformation formulas. Relativity thus "reveals a situation within which the

object must be contemporaneously in different systems to be what it is in either" (PP 63).

Now, as Arthur Murphy observes in his introduction to *The Philosophy of the Present* (xxxii), this last claim about the sense in which Einsteinian relativity entails sociality in nature is highly dubious: the special theory of relativity does not seem to assert, for instance, that the velocity a body exhibits in one inertial frame or perspective in any way *depends* upon that body's exhibiting another velocity in an alternative inertial frame. And if Mead's view is short of the truth at this juncture, then one of his main arguments for the principle of sociality in *The Philosophy of the Present* collapses. But it is not my purpose here either to explore his final cosmological speculations in detail or to assess their validity. Rather, I want simply to note that these speculations can be viewed as part of Mead's attempt to modify Whitehead's idea of nature as a system of perspectives so as to make it more congenial to his own social and functional conception of mind. By stressing emergence as a pervasive feature of nature and by grounding such emergence in sociality, he establishes continuity between nature and human mentality. For the mind in its reconstructive functioning is "a realm of continual emergence," and the emergence of novel ideas in the mind is made possible by the social interplay of alternative roles and perspectives that the mind involves (PP 85). Moreover, by emphasizing the significance of "taking the role of the other" in the formulation of the doctrine of relativity, Mead illustrates an important respect in which the social character of human thought allows nature as an organization of perspectives to appear in reflective human experience. The appearance of mind in nature, Mead concludes near the end of his Carus Lectures, "is only the culmination of that sociality which is found throughout the universe, its culmination lying in the fact that the organism, by occupying the attitudes of others, can occupy its own attitude in the role of the other" (PP 86).

Concluding Remarks

The writings of Whitehead, it should now be evident, served as a potent stimulus to Mead's thought in the years following 1921. But this stimulus did not lead Mead to abandon any of the characteristic concerns or

theses of his earlier work. Rather, the influence of Whitehead's philosophy of nature turned Mead's attention toward a variety of problems that
he had not previously explored and that he then proceeded to attack,
primarily by extensions of his own arsenal of philosophic and social
psychological ideas. Mead was not a full-fledged convert to the Whiteheadian cause, for he explicitly criticizes certain aspects of Whitehead's
program. Yet it would be a mistake to place too much emphasis upon
these criticisms, for they occur only infrequently in Mead's writings
and are almost never developed in detail. Mead was, in fact, neither
a disciple nor a systematic critic of Whitehead's thought. Instead of
making Whitehead's work the object of either adulation or extended
polemical criticism, he utilized it as a rich mine of suggestions bearing
upon his own quest for a unified view of nature and human experience.

Chapter 10

Mead's Social Pragmatism

When Mead wrote or lectured on social psychological topics, he often characterized his mature approach to human conduct as a version of psychological "behaviorism." When he sought to develop the broader implications of this same approach, however, he thought of himself as a representative of philosophical "pragmatism." Witness, for example, his participation in the 1917 cooperative volume *Creative Intelligence: Essays in the Pragmatic Attitude*[1] and his references to himself as a pragmatist, both in his correspondence and in his formal writings—most notably in his 1929 essay "A Pragmatic Theory of Truth."[2] But what was his understanding of pragmatism, and in what respects did his own work fall under the rubric of pragmatism as he conceived it? In the present chapter I conclude my examination of Mead's intellectual development by focusing upon a number of key themes in his later works that help to locate his thought with reference to the pragmatic tradition in American philosophy. And in so doing I point out what I take to be his distinctive contributions to this tradition.

Mead on Pragmatism

Charles Peirce, William James, and John Dewey are commonly regarded as the three outstanding classical figures in the history of American pragmatism. But of these three, only James and Dewey receive significant attention in Mead's historical discussions of that philosophical movement. The works of Peirce, whose posthumously edited *Collected Papers* did not begin to appear in print until the year of Mead's death (1931), seem to have had no direct influence upon the development of Mead's thought; further, they occupy no more than a minor place in his conception of pragmatism. Mead mentions Peirce only twice in his published lectures and writings, and both references occur in his 1930 essay "The Philosophies of Royce, James, and Dewey in their American Setting" in which he briefly mentions "Peirce's laboratory habit of mind" as it relates to the pragmatism of James and Dewey (sw 385, 389). Even these references, I suspect, stem from Mead's familiarity with Dewey's use of this phrase in his *Essays in Experimental Logic* rather than from any careful study of Peirce.[3] If we want to understand Mead's view of the pragmatic tradition, then, we must turn to his remarks about James and Dewey.

The pragmatic orientation in philosophy, Mead suggests in *Movements of Thought in the Nineteenth Century* and "The Philosophies of Royce, James, and Dewey in their American Setting" (1930), involves two fundamental features. One is the espousal of a "behavioristic" psychology that construes intelligence as a dimension of conduct or behavior; the other is a view of knowledge based upon the model of experimental inquiry, in which problems arising within conduct are dealt with by means of hypotheses whose test of validity consists in their capacity to resolve those problems so that action can once again proceed without confusion or conflict (MT 344–59; sw 383–84). An early expression of the psychological foundation of pragmatism, Mead notes, can be seen in James's chapter on the concept in *The Principles of Psychology* (1890). Here James locates knowledge within conduct and treats conduct as "a living physiological affair" occurring against the background of the Darwinian struggle for existence. James regards human knowledge as an elaboration of that intelligence through which an animal deals with problems encountered in the life process; its efficacy is thus to be assessed "not by its agreement with a preexistent reality but by its solution of the difficulty within which the act finds itself" (sw 383–84). Similarly, the second main feature of pragmatism can be seen in James's later claim that all ideas are hypotheses and that the test of a hypothesis is to be found in its working. According to Mead, however, James's espousal of this claim was in part motivated by a desire to justify the individual's "right to believe" in ideas that an individual found satisfying and meaningful. And this Jamesian predisposition "blurred his analysis" of the place of ideas and knowledge in human conduct. It led James to employ the ambiguous term "satisfaction" in his articulation of the pragmatic test of truth, thereby attributing evidential weight to an individual's desires and attitudes in the settlement of philosophic belief (sw 384–86).

While Mead is thus inclined to be critical of what might be called the "tender-minded" strain in James's pragmatism, his references to the pragmatism of Dewey are almost wholly sympathetic. There is a grand simplicity to the development of Dewey's thought, he points out in the 1930 essay cited above, which originates with Dewey's psychological analysis of the moral act in *Outlines of a Critical Theory of Ethics* (1891): "In the *Outlines of Ethics* we find the will, the idea, and the consequences all placed inside of the act, and the act itself placed only within the larger activity of the individual in society" (sw 387–88). Like James, Dewey subsequently turned to biological science with its dominant conception of evolution for an understanding of conduct as a life process in terms of which to analyze the nature of human intelligence. And, working with this understanding of conduct, he established at the University of Chicago an Experimental School where he developed and put to the test a philosophy of education based upon the principle that "knowing is a part of doing." Thereafter, Dewey set forth a detailed pragmatic or instrumental theory of the whole process of knowing, fully capturing the spirit of Peirce's laboratory habit of mind in his *Essays in Experimental Logic* (1916). Finally, he brought the quest begun with *Outlines of Ethics* to fruition with the publication of *Experience and Nature* (1925). In the former volume Dewey emphasized that the acts of human individuals acquire their moral character through their relationship to a larger social whole; in the latter he stressed that it is only through participation in a social life process that the individual acquires that consciousness of linguistic meanings that makes thought and knowledge possible as dimensions of conduct. Hence, in *Experience and Nature* "the parallelism between the analysis of the moral act and the cognitive act is completed" (sw 388–89).

To this brief sketch of Dewey's pragmatic intellectual journey, Mead adds a complementary account in his posthumously published essay on "The Philosophy of John Dewey." [4] Here he emphasizes the importance of Dewey's early Hegelianism as one of the foundations for his later pragmatism. Dewey's early training in the dialectic of absolute idealism, Mead contends, supplied him with several key convictions that he carried over into his mature philosophical work. Among these were: (1) the conception of reality as a developing process; (2) the

view that both human thought and its objects arise within this process and are integrally related aspects of it; (3) the notion that human
society is a culminating dimension of this process and that the human
individual can achieve self-realization only through participation with
other selves as an organic part of a larger social whole. Mead views
Dewey's subsequent pragmatism as a philosophical project in which
this initial fund of Hegelian ideas is naturalized and put to work as
a vehicle for addressing concrete human problems. Dewey natural-
izes Hegel by locating knowledge within conduct and conduct within
nature as it is understood in biological science; he treats knowing as an
active process, a finding out, which is set in motion by the presence in
conduct of conflicting impulses or tendencies to respond. The problem
of knowledge, according to Dewey, is thus "not to find out how we can
get from a state of mind to an object outside of mind, but how an intelligence that lies within nature can so reorganize its experience that the
activities of the inhibited individual can proceed." The test of knowing is the test of whether a hypothesis works—i.e., does it overcome
the conflict of impulses so that inhibited conduct can get going again?
"This is the pragmatic test of truth, not in the agreement between an
idea and an object external to it, but in the success of a plan of action." [5]

Just as knowing resides within conduct and nature, so also, according to Mead's reading of Dewey, does human conduct provide
the context within which arise conceptual meanings or universals and
consciously entertained ends, ideals, or values. For Dewey, the social
dimension of human conduct gives rise to communication through
symbols, which enable us to think abstractly, to direct our attention
to universal or recurrent features of experience. Moreover, such symbols make possible a kind of reflective intelligence enabling humans to
distill from the frustrations and fulfillments encountered in conduct a
consciously articulated set of values, ideals, or ends-in-view. Universals
and values thus have no residence in a Platonic heaven where moth
and rust do not corrupt; rather, they inhabit conduct and nature along
with all the more pedestrian objects of our experience, and we must
use our capacity of reflective intelligence to find them out. This, Mead
concludes, "is a philosophy which comes with something of the effect
of a cold shower, and it depends somewhat upon the vitality of the man
who becomes acquainted with it whether it leaves him with a chill or
a glow." [6]

Mead, of course, did not live to witness the culmination of Dewey's pragmatism in *Logic: The Theory of Inquiry* (1938). But he did have the opportunity to study its relatively late expression in *The Quest for Certainty* (1929). And his reactions to that book make it quite clear, should there remain any doubt, that he was one of those for whom repeated immersions in the cold shower of Dewey's philosophic enterprise invariably produced a glow rather than a chill. He speaks in "The Philosophies of Royce, James, and Dewey in their American Setting," for example, of the "enormous relief" to be gained from a reading of Dewey's 1929 work: "The baffled sense of the philosophic squirrel running a ceaseless dialectical round within his cage, that despairing sense of the philosophic Sisyphus vainly striving to roll the heavily weighted world of reflection up into a preexistent reality—these drop away and the philosopher can face about toward the future and join in the scientist's adventure" (SW 389–90). To which we may add Arthur Murphy's account of Mead's response when asked if he believed what Dewey had said in *The Quest for Certainty:* He drew himself up, Murphy reports, and replied, "Every word!"[7]

This is not to say, however, that Mead was wholly uncritical of Dewey's prodigious philosophic output. Student notes taken in Mead's 1926 course on the philosophy of John Dewey, for instance, show him pointing out that Dewey's philosophy was not yet in harmony with the theory of relativity—although he thought that *Experience and Nature* could be made to harmonize with that theory.[8] Moreover, in an unpublished review of Dewey's *Human Nature and Conduct* (1922), Mead objects that Dewey's foray into social psychology falls back upon "the outworn doctrine of imitation" while offering only a "sketchy and inadequate" account of the rise of the structure of the self in human social experience.[9] And in the posthumously published essay on "The Philosophy of John Dewey" he notes the logical difficulty involved in that, for Dewey, "the thinking that has its only legitimate place within conduct seems to be able to transcend that conduct, to form a judgment upon it, and yet by Dewey's criterion that judgment can only be tested by the conduct that it judges."[10] Nevertheless, such criticisms of Dewey are few and far between. Mead appears always to have seen himself as fundamentally at one with Dewey's point of view, from the beginning of their friendship at the University of Michigan until the end of his life. Consequently, he seldom raised a question of Dewey's philosophy for which he was not ready to suggest a Deweyan answer—or an answer whose details he might himself work out in terms of the broad outlines provided by Dewey's thought. He was never much interested in criticizing Dewey's work; instead, he devoted much of his philosophic energy to the patient and detailed exploratory articulation of Dewey's orientation in areas of experience whose features Dewey mapped out only on a rather large scale.

Constructive Social Pragmatism

Philosophical pragmatism, Murphy notes in his introduction to Mead's *The Philosophy of the Present* (xiii), has tended to channel the intellectual efforts of its proponents in two different directions. One is the polemical direction, in which the pragmatist wages critical battle against epistemology and other sins of the philosophic past. The other is a constructive direction, in which the pragmatist's enthusiasm for conduct or experience leads him to offer detailed analyses of its structures and objects. Some of the former can certainly be found in Mead's works, but his thought is generally much less driven by the polemical spirit than is that of Dewey. It is with the constructive sort of pragmatism, as Murphy correctly observes, that Mead is primarily concerned. What Murphy calls Mead's "constructive pragmatism" might with equal reason be labeled "social pragmatism."[11] For almost every one of his original and distinctive contributions to the pragmatic tradition in American philosophy rests upon a probing analysis of the social dimensions of conduct or experience. The survey of these contributions that follows attempts to make good this claim and, at the same time, to provide a useful concluding overview of Mead's thought.

1. *The Social Dimensions of Conduct.* One of the foundations of pragmatism, Mead claims in his discussions of James and Dewey, is a psychology that locates intelligence within conduct and conduct within nature. And it was just such a psychology, as we saw in chapter 4, that Mead took over from Dewey in the 1890s. The psychological functionalism of the early Chicago School, with its organic conception of conduct, became the basis for Mead's later pragmatism. But Mead did more than simply work out some of the implications of this new organic model of action; he transformed it by emphasizing and analyzing the social dimensions of both animal and human conduct. His delineation of such features of social conduct as the gesture, the conversation of

gestures, the significant symbol, and "taking the attitude or the role of the other" are key aspects of this analysis.

Much of the significance of Mead's analysis of social conduct derives, of course, from his use of this analysis as a basis upon which to build a number of highly original social psychological theories. Not satisfied simply to assert standard functionalist or pragmatic generalities about the place of thought within biologically construed action, Mead outlined constructive hypotheses concerning the genesis of language, self-consciousness, and reflective intelligence within human social conduct. Even if he had accomplished nothing else, these social psychological achievements are of sufficient importance to guarantee Mead a place of prominence in the history of American pragmatism.

2. *The Human Individual and the Social Process.* The details of Mead's social psychological theories have been adequately canvassed in earlier chapters, but to indicate the link between Mead's social psychology and his pragmatic naturalism, something should be said about the evolutionary conception of nature that provides the context for his social psychological theorizing. This can best be done by calling attention to Mead's discussion, in *Mind, Self and Society,* of two differing approaches to the relationship between individual human selves and the ongoing social process in which they are involved. One approach accounts for the social process in terms of the interaction of individuals whose reflective, self-conscious nature is regarded as given. It is because human individuals are rational, self-conscious beings with ideas to express, according to this view, that human social interaction takes the complex and various forms it does. The second approach takes an almost opposite tack: it explains the rational, self-conscious nature of human individuals in terms of the type of social interaction in which they participate. On this view, too, human individuals are presupposed, but only as biological organisms having certain sociophysiological capacities and tendencies to respond, not as self-conscious beings. The actual development of distinctively human mentality and personality in these organisms is held to be the product of social interaction (MSS 222–26).

In his social psychology, as in his philosophy generally, Mead is a thoroughly evolutionary thinker. It is hardly surprising, therefore, that he is not satisfied with the first or more individualistic of the two approaches to the human self mentioned above; he holds that the second approach, with its emphasis upon the primacy of sociality, yields a deeper understanding of the evolution of distinctively human behavior. If we begin with a rudimentary form of social process, Mead maintains, then we can explain human minds and selves as structures of conduct that evolve out of that process. Moreover, whereas the more individualistic approach cannot convincingly explain the existence of the minds or selves with which it begins, the second approach can explain the existence of that rudimentary social process it regards as logically prior to the development of minds and selves; it does so "in terms of such fundamental biological or physiological relations and interactions as reproduction, or the co-operation of individuals for mutual protection or for the securing of food" (MSS 223). Thus, the second approach avoids the radical discontinuity involved in the individualistic approach. It does not take mind and self-consciousness to be congenital psychical endowments that suddenly appear at the human level of evolution. Rather, it explains their nature and origin in terms of social behavior that differs primarily in complexity from that found among members of nonhuman animal species and that has its roots in the same kinds of congenital social impulses (MSS 50, 222–26).

We should note, however, that Mead's advocacy of this approach to the relationship between human nature and society does not lead him to deny the element of truth contained in the individualistic account. Where that view goes wrong is in ignoring the fundamentally *social* character of the developed human individual: "The human being's physiological capacity for developing mind or intelligence is a product of the process of biological evolution, just as is his whole organism; but the actual development of his mind or intelligence itself, given that capacity, must proceed in terms of the social situations wherein it gets its expression and import; and hence it itself is a product of the process of social evolution, the process of social experience and behavior" (MSS 226n). Nevertheless, one should not overlook the truth of the claim that individual minds or selves do influence and shape the social process. The human personality arises within a kind of social interaction similar to that exhibited in the behavior of nonhuman animals. But the individual personality is at the same time a genuine emergent, i.e., it possesses novel characteristics not reducible to properties of the biological and social factors responsible for its genesis, and as such it affects the further development of the process from which it arises. We find Mead eager to incorporate this emergent character into his social view of the human individual: "Once mind has arisen in the social process it makes possible the development of that process into much more complex forms of social interaction among the component individuals than was possible before it had arisen. But there is nothing odd about a product of a given process contributing to, or becoming an essential factor in, the further development of that process. The social process, then, does not depend for its origin or initial existence upon the existence and interaction of selves; though it does depend upon the latter for the higher stages of complexity and organization which it reaches after selves have arisen within it" (MSS 226).

In this manner, then, Mead locates his social psychological theorizing within a conception of nature involving social as well as biological evolution. And in so doing he subscribes to the same kind of evolutionary naturalism that provides the backdrop for the pragmatism of James and Dewey. He goes beyond these thinkers, however, in his emphasis upon the role of the human individual in the process of social evolution. This emphasis, as we saw in chapter 8, is central to his later writings on ethics and moral psychology: his attempts to interpret the process of moral and social reconstruction in terms of his social psychological conceptions constitute part of his contribution to the pragmatic understanding of the human personality as both social and creative. Another aspect of this same contribution can be found in his analysis of the reconstructive role of the human individual in the growth of scientific knowledge.

3. *The Temporal Dimensions of Conduct.* The striking originality of his social psychological theorizing should not lead us to overlook Mead's other important contributions to the further elaboration of that organic conception of conduct whose foundations were laid at Chicago in the 1890s. One such contribution, the analysis of the temporal dimensions of conduct, deserves emphasis here because it underlies many of the recurring pragmatic themes found in his later philosophical writings where he analyzes "the act" (his preferred term for the unit of conduct) as a dynamic whole consisting of successive and interpenetrating stages: the act is rooted in *impulse,* and it typically passes through stages of *perception* and *manipulation* toward *consummation.* We can best clarify the nature of these several stages and their relationships to each other by briefly tracing the act's passage from initiation to completion.

Every act, Mead maintains, arises from impulses that seek expression in the conduct or life process of an organism. (These impulsive tendencies, as we saw earlier, are often social in character; they always have a biological basis, but they may also have been shaped in considerable degree by the previous experience of the organism.) An organism's impulses sensitize it to certain features of its environment, which thereby become stimuli that release and guide the expression of the impulses involved. Environmental stimuli thus enter the process of conduct as functional cues, rather than as mere external influences. "The stimulus is the occasion for the expression of the impulse. Stimuli are means, tendency is the real thing" (MSS 6n).

This functional conception of environmental stimuli is further amplified by what Mead says about the place of perception within conduct. The perceptual phase of the act consists in adjustments made by the organism to features of its environment that are for the time being outside its area of contact or manipulation. Here the stimuli affecting the organism are "distance characters"—sensuous qualities such as color, sound, and odor—among which those of vision tend to play the dominant part (PA 4, 121). Impulses seeking expression in the organism's ongoing activities select and organize these distance characters so as to give them import for the control of the act. Thus, the perception of distance characters typically provides environmental stimuli initiating movement toward or away from a certain location. And the changing values of these stimuli exert a continuous control over the act as this movement proceeds (SW 289).

The perceptual phase of the act, Mead holds, often leads into a manipulatory phase, where distance characters are supplemented by those of contact. In this stage of the act the organism handles or otherwise manipulates things prior to a consummation (PA 141). And here, again, the stimuli that control conduct are means whose import is a function of the ongoing act. In this case, the manipulatory or contact characters receive attention only because they serve to release and guide the expression of impulsive tendencies driving toward an incipient consummation (PA 145, 148). A distinct manipulatory phase of conduct, Mead points out, hardly exists for most nonhuman organisms; in their experience, contact and consummation tend to be more or less inseparable. But the great flexibility of the human hand, together with the human capacity to engage in extensive manipulation prior to any kind of consummation, makes this an extremely important phase of human conduct (MSS 362–63).

Mead refers to the perceptual and manipulatory phases of conduct as "mediate" stages of the act: they occupy a temporal position between the initiation of the act and its completion. It is in the consummatory stage of the act that the impulses seeking expression in that act encounter some measure of immediate fulfillment or frustration; here things "are possessed, are good, bad, and indifferent, beautiful or ugly, and lovable or noxious." In short, "within the field of consummation all the adjectives of value obtain immediately" (PA 25). Such values, of course, have no absolute status independent of conduct. They arise within conduct, within the life process; their import, like that of distance and manipulatory qualities, is a function of ongoing activity, of modifiable impulses seeking expression. Hence, they, too, serve as a means for the continuation of activity (PA 362–63).

In setting forth this temporal or sequential analysis of the act, Mead is again building in an original manner upon Dewey's organic conception of conduct. We can properly understand Mead's analysis only if we bear in mind Dewey's claim that conduct is an affair in which responses do more than merely succeed a stimulus; they transform, mediate, or interpret that stimulus. The response, as Dewey remarks in his 1896 essay on the reflex arc concept, is not simply *to* a stimulus but *into* it. The perceptual, manipulatory, and consummatory stages Mead delineates in his analysis of the act should thus be regarded as successive phases of response, each of which further transforms or interprets an initial stimulus content. The perceptual phase of the act, for instance, brings added meaning to distance characters as the organism responds into them in terms of their significance for impulses seeking expression. Moreover, later stages of the act flow into and interpret earlier stages. When an organism responds perceptually to a distant object, it characteristically does so with habitual manipulatory and consummatory responses already aroused. The percept is in this sense a "collapsed act"; anticipated manipulatory experiences and consummatory values tend to be already implicitly present in the perceptual stage of the act (PA 3–6, 131).

4. *Conduct and the Constitution of Our Perceptual World.* It is precisely because responses mediate or interpret the stimuli that call them forth, Mead holds, that our everyday perceptual experience is populated by meaningful events and objects rather than by mere sensations: such objects are not so much *given* as *constituted* through a behavioral process in which we gradually acquire habitual patterns of

response with respect to recurring sorts of stimuli. Indeed, much of Mead's social psychological theorizing is, in fact, a creative elaboration of this key idea. According to his theory of language, for instance, it is the interpretive function of our responses that gives meaning to the gestures of the others with whom we interact; moreover, we acquire consciousness of the social meanings of our own gestures to the extent that we respond into (mediate, interpret) these gestures as others do when they interact with us. Further, according to his theory of self-consciousness, it is by importing the social attitudes or responses of others into our own behavior that we are able to constitute in our experience those important social objects we call selves. Both the selves of others and also one's own self are constructs made possible by the interpretive function of social responses.

But Mead's treatment of human perceptual experience encompasses a good deal more than these social psychological doctrines. In his later philosophical writings—especially those included in *The Philosophy of the Present* and *The Philosophy of the Act*—he uses his analysis of the perceptual and manipulatory phases of the act, together with his notion of "taking the attitude or the role of the other," to develop detailed hypotheses concerning the ways in which physical objects, space, and time are constituted as structures of our everyday perceptual world. The fundamental structure of this world, he maintains, is grounded in the manipulatory phase of human conduct. Here the tactual sensitivity and flexibility of the human hand combine with vision to facilitate extensive handling of things prior to the act's completion. Moreover, in this phase of conduct the temporal passage that normally intervenes between seeing (distance perception) and bodily contact is at a minimum; such passage can therefore be ignored by the acting organism. Thus there is present in human manipulatory experience a complex mixture of temporally congruent visual and contact characters. It is by delaying the act at this stage—and abstracting from the consummatory values that pervade this mixture in immediate or unreflective experience—that the reflective individual arrives at a field of relatively permanent implemental features in terms of which to address problems encountered in conduct (PA 143, 178, 453).

Mead furthermore understands manipulation as a variety of cooperation or social experience. It is only because things push back at us, provide us with resistance and leverage, that manipulation is possible; the things manipulated must literally do as much as the manipulator if the latter is to do anything at all (PA 109, 187). And it is just this social aspect of manipulation that gives rise in human experience to a world of physical objects. Human individuals organize their manipulatory experience with reference to a field of physical objects over against their bodies (and vice versa) when they begin to control their conduct by stimulating in their own organisms the resistance of things being manipulated or whose manipulation is anticipated. The psychological mechanism involved here is that same "taking the attitude or the role of the other" that, on Mead's view, gives rise to our awareness of selves. He thus suggests that the physical objects of our everyday perceptual experience are abstractions from what once appeared as more completely social objects. In the experience of children and primitive people, the "others" of manipulation tend to take the form of truncated personalities. But more sophisticated experience abstracts from all their social characters except resistance; this latter character is what provides the "matter" or the "inside" of physical objects in reflective experience (PA 145, 185–90, 385; PP 119–39).

The most important fact about the world of objects thus constituted by human reflection is that it is contemporaneous with the manipulatory area. By stimulating within their own organisms the anticipated resistance of objects that are still at a distance, human individuals hypothetically extend the manipulatory area to the limits of distance experience; they see things at a distance as already having the contact characteristics they would have if they were presently being handled. The resulting perceptual world is one in which the temporal passage between distance and contact characters in immediate experience is collapsed or annihilated. The reflecting individuals are thereby left with "an enduring fabric as a basis for alternative courses of action, a world of things that have identical dates, namely, the date of the manipulatory area." This enduring fabric is the "timeless space" of our everyday reflective moments; and passage, having been squeezed out of this fabric, remains only in the form of time—i.e., an abstract passage marked off and measured by recurrent motion within the field of enduring objects (PA 104, 148–52, 178, 191–92, 231).

5. *Human Conduct and the World of Physical Theory*. Not only does Mead attempt in his later writings to account for the fundamental structures of the perceptual world in terms of his temporal and social analyses of human conduct, but he also seeks to carry out a similar program with respect to the structures of the world as conceptualized in

take Role other
not nesy other
but of object

both Newtonian and post-Newtonian physics. The Newtonian view of the material world, he notes at various places in *The Philosophy of the Present* and *The Philosophy of the Act,* involves the same separation of space and time as that found in our everyday perceptual world. And we can imagine Newtonian mass particles as extremely small physical objects—so long as we deprive them of such so-called secondary qualities as color, odor, sound, taste, and temperature. Hence the basic structures of the Newtonian world-view are, in effect, refinements of those structures already present in the perceptual world; we can thus account for the constitution of both sets of structures within conduct by means of essentially the same kind of analysis (PP 37, 109, 152; PA 259–60).

But when we turn to a consideration of post-Newtonian physics we are confronted with a host of radically nonperceptual notions, chief among which are those related to Einsteinian relativity and the interpretation of mass in terms of a more general conception of energy. Einstein's special theory of relativity, for instance, requires the notion of alternative space-time perspectives as opposed to the invariant spatial and temporal containers of the perceptual and Newtonian worlds. Similarly, the electromagnetic theory of matter requires us to abandon perceptual models based upon manipulatory experience in our understanding of the ultimate physical entities (PP 37–45; PA 205–9). Clearly, these notions pose a serious challenge to anyone who wants to claim that the conceptual structures of physical science are grounded in features of human experience or conduct.

Mead devotes very little attention to twentieth-century conceptions of matter in his later writings;[12] he does, however, undertake repeated discussions of physical relativity throughout *The Philosophy of the Present* and *The Philosophy of the Act.* And these discussions, as we saw in the preceding chapter, make liberal use of ideas found in the writings of Alfred North Whitehead. Since I have already examined this use of Whiteheadian ideas in considerable detail, I here only summarize the main steps in Mead's attempts to interpret relativity in terms of his own temporal and social analyses of conduct.

a. Following the lead of Whitehead, Mead holds that the structures of space, time, and motion with which physics is concerned exist in nature only insofar as the process of nature, the natural continuum of events, is differentiated or "stratified" into alternative spatio-temporal systems by its relation to different "percipient events." This sort of relationship, which Mead calls a "perspective," underlies the selection of a "consentient set" of objects at rest with respect to a percipient event, thereby providing a space within which motion can take place. Space, time, and motion are therefore always perspectival in character, that is, they are always relative to some percipient event. Furthermore, the perspectives involved here are ingredients within nature itself; nature is, in fact, an evolving organization of entwined perspectives. Thus, the varied stratifications of nature into alternative spatiotemporal systems are not to be regarded as subjective distortions of some absolute space-time order. They are relative, but nevertheless objective, features of nature. In this fashion, both Mead and Whitehead incorporate the principle of relativity into the very texture of nature.

b. Mead links this relativistic conception of nature to his analyses of conduct by construing the ongoing life of a biological organism as a prime example of what Whitehead labels a "percipient event": the relationship between an organism and its environment, he suggests, is an example of a perspective, and the conduct of an organism stratifies the continuum of events in nature into a spatio-temporal system. Such stratification achieves the level of conscious conceptual formulation, of course, only in the case of reflective human conduct. Moreover, the alternative perspectives of different human individuals are ordinarily of sufficient similarity to allow for their unification in the form of that shared perceptual world (or its Newtonian refinement) whose basic constitution, as we saw above, Mead grounds in manipulatory experience and the capacity to "take the attitude or the role of the other."

c. For most purposes, our everyday perceptual world or its Newtonian refinement serves as an adequate guide to conduct. But there are some contexts involving exact scientific measurement in which ordinary ways of conceptualizing space, time, and motion break down: here the finite velocity of light employed in measurement requires us to assign quite different spatial and temporal values to the same objects relative to different consentient sets moving at high velocity with respect to one another. In these situations, the relativity implicit in our encounters with nature can no longer be overlooked; relativistic aspects of nature that are negligible in more usual sorts of cases now become significant and must be explicitly acknowledged. Such acknowledgment finds its precise quantitative expression in the mathematical formulations of relativistic physics. And the new conceptions of space, time, and motion these formulations force upon us, Mead suggests, are related to human conduct in two important ways. First, they involve a setting aside of the older conception of "timeless space" that was grounded in a hypothetical extension of the contact or manipulatory dimensions of the act—i.e., in that "collapsing" of the act that allows us to perceive distant objects as if they were already at hand; in its place we must substitute the conception of a space-time grounded in our more immediate experience of uncollapsed acts, in which we move out into a world of visual or distance characters infected with futurity or temporal passage relative to our actions. Second, the conceptions of relativistic physics are just as much grounded in the social character of human conduct as were their perceptual and Newtonian predecessors. It is only by a sophisticated exercise of the human social capacity to "take the attitude or the role of the other" that post-Newtonian physicists have been able to think their way into alternative spatio-temporal perspectives, correlate these by means of transformation formulas, and thereby constitute a new sort of common world within human experience.

While the preceding remarks, together with those of sections (3) and (4) above, merely scratch the surface of Mead's persistent explorations of the spatial and temporal structures of human experience in his later writings, they do at least indicate the overall thrust of his endeavors in this area. They indicate also what Mead had in mind when he observed in his 1926 class lectures that Dewey's general orientation in *Experience and Nature* could be made to harmonize with the theory of relativity. Mead's repeated efforts to develop this line of thought, despite their often tentative and incomplete character, are of sufficient originality and significance to merit recognition as another of his distinctive contributions to American pragmatism.

6. *The Growth of Scientific Knowledge.* Mead's pragmatic attempt to ground the world as portrayed by scientific knowledge in an analysis of human conduct is one of two main projects undertaken in his mature writings on the philosophy of science. The other project takes the form of a similarly pragmatic analysis of the reconstructive process exhibited in the growth of scientific knowledge. His efforts to carry out this second project, as might be expected, involve further variations on a theme that had occupied him in one way or another almost from the start of his career at Chicago. We saw in chapter 4, for instance, that he began to analyze the way in which the reflective consciousness of the human individual functions to bring about reconstruction of experiential problems in such early essays as "Suggestions Toward

a Theory of the Philosophical Disciplines" (1900) and "The Definition of the Psychical" (1903). Moreover, we had occasion to observe in chapter 8 how this analysis, given additional articulation in the development of his social psychology, provides the central thrust of his work in the area of ethics and moral psychology. But it is in his later writings on the philosophy of science that this line of analysis is brought most fully to fruition. And it is here that we see most clearly how it informs Mead's pragmatic understanding of such notions as inquiry, knowledge, and truth.

Now there is nothing especially novel or original about the broad outlines of the pragmatic framework Mead uses when he devotes his attention to the growth of scientific knowledge in "Scientific Method and Individual Thinker" (his contribution to the 1917 cooperative volume *Creative Intelligence: Essays in the Pragmatic Attitude*), "A Pragmatic Theory of Truth" (1929), and various sections of the posthumously published volumes of his work.[13] His general view of scientific inquiry, for instance, is exactly the one made familiar by the work of Dewey. Such inquiry, Mead assumes, is at bottom simply the use of reflective intelligence and an experimental method to deal with problems arising within human conduct or experience. In unproblematic experience we act with respect to a world of objects whose already established meanings guide our conduct more or less adequately. But from time to time we encounter situations in which these meanings prove inadequate to their functional task; we are faced with objects whose meanings are uncertain or ambiguous, and our conduct accordingly breaks down in hesitancy or vacillation. It is the function of scientific inquiry to analyze such situations, distinguish what is problematic from what is unproblematic in them, propose a hypothesis that tentatively revises the problematic meanings thus identified, and then put this hypothesis to the test by seeing whether it can successfully guide the conduct that has broken down (PA 45, 48, 59, 82–83).

Similarly, Mead agrees with Dewey in the way he relates the concepts of knowledge and truth to the preceding account of inquiry. The problem of knowledge for the practicing scientist, he holds, is never one of trying to establish a bridge between human experience and some absolute reality lying outside experience. This road leads only to insoluble difficulties and the "philosophic riffraff known as epistemology" (SW 341–42; PA 94). Rather, scientific knowing is a matter of solving problems residing within experience. Scientific inquiry is always localized inquiry: it addresses specific problems within the context of a largely unproblematic experiential world. Scientists can intelligently analyze certain puzzling features of the world only by using or appealing to other features of the world that, for the time being, are not puzzling and do not themselves require analysis; they can devise experiments and test their hypotheses only by means of perceptual objects whose meaningful characters are, for the time being, taken for granted (PA 29–32, 45; SW 205, 333). Mead refers to all those unproblematic features of the world that are taken for granted in the context of a given inquiry as "the world that is there" with respect to that inquiry (PA 45–48, 63–64). This "world that is there," he emphasizes, is not the object of scientific knowledge; instead scientific knowing has to do with the problematic aspects of experience. The latter become objects of scientific knowledge and are known when they have been analyzed and more adequately conceptualized by means of a hypothesis that overcomes their problematic character (PA 28, 45). Further, the term "truth" applies to a hypothesis just insofar as it successfully performs this reconstructive task. In the context of scientific inquiry, therefore, "there is no such thing as Truth at large. It is always relative to the problematic situation" (SW 324).

Mead's general views about scientific inquiry, knowledge, and truth thus echo those of Dewey at nearly every point. He goes beyond Dewey and begins to make contributions of his own, however, as soon as he turns to a detailed analysis of the reconstructive process involved in the growth of scientific knowledge. These contributions result from a further elaboration of Dewey's views on scientific inquiry by means of Mead's distinctive social psychological ideas and his adoption of a modified Whiteheadian view of nature.

Embracing a version of Whitehead's view of nature, Mead maintains that nature takes on certain structures and qualities in its relationship to each human individual and that such structures and qualities are objective aspects of these perspectives existing within nature. At the same time, he urges us to bear in mind that human individuals are always members of a human community. Through communication and the capacity to "take the attitude or the role of the other," they acquire a socially structured language, a socially structured self, and a socially structured thought. Mature human individuals are thus social through and through, and the world in which they ordinarily live, move, and have their being is a shared or common world corresponding to the social organization of perspectives they have taken up into their conduct (PA 202–4, SW 340–41). "The world that is there" with respect to any scientific inquiry is just such a common world: it is a common world of unproblematic meanings or objects grounded in the shared structures of social conduct, the shared universe of discourse and thought, ingredient in the community of scientific inquirers. The problematic meanings that call forth scientific inquiry, on the other hand, appear as anomalies or exceptions that do not fit into the accepted structures of the common world (PA 33–34, 58, 70; SW 341). One of the great strengths of modern scientific inquiry, Mead holds, is that it makes use of these anomalies or exceptions as transitional guides in the growth of scientific knowledge. And the mechanisms of conduct by means of which it does this are part and parcel of the social character of human intelligence.

To begin with, Mead suggests, the exceptional or anomalous features of a problematic situation can function as useful material for inquiry only if the individual inquirer can hold on to them and accord them some kind of objective status. The social structure of human experience makes this possible because it gives rise to self-consciousness: the mature human individual experiences his self as an object that is part of a socially common world. He can, therefore, refer exceptional features of experience, in the first instance, to that self; he can give them at least a marginal status in the common world by treating them as items in his own biography. But this, of course, is only a first small step in the direction of that reconstruction needed to overcome the problematic situation. The next step is for the inquirer to make additional use of his socially based reflective intelligence to analyze further the exceptional elements of the situation, stating them so far as possible in such a manner that they can be observed and confirmed by other inquirers. To the extent that this is accomplished, the problematic elements involved gain a further foothold in the common world: they now become data observable by a number of competent observers (PA 33–35; SW 196–97, 341).

If we look carefully at the part scientific data play in the process of inquiry, Mead argues, we will find that they bear little resemblance to those private "sense data" that certain empiricist philosophers take to be the foundation of scientific knowledge. Nor do they resemble the other kinds of indubitable foundational facts so often sought by epistemologists. Rather, they are presently unproblematic aspects of meaning that scientific analysis ferrets out of the problematic situation and precisely identifies in its statement of the problem to be overcome. The meaningful aspects of the situation recorded in these data are incomplete in that they provide only certain conditions to be met by any acceptable solution to the problem at hand; if they were not thus incomplete, if they were wholly adequate to the situation, there would be no problem to be solved (sw 173, 189–95, 328, 341). To the extent that such data are specified so that they can be observed by any competent inquirer, they belong to the common world of the scientific community. But they lack full membership in the unproblematic "world that is there" for that community due to the incomplete and anomalous character of the meanings they involve. The primary aim of scientific inquiry is to overcome the incompleteness of these meanings by so reconstructing the problematic situation that their exceptional character is overcome and they are taken up into a more complete set of meanings constituting a new common world (sw 196–97, 328; pa 34–35, 46–48). Because the rigorously ascertained data used to guide this reconstructive process are identified in relative isolation from the various hypotheses that may be used in attempts to interpret them, they are sometimes misconstrued as characters residing in a reality independent of all human thought and experience. In fact, however, they are as much ingredients of human experience as are the more complete meanings into which they are absorbed once they are integrated into a successful working hypothesis (pa 276–80).

The chief conceptual vehicle for such reconstruction is, of course, a hypothesis that reinterprets the anomalous features of a problematic situation so as to make them instances of a revised version of the natural order. And, here again, Mead emphasizes the significance of the social character of the human individual as an underlying condition for the possibility of scientific inquiry. It is the social structure of human intelligence, he claims, that makes it possible for the human individual not only to analyze a scientific problem in the manner described above but also to envision new hypotheses that might bring about a resolution of that problem. Such hypotheses arise within human experience just insofar as creative human individuals use socially significant symbols and their socially grounded capacity of reflective intelligence to devise new interpretations of scientific data. And these hypotheses gain an initial foothold in the common world by being located in the biographies of the socially constituted selves of those individuals who devise them.

Hypotheses that fail in their attempt to provide the needed reconstruction of a scientific problem remain simply items in the biographies of their creators. But hypotheses that succeed in this task acquire a larger status: they become socially accepted structures of a new common world (PA 68–71, 78, 274; SW 211, 331, 341–42).

Thus the rational solution of scientific problems "takes place through minds which have arisen in social evolution" (SW 342). And the growth of scientific knowledge involves a reconstructive social process in which new common worlds succeed one another as new problems arise and are for the time being successfully overcome. The provisional common world of the scientific community at any moment in this process, however, is at best only a partial world: it consists of those accepted objects and structures that correspond to the shared interests and activities of the scientific community. Suppose, then, that one wishes to go beyond these limitations and "see the world whole." Mead views this as a legitimate task for philosophy, which can be successful only if it does not pretend to grasp some absolute reality independent of all human conduct. The philosophical attempt to see the world whole, he suggests, should be understood as an attempt on the part of reflective human intelligence to give articulation to the widest possible common world— a world corresponding to the widest possible set of shared human interests and activities, including but not restricted to those peculiar to the scientific community. Seeing the world whole is thus possible only for human individuals who use the capacity to take the role of "generalized others" so as to import into their own conduct or experience "the most highly organized logical, ethical, and aesthetic attitudes of the community, those attitudes which involve all that organized thinking, acting, and artistic creation and appreciation imply" (SW 337).

If the philosophers seeking to see the world whole are pragmatists, Mead would hasten to add, they will steadfastly abjure any "yearning to rest in the arms of finality" or to find repose for their perturbed spirits "in the everlasting arms of an absolute of one sort or another" (SW 324). They will quite reasonably expect their vision of a larger common world to give them guidance in the social, ethical, and aesthetic dimensions of their lives, just as the common world of the scientific community informs the inquiries of individual scientists. At the same time, they will recognize that their larger common world is as provisional and as subject to reconstruction in the face of problematic situations as is that of the scientific community. They will acknowledge that even the most all-encompassing vision of a common world must allow for its own revision; no such vision can obviate the need for an intelligent method of dealing with the new sorts of problems that continually emerge within ongoing human experience. It is Mead's view, of course, which he regards as central to pragmatism, that the best such method so far devised for the solution of experiential problems is the method of experimental intelligence as this is practiced in scientific inquiry. And it is one of his distinctive pragmatic contributions to have supplied an analysis of this method in terms of the social structures of human conduct.

Concluding Remarks

Mead's later contributions to the pragmatic tradition, like their precursors in his early contributions to the development of functional psychology, are best understood as elaborations of ideas he began to share with Dewey in the late 1890s. What stands out above all else in these contributions is his analysis of the social dimensions of human conduct and his use of this analysis to construct suggestive hypotheses concerning the underlying social structures of such important aspects of human experience as self-consciousness, language, thought, perceptual objects, space and time, scientific objects, and scientific inquiry. It is this fruitful attempt to explore the many philosophical implications of the pervasive sociality of human conduct that led Dewey to speak of Mead as "a seminal mind of the very first order" (PP xl). And it is this central intellectual project of his mature philosophical writings that I have sought to acknowledge by referring to him as a social pragmatist.

Epilogue

Mead and the Hutchins Controversy

George Herbert Mead was sixty-five on February 27, 1928, and thus became eligible for retirement from the University of Chicago at the end of the 1927–28 academic year. But the president and board of trustees annually invited him to continue in the service of the university throughout the remainder of his life.[1] In 1929 he was honored by the American Philosophical Association with an invitation to deliver the Carus Lectures (subsequently edited by Arthur E. Murphy and published in *The Philosophy of the Present*) at the Pacific Division American Philosphical Association meetings held in Berkeley in December 1930. Further, following the retirement of his long-time colleague, James H. Tufts, Mead was asked to serve as chairman of the department of philosophy at Chicago beginning in the fall of 1930. Unhappily, the final months of Mead's short tenure as chairman were marred not only by the rapid deterioration of his health but also by a monumental conflict between the department of philosophy and the new president of the university, Robert Maynard Hutchins. It was this conflict that Murphy had in mind when he explained, in his preface to *The Philosophy of the Present,* why Mead was never able to complete the elaboration of those ideas he began to set forth in his Carus Lectures: "Unfortunately, Mr. Mead, in his capacity as chairman of the department of philosophy at the University of Chicago, was forced to surrender the time he had set aside for the completion of the lectures to administrative concerns of an unexpected and disturbing character. As a consequence the lectures were written hurriedly, in large part on the journey from Chicago to Berkeley; and he had no opportunity in the weeks immediately following their delivery to begin the revisions he had in mind. By the end of January he was seriously ill and he died within a few weeks."[2] Because this controversy eventually led to

Mead's resignation and marked the end of an era in philosophy at Chicago, and because its story has never been fully told in print, I want to supplement my examination of Mead's intellectual career by exploring its course in some detail.[3]

The controversy seems to have had its origin in a conversation between Hutchins and Mortimer J. Adler sometime in May 1929, shortly after Hutchins had been selected as the next president of the University of Chicago. Adler was at that time a young instructor in the department of psychology at Columbia University, where he had done his graduate work in philosophy and psychology; Hutchins was an almost equally young dean of the Yale Law School. The two men had earlier become good friends as the result of their collaboration in a study dealing with the rules of the law of evidence. During the course of the conversation in question, Adler, as he recalled it many years later in his autobiography, proposed that Hutchins take steps to create at the University of Chicago a philosophy department that might rival in greatness the earlier Harvard department of William James, Josiah Royce, George Santayana, and George Herbert Palmer. And to this exuberant proposal Adler added the immodest suggestion that Hutchins might begin the process by hiring him and several of his close philosophical friends—Scott Buchanan, Richard McKeon, and V. J. McGill.[4]

Hutchins, somewhat surprisingly, took Adler's suggestion quite seriously. A week later he wrote to request that Adler and his friends send him their complete academic biographies; he was, he said, "most optimistic about the possibilities" with respect to their employment at Chicago. And in July he wrote Adler further to say that he "found the budgetary situation in Philosophy not impossible. What the reaction of the members of the staff would be to the appointment of the three or four of you, I do not know." Finally, Hutchins wrote Adler in October from Chicago that "the chairman of the Philosophy Department [then James H. Tufts] has been informed of my interest in you three gentlemen [Adler, Buchanan, and McKeon—the name of McGill having by this time been eliminated from the list of possible candidates], and the most important member of the department, who is not the chairman, has enthusiastically endorsed my proposals."[5]

Given the battle that ensued between Hutchins and the department over this matter in the following year, it would be interesting to know which member of the department "enthusiastically endorsed" Hutchins's proposals in the fall of 1929, or, to put the question in another way, whom Hutchins considered "the most important member of the department" at that time. A reasonable guess would be that it was not Mead, E. A. Burtt, Arthur Murphy, or Edward Scribner Ames, but rather T. V. Smith. (The other two regular members of the department, Charles Hartshorne and Everett W. Hall, held only junior status in 1929 and were clearly not in the running for the "most important member" label.) Smith had already authored several books, had served as an associate dean, and was well known outside the university as a public speaker; furthermore, there is strong evidence in his correspondence that he enjoyed a friendly relationship with Hutchins from the time of the latter's arrival at Chicago. Unlike most other members of his department, Smith succeeded in maintaining this kind of relationship with Hutchins even after 1931—an accomplishment helped out considerably by the fact that he was away on leave at Cornell University when the controversy between Hutchins and the department broke out in earnest.[6]

Shortly after Hutchins approached Tufts concerning the possible addition of Adler, Buchanan, and McKeon to the Chicago faculty, Tufts discussed the matter with members of his department; he then summarized the results of this departmental consultation in a three-page memorandum to the president, dated October 28, 1929. Tufts's memorandum was diplomatic but unenthusiastic in its response to the president's suggestions. After expressing the philosophers' "high appreciation for your interest in the department, which is shown in your request for information as a preliminary to possible additions to the department," it continued with brief and generally favorable reviews of the published work of Adler, Buchanan, and McKeon. Next Tufts discussed the staffing needs perceived by members of his department. Finally, he closed the memorandum by summarizing the department's position concerning the three candidates suggested by Hutchins: "While we believe that the three men in question are men of scholarly promise, we are not prepared to say, without further consideration, whether if we were to take into account all the possibilities in Philosophy, we should settle upon the three men in question as the best available for the needs and purposes of the department."[7]

There is some evidence that in composing this tactfully worded reply to the president, Tufts was diplomatic to a fault. Tact, in this case, may have been a poor tactic, or so it must have seemed to the department in hindsight. For witness the much stronger language of a document titled

"A Statement from the Department of Philosophy" that was circulated among the faculty somewhat more than a year later. This document, whose chief author was probably Professor Burtt, recalls the department's reaction to Hutchins's suggestions as follows:

> The department replied that Mr. McKeon had been considered in its program for expansion in the future, but was regarded as less imperatively needed than other men the department had in mind, in view of phases of its work that needed development more than the phase of medieval philosophy. As for the other two, its position was that Mr. Buchanan had yet to demonstrate his promise in the field of philosophy, and that it entertained grave doubts as to Mr. Adler's competence in the field. After some years of study in the department of philosophy at Columbia he had finally taken his degree in psychology instead, and his one published book in the field of philosophy had raised rather serious questions as to his philosophical scholarship. In any case there were other men whom the department had complete confidence in and would be eager to add to its ranks if the president would permit it to make them an offer.[8]

Hutchins made no immediate response to Tufts's memorandum, choosing instead to postpone further negotiations with the department of philosophy until after his official inauguration in late November. Then, on December 4, he wrote Adler that "our present plan is to re-tire two men [presumably Tufts and Mead] and appoint you in their place. It should give you a feeling of satisfaction to learn that you are regarded as the moral equivalent of two individuals of the combined age of 135. By the time I talk to you on the phone I hope that this will be absolutely definite. The financial situation is such that we probably can't swing Buchanan and McKeon this year. I have great hopes however that we can bring them in the year following."[9] At about the same time, Hutchins again contacted Tufts and, without mentioning either Buchanan or McKeon, asked whether the department of philosophy would be willing to accept the appointment of Adler under certain conditions. These conditions were that the appointment would not nec-essarily be permanent and that the department would be its own judge as to how long Adler's membership in the department was to continue. Furthermore, while the appointment would bear the title of a position in philosophy, it would be interdisciplinary in character: Adler would devote only a third of his teaching time to philosophy, the remaining two-thirds being allocated to the department of psychology and the law school. Hutchins explained his request, according to the later recollections of the department, by saying that "there were important tasks in the university that he thought Mr. Adler eminently fitted to perform, that if he were to come he had to be housed in some department, and that Mr. Adler's strong preference was to be closely connected with philosophy."[10]

With this understanding, and given the conditions specified by the president, the department somewhat reluctantly gave its approval to Hutchins's request. Hutchins then recommended Adler's appointment to the board of trustees and near the middle of December the secretary of the board sent Adler a formal notification of his appointment as associate professor of philosophy for three years at a salary of $6,000 a year.[11] The rank and salary connected with this appointment may well have come as a surprise even to Adler. (At that time he held the rank of instructor in the department of psychology at Columbia, where he received a yearly salary of only $2,400.[12]) Certainly they came as a surprise to Tufts and the Chicago department of philosophy, who learned of them shortly before the Christmas holidays. Tufts subsequently urged the president to make appropriate adjustments in the salaries of other members of the department, on the ground that the salary to be paid Adler was nearly a thousand dollars more than that being paid any full professor in the department with the exception of Tufts himself. This request, however, was politely rejected.[13]

The events surrounding Adler's appointment had by this time led Tufts to feel that the administration lacked confidence in his leadership of the department. And this feeling was intensified by rumors that began to reach Chicago from Columbia, to the effect that Adler had little respect for either the philosophers or the brand of philosophy found at Chicago and that he was planning (perhaps with Hutchins's blessing) to use his new position in the department to bring about a radical change in its make-up.[14] Tufts therefore decided that the time had come for him to retire; he accordingly resigned from the chairmanship of the department—agreeing, however, to do a limited amount of teaching during the 1930–31 academic year.[15]

Tufts's resignation from the departmental chairmanship led the president to adopt what the philosophers perceived as "a milder attitude toward the department."

Through one of our members he gave us assurances again that we need not continue Mr. Adler in the department if we did not find his work sufficiently valuable to us, and added that he had no further designs in connection with the departmental program, that we were to determine our own future in accordance with accepted departmental rights and privileges, and that he would approve our selection as chairman to succeed Mr. Tufts. Mr. Mead was reluctantly prevailed upon to undertake this responsibility, and resting upon the president's complete assurances as to our future, we concluded that our earlier fears had been exaggerated and went ahead with our work.[16]

This, then, is where matters stood between Hutchins and the department of philosophy when Mead, at age sixty-seven, assumed the chairmanship in the summer of 1930.

Mortimer Adler joined the faculty in the fall of 1930 but did not teach any courses in the philosophy department during his first quarter at Chicago. He chose instead to accept Hutchins's invitation to cooperate with him in the joint teaching of twenty selected freshmen in an experimental general honors course dealing with the great books of Western literature. In addition, Adler played an active role on a special Curriculum Committee set up by Hutchins to consider possible reform of the program of undergraduate studies at the university.[17] While this arrangement was to Adler's liking, it did little to integrate him into the department of philosophy; moreover, the other members of the department seem to have done little to make Adler a part of their program. Indeed, the dean of the humanities division later criticized the department in general, and Mead in particular, for "a serious error in their attitude toward Mr. Adler" at the outset of his career at Chicago: "They hardly treated him as a new member of the Department might expect to be treated; they did not ask him to join them in their departmental luncheon conferences at the Quadrangle Club. . . . When I discussed this point with Mr. Mead, he said that insomuch as Mr. Adler was not actually giving any courses in the Department during the Autumn Quarter, he and his colleagues had not thought it necessary to have him with them. It seems to me that this contention is wholly lacking in validity. In view of the tension that already existed, this attitude was sure to make matters worse."[18] Nevertheless, Adler must have been in attendance at some of the departmental luncheons here mentioned, perhaps at a later date. For he records in his autobiography an unfortunate verbal exchange at just such an occasion when "I angered Professor Mead by my blithe espousal of what he regarded as the undemocratic elitism of President Hutchins' proposal of small-class instruction only for honor students, and large lecture classes for the rest." [19]

Adler's nominal membership in the department of philosophy during the fall of 1930 was no doubt a significant irritant in the minds of the department's senior members. And so, also, was the administration's continuing refusal (on the ground of general financial stringency) to grant approval for the department's request that it be allowed to secure new staff members of its own choosing—staff it was convinced it badly needed due to the retirement of Tufts and the imminent retirement of Mead. But something more than either of these irritants was required to precipitate the crisis that shortly ensued. This additional factor was supplied when Hutchins approached Mead to request departmental approval for the appointment of Scott Buchanan (then in the philosophy department at the University of Virginia) as one of its members. Once again the appointment was to be interdisciplinary (Buchanan was to work in the departments of mathematics and biology as well as philosophy) and not necessarily permanent; Hutchins wanted to locate Buchanan in the department of philosophy because it was necessary to house him in some department and it was Buchanan's desire to be attached to the department of philosophy.[20]

Not surprisingly, this request served as a spark to ignite an already volatile situation. The request was, in the minds of Mead and his colleagues, all too similar to that which had preceded the appointment of Adler; it also seemed to run counter to all the assurances the president had given the department following the resignation of Tufts as chairman. Worse yet, it was seen by the Chicago philosophers as confirming persistent rumors that Hutchins had a hidden agenda with respect to their department: that he was unsympathetic to the orientation of the department and that he was intent upon radically changing its character by bringing in Adler, Buchanan, and McKeon. The department therefore communicated to the administration through Mead its disapproval of Hutchins's request and further asked the president to state definitely what his position was with respect to the present status of the department and its program for the future. The president's response, given to the philosophers in December 1930, was hardly flattering. He was understood by them as saying that "he did not know whether or not he wished to commit himself to a department in the future built up on the basis of its present membership, but that he would supplement his own judgment on the matter by enquiries of people in philosophy elsewhere as to the relative merits of his favored group and of those already in the department."[21]

This response, quite understandably, did nothing to allay the growing tension between Hutchins and the philosophy department. Nevertheless, the members of the department decided not to object to Hutchins's apparent desire for an external evaluation of their professional standing. Instead, they prepared a list (variously described in existing documents as containing either eight or twelve names) of highly regarded American philosophers whom they thought qualified to serve as external evaluators. This list Mead passed on to Hutchins with the suggestion that the president might write the individuals therein named to secure the kind of external evaluation for which he felt a need. Finding this to be a reasonable suggestion, Hutchins proceeded to act upon it—but in so doing he further aroused the ire of almost everyone involved. He first prepared on his own, without further consulting Mead, a letter or questionnaire asking the evaluators to rank in order of merit a number of younger American philosophers including Buchanan, McKeon, and various members of the Chicago department.[22] He then sent the letter, again without consulting Mead, to four individuals selected from the department's list and four additional evaluators.[23] The Chicago philosophers subsequently objected to this lack of consultation and charged also that Hutchins had not seen fit to show the replies he had received either to the chairman of the department or to the dean of the humanities division. They further complained that Hutchins's questionnaire, together with the "indiscretion of those who believed themselves in a position to speak for him on matters pertaining to the department of philosophy," had broadcast their plight throughout the country and had led to a consequent lowering of the prestige of their department.[24] Nor were Buchanan and McKeon especially happy to learn that their names had been placed in a questionnaire without their consent. The latter, in fact, expressed his displeasure in no uncertain terms: "In the future when you send out lists of 'candidates' for ratings, leave my name out of them. I resent having my friends asked to pass on them."[25] Even the dean of the humanities division, who later did his best to defend the president's procedure against the criticisms of the philosophy department, admitted that the letter had been a bad idea—but an idea, he wanted it understood, that Hutchins had pursued at Mead's suggestion: "Personally I regret that he ever adopted Mr. Mead's suggestion to send out the letter."[26]

The replies to Hutchins's letter, it turned out, were strongly supportive of the members of the Chicago department, but this fact seems to have had little impact upon the controversy between Hutchins and the department. For even as the letter was being circulated three of the five remaining senior members of the department were already considering the possibility of resigning. Burtt had received an offer from Cornell University, Murphy from Brown University, and Mead had been invited to Columbia University for the following year at twice the salary Chicago had been paying him.[27] Sometime around the middle of January 1931, the three men apparently decided that given these favorable prospects elsewhere, they no longer had to accept what they regarded as the intolerable treatment of their department by the Hutchins administration. They therefore resolved to give the administration a kind of ultimatum, listing the conditions that would have to be met if they were to continue in the service of the university. These conditions, which Mead communicated orally to the dean of the humanities division, were that Adler and Buchanan would not be included in the department of philosophy, that the administration make certain salary adjustments for members of the department along the lines suggested by Tufts during the preceding year, that the administration grant the department's request to offer an appointment at the rank of full professor to Albert P. Brogan (then at the University of Texas), and that the president should give them his response to these conditions by 10:00 A.M. the following morning.[28]

Hutchins did meet with Mead at the designated time on the following day. And what transpired was later summarized by G. J. Laing, dean of the humanities division, in the following words:

I was present at the meeting at ten o'clock the next morning and Mr. Mead repeated the same terms. Mr. Mead regretted that his statement had the appearance of an ultimatum and said that they had mentioned a definite time for a reply because they felt they must give an answer to the three institutions which had called them. . . . The President replied: (1) that he fully recognized the right of a department to pass on its personnel; (2) that if they so desired, he would see that neither Mr. Adler nor Mr. Buchanan were members of the Department; (3) that he would take care of the salary adjustments mentioned. On the fourth point, however, that he should appoint Mr. Brogan to a full professorship, he declined to accede to the wishes of the Department. He stated that Mr. Brogan's name had hardly appeared in all the previous negotiations; that in dealing with all the departments he had adopted the policy which he believed to be traditional in the University, of appointing no one to a full professorship until he had assured himself of his qualifications; no brief of Mr. Brogan's accomplishments in writing or teaching had ever been presented to him; he had never seen a bibliography of his contributions; he knew almost nothing about him. If the Department wished to recommend Mr. Brogan for a term appointment, he was willing to appoint him, but he couldn't on the information he then had offer him a full professorship. . . . That ended the interview. When Mr. Mead, Mr. Woodward [dean of the college] and I had a further conference in Mr. Woodward's office, both the latter and I thought that Mr. Mead, in view of the President's concessions, was inclined to take a much more favorable view of the situation.[29]

Immediately after his meeting with Mead, Hutchins left Chicago on a trip to Arizona necessitated by his wife's need for rest and medical treatment. He remained there until mid-February but in the meantime kept in touch with the situation in the philosophy department through Dean Frederic C. Woodward. On January 22 Woodward wrote that his continued conversations with members of the department had led him to believe that Mead and Murphy would stay at Chicago, but that Burtt would probably go to Cornell. Six days later, however, he was less hopeful about the situation. He cabled Hutchins on January 28 that he had been unable to convince Murphy to stay at Chicago: "He feels that in view of difficulty in satisfactorily filling vacancies here he will find more congenial atmosphere for his own study and writing at Brown." Burtt, he reported, "seems to be irreconcilable." Then, on February 6, Woodward sent Hutchins a final telegram saying "Morning papers carry news of resignation of Mead, Burtt, Murphy. We had fair success in preventing sensational story but faculties seriously disturbed."[30]

That same day Mead wrote Hutchins from St. Luke's Hospital, where he had been confined for a week due to a high fever, that he was declining his appointment as professor of philosophy for the coming year and "electing to retire at the end of my scholastic year, which will be October first, next." On February 17, immediately after his return from Arizona, Hutchins wrote Mead that he was very much distressed by the latter's resignation: "I have not presented it to the Board and shall not do so unless you insist until I have had an opportunity to talk with you. I hope that when you are ready to discuss the matter we may meet and that I may persuade you to reconsider." Two weeks later Mead replied that he was still in the hospital and expected to remain there for several weeks longer. "I should therefore be unable to have an interview with you until early in April. But no interview is necessary as my mind is made up that I will retire at the end of my academic term. I desire therefore that you will submit my request for retirement to the Trustees at the earliest opportunity."[31]

Mead was dismissed from St. Luke's Hospital on the last Saturday of April and went from there to the home of his son, Henry Mead, for a period of further convalescence. But one day later, on April 26, 1931, he died suddenly and quite unexpectedly of heart failure. At a memorial service held in Bond Chapel during the following week he was eulogized by John Dewey, James H. Tufts, and Edward Scribner Ames. None of these longtime friends and colleagues mentioned the controversy with Hutchins that had troubled Mead's final year at the university, but together they called attention to almost all the salient aspects of his thought and character: his love of literature—especially the English poets; his genius for conversation and friendship; his involvement in civic reform activities; his successful career as a teacher at Chicago; and the power and originality of his ideas. It was perhaps fitting that Dewey, the one thinker chiefly responsible for shaping Mead's early intellectual development, should acknowledge his own indebtedness to Mead and offer high praise of Mead's originality. "One would have to go far to find a teacher of our own day," Dewey said, "who started in others so many fruitful lines of thought; I dislike to think what my own thinking might have been were it not for the seminal ideas which I derived from him." In particular, Dewey noted that Mead's social psychological ideas, his social interpretations of life and the world, had "worked a revolution in my own thinking though I was slow in grasping anything like their full implications." A certain measure of diffidence, Dewey thought, had kept Mead from extensive publication and consequent wide recognition, but his mind was deeply original—"in my contacts and my judgment the most original mind in philosophy in the America of the last generations."[32]

Notes

Introduction

1. See, for instance, Lewis and Smith, *American Sociology and Pragmatism;* Bulmer, *Chicago School of Sociology;* Shalin, "Mead, Socialism, and the Progressive Agenda"; Deegan, *Jane Addams and the Men of the Chicago School.* See also the numerous discussions of Mead's thought in various recent numbers of *Symbolic Interaction.* Baldwin's *George Herbert Mead* is an attempt by a sociologist to provide an overview of Mead's contributions to both sociology and philosophy.

2. See Thayer, *Meaning and Action;* Rucker, *Chicago Pragmatists;* Miller, *George Herbert Mead;* Scheffler, *Four Pragmatists;* Aboulafia, *Mediating Self.*

3. See Tugendhat, *Self-Consciousness and Self-Determination;* Joas, *G. H. Mead;* Joas, ed., *Das Problem der Intersubjektivität;* Habermas, *Theory of Communicative Action,* vol. 2; Wenzel, *George Herbert Mead.* For a work by an American writer who combines several of the perspectives mentioned above, see Rochberg-Halton, *Meaning and Modernity.*

4. Mead, to Irene Tufts Mead, July 11, 1923, box 1a, folder 10.

5. Dewey, "George Herbert Mead as I Knew Him," 174.

6. SW.

7. ESP.

8. University of Chicago Settlement: Board Minutes and Reports, located in the Mary McDowell and the University of Chicago Settlement Papers.

9. *The City Club Bulletin,* published by the City Club of Chicago, available at the Regenstein Library, the University of Chicago.

10. See the 1931 correspondence between Charles W. Morris and Irene Tufts Mead, Mead Papers, box 11, folder 3. See also Merritt H. Moore's comments in the prefatory note to MT vi–vii.

11. For student notes taken in Mead's course in Elementary Ethics, see Mead Papers, box VII, folders 3 and 4.

12. The material that Miller entitles "1914 Lectures in Social Psychology" is based upon student notes now preserved in the Mead Papers, box III, folder 2. These student notes bear the later handwritten notation "About 1912" on the first page. But they can be dated more reliably in the following manner. In preparing the manuscript for Mead's *Mind, Self and Society,* Charles Morris recorded selected passages from various sets of student notes so that he could subsequently insert

some of these passages in the main text provided by a stenographic set of notes from Mead's 1928 course in advanced social psychology. The Mead Papers, box IV, folder 8, contain a set of passages that Morris extracted from notes he identifies as those of a student named Queen, who took them in Mead's course on social psychology in the autumn of 1912. These passages are identical with, or correspond very closely to, material contained in the student notes found in the Mead Papers, box III, folder 2, and reproduced in Miller's book. Further, the archival research reported by J. David Lewis and Richard L. Smith indicates that S. A. Queen was indeed enrolled in Mead's course on social psychology during the fall quarter of 1912. For this latter bit of information, see Lewis and Smith, *American Sociology and Pragmatism*, 276.

Chapter 1: "Early Life and Letters: Part 1"

1. Information on Hiram Mead (1827–81) appears in an obituary prepared by President James H. Fairchild of Oberlin College, *Oberlin Review* 8 (no. 18) (May 28, 1881): 212–14.

2. Cowles, "Mrs. Elizabeth Storrs Mead."

3. Mead's letters are in the George Herbert Mead Papers. Castle's letters are in the Castle Papers. Many of Castle's letters also appear in *Henry Northrup Castle: Letters,* a volume edited by George and Helen Mead (London, 1902). Fifty copies of this volume were privately printed for the Castle family.

4. Information on Castle's family can be found in Taylor, Welty, and Eyre, *From Land and Sea.*

5. Mead, "Recollections of Henry in Oberlin, and After," *Henry Northrup Castle: Letters,* 807.

6. The letters of Mead and Castle refer to this course as "Mental Philosophy" or the class in "Porter." Porter's *The Elements of Intellectual Science* is included in Castle's undated listing of the volumes in his personal library, found in box VII, folder 2, of the Castle Papers.

7. Castle to his parents, May 24, 1882.

8. Mead, "Recollections of Henry in Oberlin, and After," 810.

9. Castle to his mother, Oct. 28, 1882. The masthead of the *Oberlin Review* 10 (no. 1) (Sept. 23, 1882), lists Henry N. Castle as editor-in-chief and George H. Mead as the representative of the Phi Kappa Pi literary society on the editorial board.

10. Castle to his mother, Oct. 28, 1882.

11. Information on Ellis and Fairchild, as well as a description of Oberlin College during the Fairchild administration, can be found in Barnard, *From Evangelicalism to Progressivism at Oberlin College.*

12. Mead, "Recollections of Henry in Oberlin, and After," 810–11.

13. Castle to his parents, Oct. 13, 1882.

14. Castle to his parents, Nov. 4, 1882.

15. Mead, "Recollections of Henry in Oberlin, and After," 811.

16. Mead to Castle, Sept. 14, 1883.

17. Mead to Castle, Oct. 7, 1883.

18. Mead to Castle, Feb. 23, 1884. See also the letter of Nov. 15, 1883.

19. Mead to Castle, undated letter. See also his letters of Nov. 15, 1883, and Feb. 23, 1884.

20. Mead to Castle, undated letter.

21. Mead to Castle, Feb. 23, 1884.

22. Mead to Castle, Mar. 5, 1884.

23. Mead to Castle, Mar. 7, 1884.

24. Ibid.

25. Mead to Castle, Mar. 12, 1884.

26. Mead to Castle, Apr. 23, 1884.

27. Mead to Castle, Aug. 7, 1884.

28. Ibid.

29. Mead to Castle, July 18, 1884. See also his letter of Sept. 14, 1884.

30. Mead to Castle, Aug. 16, 1884.

31. See Mead's letters of Sept. 14 and Oct. 26, 1884, and Jan. 31, 1885.

32. Mead to Castle, Jan. 31, 1885.

33. Mead to Castle, Oct. 29 and Nov. 30, 1885, and Feb. 28, 1886. That Castle took some steps toward making a formal application for this position is indicated in Castle's letter of Jan. 19, 1886, to his sister Helen. This position was later held by John Dewey for a single academic year, 1888–89; at the end of that year Dewey resigned to accept an appointment as head of the department of philosophy at the University of Michigan. See Dykhuizen, *Life and Mind of Dewey*, 57–63.

34. Mead to Castle, Feb. 28, 1886.

35. Mead to Castle, May 2, 1886.

36. Mead to Castle, Oct. 26, 1886.

37. Ibid.

38. Castle to Helen, Jan. 9, 1887.

39. Mead to Castle, Apr. 14, May 5, June 17, July 24, and Aug. 21, 1887.

40. Castle to Mead, July 30, 1887.

41. Mead to Castle, Sept. 7, 1887.

42. Castle to Helen, Oct. 9, 1887.

43. Castle to his parents, Jan. 22, 1888.

44. Ibid.

45. Castle to his parents, Feb. 1, 1888.

46. Castle to his sister Carrie, Feb. 12, and Mar. 11, 1888; Castle to his parents, Feb. 15 and Mar. 18, 1888. By mid-July Castle had been admitted to the bar, was working in his brother's law office, and was writing editorials for two local newspapers. At the same time, he spoke of being "anxious to return to Harvard in September and complete my course." See Castle to Carrie, July 18, 1888.

47. Mead to Castle, May 10, 1888.

48. Mead to Castle, May 23, 1888.

49. Mead to Castle, June 19, 1888.

50. In spite of his Oberlin College degree, Mead was required to spend a year completing a B.A. degree at Harvard before he could attain graduate status at that institution. See Castle to Mead, Apr. 7, 1887.

51. Mead to Castle, July 1 (or perhaps July 10—the date is indistinct), 1888.
52. Ibid.
53. Mead to Castle, July 18, 1888.
54. Ibid.
55. Mead to Castle, Oct. 24, 1890.
56. James to his wife, Sept. 12, 1888, the James Papers. Unless otherwise cited, all of the James letters come from this collection.
57. James to his wife, Sept. 23 and 16, 1888.
58. The evidence comes from Dr. Irene Tufts Mead, Mead's daughter-in-law, with whom I had a conversation on July 26, 1977. She reported having heard from Mead that he had developed a "youthful infatuation" (Mead's term, she suggested) while he was a tutor at the James summer home and that, as a result, he had been asked by James to leave. It was this story that led me to examine the James letters for the summer of 1888. The letters confirm the infatuation but do not confirm the report that James asked Mead to leave the Chocorua residence early. The letters do indicate, however, that Mead was back in Cambridge prior to September 12, at least two weeks before the beginning of the fall term at Harvard.
59. James to his wife, Sept. 28, 1888.
60. James to his wife, Sept. 13, 1888.
61. See Castle to Carrie, Oct. 18, 1888. On Mead's lack of Harvard scholarship aid, see Castle to his parents, June 3, 1889. Mead apparently borrowed money from a family friend named Abbot to help finance both his studies at Harvard and in Germany. See Mead to Castle, June 24, 1887; see also James to his wife, Sept. 25, 1888.
62. Mead, unpublished and untitled essay on Royce and James, contained in the Mead Papers, box IX, folder 19, 6.
63. Mead, "Josiah Royce—A Personal Impression" (1917), 170.
64. Mead, unpublished essay on Royce and James, 5.

Chapter 2: "Early Life and Letters: Part 2"

1. Castle to his parents, Nov. 6, 1888.
2. This information was obtained from the Archives of the Karl-Marx-Universität in Leipzig and published in Joas's *G. H. Mead*, 18.
3. Castle to his parents, Feb. 6, 1889. Castle's view of the current status of philosophical studies in America (which this letter attributes also to Mead) closely resembles the position G. Stanley Hall had earlier presented in his "Philosophy in the United States."
4. Mead to Castle, July 13, 1889.
5. Joas, *G. H. Mead*, 218, n15.
6. Ibid.
7. Castle to Helen, June 27, 1890.
8. Castle to Mead, Aug. 24, 1890.
9. Henry C. A. Mead, "Biographical Notes," in PA lxxix.
10. Mead to Castle, Oct. 21, 1890.

11. Mead to Castle, undated letter whose references to Frida Castle's recent death indicate that it was written during the fall of 1890.

12. Joas, *G. H. Mead*, 218, n15.

13. Mead to Castle, Apr. 26, 1891.

14. Mead to Castle, July 22, 1891.

15. Mead to Castle, Apr. 26, 1891; see also H. Mead, "Biographical Notes," in PA lxxix.

16. Mead to Castle, July 13, 1891.

17. Mead to Castle, Oct. 20, 1891.

18. Mead to Castle, Mar. 12, 1893.

19. Mead to Castle, Dec. 19, 1891. Mead's letters of this period do not mention Charles Horton Cooley, who began teaching at the University of Michigan in the fall of 1892, a year after Mead's arrival. Nor do these letters indicate that Mead was in any way influenced by Cooley's thought during his stay in Ann Arbor. This is hardly surprising, however, since Cooley did not begin to teach sociology until the academic year 1894–95, by which time Mead had moved to Chicago. Given the small size of the faculty at Michigan during the 1890s, however, it is almost certain that Mead was acquainted with Cooley. Indeed, in a letter written many years later, Mead remarked that he had been "peacefully floating down the current of Mr. Cooley's *Social Process* and enjoying with the book . . . the pictures of the mind that recur from Ann Arbor—of faculty meetings and buildings and meetings of bodies and minds and of ourselves as we were in those days" (Mead to Irene Tufts Mead, Aug. 15, 1919, Mead Papers, box 1, folder 19). For biographical information on Cooley, see Richard Dewey, "Charles Horton Cooley," 833–52. For Mead's critical evaluation of Cooley's thought, see Mead, "Cooley's Contribution to American Social Thought" (1930).

20. See White, *Origin of Dewey's Instrumentalism;* Buxton, "The Influence of William James on John Dewey's Early Work"; Reck, "The Influence of William James on John Dewey in Psychology"; Welchman, "From Absolute Idealism to Instrumentalism: The Problem of Dewey's Early Philosophy."

21. Dewey, "Introduction to Philosophy: Syllabus of Course 5," in *John Dewey: The Early Works*, 3:211–35.

22. Ibid., 211–12.

23. Ibid., 212–14; James, *The Principles of Psychology*, 1:23–25.

24. Dewey, "Introduction to Philosophy: Syllabus of Course 5," 215–17.

25. Ibid., 220, 229.

26. Ibid., 225, 229–30.

27. For an account of Dewey's involvement in the *Thought News* project, see Coughlan, *Young John Dewey*, ch. 6.

28. Mead to Castle, Feb. 28, 1892.

29. Mead to Mr. and Mrs. Samuel Northrup Castle, June 18, 1892.

30. Dewey, "Christianity and Democracy," in *John Dewey: The Early Works*, 4:3–10.

31. Mead to Castle, Dec. 1, 1892.

32. Mead to Mr. and Mrs. Samuel Northrup Castle, July 9, 1893.

33. See Mead to Samuel Northrup Castle, Nov. 7, 1893. Mead's research during this period was closely tied to the courses he was teaching. The *Calendar of the University of Michigan* (1891–94) lists him as the instructor for the following courses in the area of psychology: (a) General psychology. Textbook: Dewey's *Psychology;* (b) Physiological psychology. Lectures and laboratory work; (c) Advanced physiological psychology. Lectures and laboratory work; (d) Experimental psychology. Statement of psychological problems in terms of the organism. Lectures, demonstrations, and experiments; (e) Seminary. Investigations into psychical phenomena of living organisms. Laboratory work and lectures; (f) Seminary. Continuation of preceding course, with study of pathological psychology in asylums and hospitals; (g) English psychology: from Locke through Hartley and Mills to Bain; (h) Special topics in psychology. Sense-perception, attention, memory, localization of brain functions, etc. Lectures and demonstrations. James's and Ladd's larger works will serve as collateral reading; (i) Special research in the laboratory of experimental psychology. In addition, Mead is listed as the instructor for the following courses in philosophy: (a) History of ancient and mediaeval philosophy. Lectures and readings in Plato and Aristotle; (b) History of modern philosophy. Lectures, with readings from Descartes, Spinoza, Locke, Berkeley, Hume, and Kant; (c) Philosophy of evolution. Spencer's *First Principles,* with lectures and assigned readings; (d) Matter and motion. The net results of the concepts of modern science. The starting point will be found in the writings of Spencer and Clifford. (This information is found in the Michigan Historical Collections, Bentley Historical Library, University of Michigan, Ann Arbor.)

34. Mead presented this address on Sunday, Feb. 26, 1893. For a brief report of this talk, see the *Michigan Daily,* vol. 3, no. 106, Feb. 28, 1893, 3. The manuscript of Mead's address is preserved in the Mead Papers, box x, folder 1. See especially pages 12–13, 25–38 of the essay.

35. Castle to his parents, Nov. 7, 1893. A letter written by Mabel Wing Castle to Henry Castle, Dec. 7, 1893, provides an amusing anecdote related to Mead's research and teaching in the area of physiological psychology at Michigan: "George had a sad affair at his laboratory this morning—he had left something to harden, a brain, and the flame of the light had spread and set fire to a valuable microscope and some other things which make a loss of a hundred dollars about. George felt rather badly as it was so hard to get any money for his tools from the regents, and he has not as much apparatus as he would like to have and who knows when he will ever get any more? The night-watchman on his rounds discovered the fire before it had spread, but it was a careless thing to do, and I do not believe he will leave any more brains to harden over night." Elinor Castle Nef Papers, box 17, folder 10.

36. Castle to his parents, June 10, 1893.

37. See John Dewey to President William Rainey Harper of the University of Chicago, Mar. 27 and Apr. 10, 1894, University Presidents' Papers, box 17, folder 11. In these letters Dewey urges the appointment of Mead as a member of the department Dewey had been hired to chair at Chicago.

38. Elinor Castle (1894–1953) later took her bachelor's degree at the University of Chicago and became the wife of John U. Nef, professor of economic history

at that university. A collection of her writings appears in Nef, *Letters & Notes*. See also Elinor Castle Nef Papers. Interesting biographical information concerning Mabel Wing Castle (1864–1950) can be found in Nef, *My Mother's Reminiscences*.

39. Castle to his wife, Jan. 4, 8, 20, and 22, 1894.

40. San Francisco *Chronicle*, Jan. 31, 1895.

41. Helen Castle Mead to her sister Hattie, Feb. 2, 1895.

42. Mead to his wife, Jan. 31, 1895.

Chapter 3: "From Hegelianism to Social Psychology"

1. Other members of Dewey's department in 1894 included Charles A. Strong, associate professor of psychology, who left Chicago for Columbia University the following year, and Julia E. Bulkley, associate professor of pedagogy, who had been appointed by Harper in 1892 but who was on a leave of absence for advanced study at the University of Zurich until the fall of 1895. Addison W. Moore and Edward Scribner Ames, both of whom served as graduate student teaching fellows during the 1894–95 academic year, became regular members of the departmental faculty in 1895 and 1900, respectively. See McCaul, "Dewey's Chicago," 258–59; Dykhuizen, *Life and Mind of Dewey*, 77–78.

2. Angell, autobiographical essay, in *History of Psychology in Autobiography*, ed. Murchison, 3:1–38.

3. Mead to his wife, June 12, 1901, Mead Papers, box 1, folder 5. In his quest for a promotion Mead may well have been thankful not only for Dewey's strong support but also for the fact that Harper was inclined to place more emphasis upon research and graduate teaching than undergraduate teaching in his evaluation of faculty. Mead's performance as a teacher of undergraduates during his early years at Chicago evidently left something to be desired, as is indicated in a letter Harper sent him on May 20, 1898: "I am wondering whether it would be possible for you to make your Tuesday lectures more interesting to the students. A great many complaints have come that they are so thoroughly dry that nobody has any interest in them and the attitude, I am afraid, is one of general lack of interest. This being true on the part of good students as well as poor students. Of course the statements that come to my attention may have been all one-sided, but I have thought you should know that this feeling existed." William Rainey Harper Papers, box 4, folder 7. According to the annual *Register of the University of Chicago*, Mead's lecture courses for the spring quarter of 1898 were logic and movements of thought in the eighteenth and nineteenth centuries. Harper's letter probably refers to the latter course.

4. *John Dewey: The Early Works*, 4:167n. The abstract of Mead's paper appears in *Psychological Review* 2 (1895): 162–64.

5. Mead, "A New Criticism of Hegelianism: Is It Valid?" (1901), 87, 88, 96.

6. Ibid., 96, 93.

7. See Mayhew and Edwards, *Dewey School*. On Dewey's relations with Harper, see McCaul, "Dewey and the University of Chicago," 152–57, 179–83, 202–6.

8. Mayhew and Edwards, *Dewey School*, x; Dewey, *School and Society*, 2d ed., xi–xii.

9. G. H. Mead to Helen Mead, May 13 and June 8, 1901, Mead Papers, box 1, folder 5. Mead, "The Basis for a Parents' Association" (1903), 337–46, reprinted in ESP 63–70. During this same period, Mead served (along with Dewey and Angell) on the board of trustees of the Chicago Physiological School—a school for children with severe physiological handicaps. The school was affiliated with Rush Medical College and was supervised by the departments of philosophy and neurology at the University of Chicago from about 1900 to 1904. See Deegan and Burger, "George Herbert Mead and Social Reform," 363–65. Documents relevant to Mead's involvement with this school can be found in University Presidents' Papers, 1889–1925, box 39, folder 6.

10. Mead, "The Relation of Play to Education" (1896), 140–45, reprinted in ESP 27–34. Mead, "The Child and His Environment" (1898), 1–11.

11. Mead, "The Child and His Environment" (1898), 7–8.

12. "The Working Hypothesis in Social Reform" (1899), 367–71, reprinted in ESP 125–29; review of Gustav Le Bon's *The Psychology of Socialism* (1899), 404–12.

13. "The Working Hypothesis in Social Reform" (1899), in ESP 128.

14. Ibid., 127.

15. Review of Le Bon's *The Psychology of Socialism* (1899), 409.

16. "The Working Hypothesis in Social Reform" (1899), in ESP 128.

17. Ibid., 127–28.

18. *Register of the University of Chicago* for 1893–94 and subsequent years. For information on Mead's courses at the University of Michigan, see ch. 2, n. 33.

19. Watson, autobiographical essay, in *History of Psychology in Autobiography*, ed. Murchison, 3:274.

20. See the annual *Register of the University of Chicago* for the years 1893 to 1931. A fairly full, but by no means complete, listing of Mead's yearly course offerings can be found in appendix 2 of Lewis and Smith, *American Sociology and Pragmatism*.

21. "Concerning Animal Perception" (1907), 383–90, reprinted in SW 73–81. Mead also presented a paper on "The Relation of Imitation to the Theory of Animal Perception" at the annual meeting of the American Psychological Association in 1906. For the abstract of this paper see *Psychological Bulletin* 4 (1907): 210–11.

22. See, for instance, his "The Genesis of the Self and Social Control" (1925), reprinted in SW 267–93. See also his *Mind, Self and Society*, 119–20, 227–44, 278–80, 347–51, 354–65.

23. Review of C. L. Morgan's *An Introduction to Comparative Psychology* (1895), 401.

24. Review of G. Class's *Untersuchungen zur Phaenomenologie und Ontologie des Menschlichen Geistes* (1897), 790–91.

25. "A New Criticism of Hegelianism: Is It Valid?" (1901), 95.

26. Royce, "The External World and the Social Consciousness," 513–45; "Self-Consciousness, Social Consciousness, and Nature," 465–85, 577–602; "Some Ob-

servations on the Anomalies of Self-Consciousness," 433–57, 574–84. The last two of these essays are reprinted in Royce's *Studies of Good and Evil*. See also Baldwin, *Mental Development in the Child and the Race* and *Social and Ethical Interpretations in Mental Development*.

27. Royce, "The External World and the Social Consciousness," 535–40, 532–33.

28. Baldwin, *Social and Ethical Interpretations in Mental Development*, 87.

29. Mead, Review of D. Draghiscesco, *Du role de l'individu dans le déterminisme social* and *Le problème du déterminisme, déterminisme biologique et déterminisme social* (1905), 403–4.

30. Royce, "The External World and the Social Consciousness," 532.

31. See *Psychological Review* 2 (1895): 305–9, 407–8, 616–18; 4 (1897): 316–18; 6 (1899): 533–36.

32. For Tufts's review of Baldwin's book, see *Psychological Review* 5 (1898): 313–21. Two reviews by Dewey appear in *John Dewey: The Early Works*, 5: 385–422. On the discussion of Baldwin at the University of Chicago sociology club, see Lewis and Smith, *American Sociology and Pragmatism*, 311n.

33. Mead to Henry Mead, Jan. 21, 1915, Mead Papers, box 1, folder 8. For information on Mead's course offerings at the University of Chicago, see *Register of the University of Chicago, 1894–1931*.

34. The present study is concerned with Mead's intellectual development, rather than with his influence upon other thinkers. Nevertheless, I cannot resist quoting a letter Ellsworth Faris wrote to Mead's son shortly after Mead's death (May 4, 1931), which indicates the impact Mead's teaching had upon at least some of his students, in this case a student who subsequently taught at the University of Chicago during the 1915–16 academic year and then returned to serve as a regular member of Chicago's department of sociology from 1919 until his retirement in 1939. "Will you allow me, please, to put on paper the feeling of obligation and admiration I have never ceased to feel since I met your father, twenty years ago. I was his student then, I became his colleague later, but I have been his disciple ever since and shall always acknowledge him as the source of my philosophy of life and of my scientific organization. There is no one to whom I owe more—no one in all the world. The debt is personal, his kindness and friendship when I was so much in need of friends. The debt is also intellectual. I have for years regarded it as one of my chief aims to interpret and, if possible, extend the ideas which his great mind originated. Many others have written you. None have more cause than I to love him, thank him, honor him. For in an academic sense I call myself his son." Mead Papers Addenda, box 1, folder 8. For information on Ellsworth Faris, see Faris, *Chicago Sociology, 1920–1932*.

Chapter 4: "The Development of Mead's Social Psychology"

1. Charles W. Morris, the editor of Mead's *Mind, Self and Society*, claims in his preface that stenographic student notes of Mead's "1927 course in social psychology" were used as the basis for this volume (vi). But the date Morris mentions

here appears to be inaccurate. An examination of the materials from which Morris constructed the book reveals that the basic set of notes was taken by W. T. Lillie in Mead's course philosophy 321, advanced social psychology, during the winter quarter of 1928. See Mead Papers, box 11, folders 4–13.

2. PP xxxvi–xxxvii.

3. Rucker, *Chicago Pragmatists*, 59–60.

4. Dewey, "The Reflex Arc Concept in Psychology," reprinted in *John Dewey: The Early Works*, 5:96–109.

5. *John Dewey: The Early Works*, 5: 104, 102, 98–99.

6. Ibid., 107, 108–9.

7. All of the Mead essays discussed in this chapter are reprinted in SW, and the page references indicated in the text are to this book.

8. In later years Mead preferred the term "impulse" when referring to the root tendencies of human conduct. "They are best termed 'impulses' and not 'instincts,' because they are subject to extensive modifications in the life-history of individuals." MSS 337.

9. Mead's use of the term "fictitious" in this passage is puzzling, but it may suggest that he himself was aware of the somewhat misleading character of the term "I" as applied to the immediate act. The "I," he says several lines earlier, is the transcendental self of Kant. But this remark does nothing to render the use of a personal pronoun here less questionable.

10. MSS 174.

11. "Now, it is this living act which never gets directly into reflective experience. . . . It is that 'I' which we may be said to be continually trying to realize, and to realize through the actual conduct itself." Ibid., 203. Also, "The act itself which I have spoken of as the 'I' in the social situation is a source of unity of the whole, while the 'me' is the social situation in which the act can express itself." Ibid., 279.

12. Kolb, "A Critical Evaluation of Mead's 'I' and 'me' Concepts," reprinted in *Symbolic Interaction: A Reader in Social Psychology*, ed. Manis and Meltzer, 241–50.

Chapter 5: "Behaviorism and Mead's Social Psychology"

1. Page references to *Mind, Self and Society* are indicated in the text by the abbreviation MSS and the relevant page number.

2. Watson, "Psychology as the Behaviorist Views It," 158–77.

3. Heidbreder, "Functionalism," in *Schools of Psychology*, ed. Krantz, 39–40.

4. Ibid., 67.

5. Angell, "The Province of Functional Psychology," 66, 67.

6. *History of Psychology in Autobiography*, ed. Murchison, 3:25.

7. SW xxiv–xxv.

8. Miller, *George Herbert Mead*, xxix.

9. Morris admits in his introduction to *Mind, Self and Society* that Mead himself did not use the term social behaviorism (xvi).

10. *History of Psychology in Autobiography*, ed. Murchison, 23.

11. MT 390–95.

12. Boring, *A History of Experimental Psychology,* 2d ed., 645.

13. Dewey, "Conduct and Experience," in *Psychologies of 1930,* ed. Murchison, 409–22.

14. PA, especially 3–25, 125–39.

15. See, for instance, PA 140–53; PP 119–39, 172–73.

Chapter 6: "Taking the Attitude or the Role of the Other"

1. See "What Social Objects Must Psychology Presuppose?" (1910), SW 111, and "Social Consciousness and the Consciousness of Meaning" (1910), SW 132, for early hints of this concept. See "The Mechanism of Social Consciousness" (1912), SW 139–40, and "The Social Self" (1913), SW 145–46, for Mead's first explicit use of the concept in his published work. The concept also appears frequently in student notes from Mead's 1912 class lectures on social psychology, reproduced in Miller, ed., *The Individual and the Social Self.* Miller incorrectly assigns the date of 1914 to these notes.

2. This definition is borrowed from Coutu, "Role-Playing vs. Role-Taking," 180.

3. See MSS 5, 100, 362; "A Pragmatic Theory of Truth" (1929), SW 336; PA 130.

4. I agree with Dmitri N. Shalin's observation that Mead tends to move back and forth in a somewhat confusing manner between a phylogenetic and an ontogenetic perspective in his accounts of such phenomena as language, thought, and self-consciousness. That is, sometimes he is offering an evolutionary account of the development of these phenomena in the human species; at other times he is offering a genetic account of the development of these capacities in a human individual. Unfortunately, he seldom makes any distinction between these two perspectives. See Shalin, "Mead, Behaviorism and Indeterminacy," 38–39.

5. See "Social Psychology as Counterpart to Physiological Psychology" (1909), SW 97–98; MSS 337.

6. Other references to this selective mechanism appear in Mead's 1912 class lectures in social psychology (Miller, ed., *Individual and Self,* 57–58), in his 1927 class lectures in social psychology (ibid., 152), and MSS 359–60.

7. The idea of distinguishing between the anticipatory, reflexive, and appropriative functions was suggested to me by my reading of Lauer and Boardman's "Role-Taking: Theory, Typology, and Propositions," 137–48. However, my way of distinguishing various functions of attitude-taking differs somewhat from their attempt to distinguish different types of role-taking.

8. "The Genesis of Self and Social Control" (1925), SW 278–93; MSS 155, 227ff., 253.

Chapter 7: "Mead and the City of Chicago: Social and Educational Reform"

1. For background information on the social settlement movement and the University of Chicago Settlement, see Davis, *Spearheads for Reform,* and Wilson, *Mary McDowell, Neighbor.* For a discussion of important aspects of Mead's involvement

in the University of Chicago Settlement, see Diner, *A City and Its Universities*, 124–27.

2. For Dewey's service on the Hull-House board of trustees, see Hull-House Association Board of Trustees: Minutes 1895–1970. According to *Hull-House Bulletin*, vols. 2–3, Mead gave the following lectures under Hull-House auspices: "The Story of the Brain" (jointly sponsored by Hull-House and the Chicago Board of Education on Feb. 26, 1897), "The Evolution of Intelligence" and "The Present Evolution of Man" (Mar. 7 and 21, 1897, as part of a Sunday evening lecture series in the Hull-House gymnasium), and "The Hawaiian Islands" (stereoptican lecture at Hull-House on Nov. 13, 1899). See Hull-House Association Papers.

3. See the *Daily Maroon,* Oct. 29, 1907; "The Social Settlement: Its Basis and Function" (1908), 108–10.

4. "The Social Settlement: Its Basis and Function" (1908), 110.

5. Ibid., 108, 110.

6. Ibid., 110.

7. See "University of Chicago Settlement: Board Minutes and Reports," in the Mary McDowell and the University of Chicago Settlement Papers.

8. University of Chicago Settlement Board Minutes of Apr. 14 and May 12, 1909. On the social survey movement, see Bulmer, *Chicago School of Sociology,* 65–68.

9. See the letters of July 25 and Dec. 1, 1910, drafted by William Scott Bond on behalf of the Settlement Board. These are included in the University of Chicago Settlement Board Minutes. See also John C. Kennedy's outline of the nature and purpose of the proposed survey included with the minutes of Dec. 8, 1909.

10. University of Chicago Settlement Board Minutes from June 1909 to Nov. 1914. For the published results of the Chicago stockyards survey, see University of Chicago Settlement, *A Study of Chicago's Stockyards Community,* 3 vols: vol. 1, *Opportunities in School and Industry for Children of the Stockyards District,* by Ernest L. Talbert; vol. 2, *The American Girl in the Stockyards District,* by Louise Montgomery; vol. 3, *Wages and Family Budgets in the Chicago Stockyards District,* by John C. Kennedy.

11. See Diner, *A City and Its Universities,* 124–29. A draft of Mead's proposal for a central research bureau appears in the Mead Papers, box IX, folder 23. For McDowell's work with the Department of Public Welfare (1923–27), see Wilson, *Mary McDowell,* ch. IX.

12. See the Annual Reports of the Immigrants' Protective League in the Immigrants' Protective League of Illinois Papers. See also Diner, *A City and Its Universities,* 129–31; Buroker, "From Voluntary Association to Welfare State," 643–60.

13. "Concerning the Garment Workers' Strike: A Report of the Sub-Committee to the Citizens' Committee, Nov. 5th, 1910." The published version of this report can be found in the Graham Taylor Papers. For Mead's typed copy, see Mead Papers, box IX, folder 22.

14. Mead's handwritten draft of "Grievances against the Association Houses" is found in Mead Papers, box IX, folder 22.

15. For further discussion of Mead, the Citizens' Committee, and the 1910 garment workers' strike, see Diner, *A City and Its Universities,* 148–50.

16. *City Club of Chicago Yearbook,* 1904, 7; *City Club Bulletin* (hereafter abbreviated CCB) 13 (Apr. 19, 1920): 94.

17. CCB 1 (May 8, 1907): 131–38; 11 (Apr. 8, 1918): 125.

18. "Report on Chicago's Public Library Service, by the Sub-Committee on Libraries, of the Committee of the City Club of Chicago, on Public Education," CCB 2 (Apr. 21, 1909): 381–88. See also Joeckel and Carnovsky, *Metropolitan Library in Action,* 38–47; "The Civil Service Commission and the Appointment of a Librarian of the Chicago Public Library," CCB 2 (June 19, 1909): 479–82.

19. These last two subcommittees and their reports will be more fully discussed in the next section of the present chapter.

20. CCB 12 (Apr. 7, 1919): 87; 8 (Dec. 16, 1915): 164–66.

21. CCB 10 (July 20, 1917): 212; 12 (Apr. 7, 1919): 87.

22. CCB 9 (July 17, 1916): 131–32. See also Mead Papers Addenda, box 2, folder 17; CCB 9 (July 17, 1916): 126.

23. Herrick, *Chicago Schools,* 128–31; The Public Education Association of Chicago, *Bulletins* 1–4 (1916).

24. CCB 10 (Dec. 10, 1917): 229.

25. CCB 9 (July 17, 1916): 126–27.

26. CCB 10 (Mar. 27, 1917): 104–8.

27. CCB 11 (Apr. 22, 1918): 139; 12 (Apr. 21, 1919): 98.

28. Chicago *Evening Post,* Mar. 7, 1919; CCB 12 (Mar. 10, 1919): 69–71. 12 (Mar. 17, 1919): 74.

29. CCB 13 (Apr. 19, 1920): 93; 14 (Apr. 25, 1921): 70; 24 (May 4, 1931): 88.

30. *Annual Register of the University of Chicago,* 1906–11. *Elementary School Teacher* 8 (1907–8): 281–84.

31. Mead, "Science in the High School" (1906), 240–41; "The Teaching of Science in College" (1907), reprinted in SW 63–64. Compare Dewey, *School and Society,* ch. III, and *The Child and the Curriculum.*

32. "Science in the High School" (1906), 243–44. Compare Mayhew and Edwards, *Dewey School,* ch. XV.

33. Mead, "The Psychology of Social Consciousness Implied in Instruction," SW 116–17. Compare Dewey, "My Pedagogic Creed" (1897), reprinted in *John Dewey: The Early Works,* 5 : 84–95.

34. "The Educational Situation in the Chicago Public Schools," CCB 1 (May 8, 1907): 134–35.

35. "Editorial Note on the School System of Chicago" (1907), 162–63.

36. Ibid., 164.

37. Ibid., 163–64.

38. "Educational Aspects of Trade Schools," *Union Labor Advocate* 8 (1908): 1920, reprinted in ESP 44–49. "Industrial Education, the Working-Man, and the School," *Elementary School Teacher* 9 (1908–9): 337–46, reprinted in ESP 50–62. See also the following editorial notes in *Elementary School Teacher:* "Industrial Education and Trade Schools," 8 (1907–8): 402–6; "Resolution on Industrial Education," 9 (1908–9): 156–57; "Industrial Training," 9 (1908–9):212–14.

39. "Educational Aspects of Trade Schools," ESP 45.

40. "Industrial Education and Trade Schools," 406.

41. "Educational Aspects of Trade Schools," ESP 47.

42. "Industrial Education, the Working-Man, and the School," ESP 53–58; "Resolution on Education," 157.

43. *A Report on Vocational Training in Chicago and in Other Cities,* by a committee of the City Club of Chicago, George H. Mead, Chairman (Chicago, 1912).

44. Ibid., 9–10.

45. For a summary of the report and its recommendations, see the review by Leavitt, 402–4. See also Diner, *A City and Its Universities,* 92–94.

46. "A Report of the Public Education Committee of the City Club of Chicago upon issues involved in proposed legislation for vocational education in Illinois," CCB 5 (Dec. 4, 1912): 373–83.

47. Ibid., 375, 376.

48. Mead, "The Larger Educational Bearings of Vocational Guidance," in *Readings in Vocational Guidance,* ed. Bloomfield, 43–55.

49. Ibid., 55.

50. *Bulletin of the Vocational Supervision League* (Apr. 15, 1919), Mead Papers Addenda, box 2, folder 5. See also Diner, *A City and Its Universities,* 92–99.

51. For another writer's interpretation of Mead's theory and practice of social reform, see the excellent essay by Shalin, "Mead, Socialism, and the Progressive Agenda," 913–51.

Chapter 8: "Moral Reconstruction and the Social Self"

1. Mead to his son Henry Mead, July 28, 1914. Mead Papers, box 1, folder 7.

2. Mead to Henry Mead, Jan. 30, 1919, Mead Papers, box 1, folder 9.

3. Mead, "Democracy's Issues in the World War," Chicago *Herald,* Aug. 4, 1917; "War Issue to U.S. Forced by Kaiser," ibid., Aug. 2, 1917; "Germany's Crisis—Its Effect on Labor, Parts I and II," ibid., July 26 and 27, 1917.

4. Joas, *G. H. Mead,* 25. Joas quite correctly notes that Mead was thoroughly supportive of President Woodrow Wilson's wartime foreign policy. Hence any fundamental criticism of this policy also applies to Mead's position with respect to World War I.

5. Mead, "Germany's Crisis—Its Effect on Labor, Part I"; "America's Ideals and the War," Chicago *Herald,* Aug. 3, 1917.

6. Mead, "Democracy's Issues in the World War."

7. Mead also discusses the hostile impulses in "The Psychology of Punitive Justice" (1918).

8. Review of G. Le Bon's *The Psychology of Socialism* (1899), 409.

9. Student notes on Mead's lectures in the course elementary ethics, autumn quarter, 1927, Mead Papers, box VII, folders 3 and 4. References to these notes are hereafter indicated by the abbreviation LE and the relevant page number. Whenever I refer to a passage from these notes that is reproduced in the supplementary essay "Fragments on Ethics" included in *Mind, Self and Society,* I give page references to both MSS and LE.

10. In the discussion that follows, I have chosen not to address Mead's occa-

sional references to the concept of rights. Despite the promising title of one of his published essays, "Natural Rights and the Theory of the Political Institution" (1915), Mead's writings contain nothing even approximating a careful analysis of rights. This is disappointing, not only because of current interest in this topic but also because Mead's social psychology appears to contain the conceptual resources for such an analysis. For two recent attempts to work out a Meadian theory of rights, see Betz, "George Herbert Mead on Human Rights," 199–223, and Beth J. Singer, "Rights and Norms," a paper presented at the international conference on "Frontiers in American Philosophy," Texas A & M University, June 1–4, 1988.

11. For a reading of Mead's ethics that places considerable emphasis upon the significance of this suggestion, see Joas, *G. H. Mead,* 135–37. For a further and more recent development of this line of thought, see Habermas, *Theory of Communicative Action,* 2:sec. V.3.C.

12. For a recent and insightful attempt to build upon Mead's contributions to moral psychology, see Schwalbe, "Toward a Sociology of Moral Problem Solving," 131–55.

Chapter 9: "Whitehead's Influence on Mead's Later Thought"

1. The program for this congress appears in the *Journal of Philosophy* 23 (Sept. 16, 1926): 526–32. Mead and Whitehead spoke at a session titled "Physics and metaphysics, with special reference to the problem of time."

2. Mead to Irene Tufts Mead, Sept. 14, 1926, Mead Papers, box 1a, folder 14. In the interest of clarity, I have inserted the dashes and the comma in the second sentence quoted. Mead was inclined to neglect punctuation in his handwritten letters.

3. Mead had earlier published a review of Bergson's *L'Evolution creatrice* (1907), 379–84. In this review he had also made reference to Bergson's *Matière et Mémoire* and *Essai sur les données immédiates de la conscience.* But in a letter of Aug. 2, 1920, he admits finding, with respect to *Creative Evolution,* that "my reading and rereading of it years ago have left almost no impression on my mind." Mead Papers, box 1a, folder 4.

4. Mead to Irene Tufts Mead, July 17, 1920, Mead Papers, box 1a, folder 1. While Bergson's influence on Mead is not as obvious as is the influence of Whitehead, Mead apparently turned frequently to Bergson's work for stimulation. Arthur Murphy reports, for instance, that "at the time of my last conversation with him, in the week before his death, he was at work on Bergson's *Durée et Simultanéité* in its relation to his own account of relativity." PP viii.

5. This interest in relativity led Mead to offer a graduate course on relativity from the standpoint of pragmatism in the spring quarters of 1922 and 1923. And in the winter quarter of 1925 he taught a similar course on the metaphysics of relativity. (See the *Register of the University of Chicago* for these years.) Student notes that Van Meter Ames took in the 1923 course, and that he was kind enough to share with me, indicate that Mead focused much of his discussion around the contrasting

interpretations of relativity found in the writings of Einstein and Whitehead. These notes can now be seen in Mead Papers Addenda, box 4, folder 10.

6. Mead to Irene Tufts Mead, July 26, 1921, Mead Papers, box 1a, folder 8. For a discussion of what Mead has in mind when he refers to "visual and contact space," see chapter 10 below. Professor Albert Einstein gave a series of three lectures on the theory of relativity at the University of Chicago on May 3, 4, and 5, 1921. The dinner to which Mead refers in the quoted passage was a dinner in honor of Einstein held at the Quadrangle Club on the evening of May 3. According to the report of the Einstein lectures in the *University Record* 7 (July 1921): 184: "Professor Einstein spoke in German with a simplicity and skill of presentation which were commented upon by many—among others, editorially, by the *Chicago Evening Post*."

7. Mead to Irene Tufts Mead, Aug. 2, 1921, Mead Papers, box 1a, folder 8.

8. Mead to Irene Tufts Mead, Sept. 12, 1921, Mead Papers, box 1a, folder 9.

9. MT 340.

10. SW 340.

11. David L. Miller reports in this connection that "when in early 1931 a few of Mead's students asked him what he thought of Whitehead's *Process and Reality*, he told us that he was reading it but had not come to a clear understanding of it." Editor's introduction (512) to Mead, "Two Unpublished Papers."

12. This essay and the three others to be discussed below are reprinted in SW.

13. Whitehead, *The Concept of Nature*, 53–60; hereafter, references to this volume are indicated by the abbreviation CN.

14. Whitehead, *An Enquiry Concerning the Principles of Natural Knowledge*, 68–71; hereafter, references to this volume are indicated by the abbreviation PNK. See also CN 107–10, 187–89.

15. PNK 31–32, 70–71.

16. CN 187, 194–95; Whitehead, *The Principle of Relativity*, 66–67.

17. Whitehead, *The Principle of Relativity*, 25.

18. See chapters 4 and 5 of this study.

19. CN 29.

20. Ibid., 4–5.

21. Examples of such "dark hints" in Whitehead's writings can be found on the following pages: CN 56; PNK 67, 78–79, 89, 93–94; *The Principle of Relativity*, 66.

22. See, for instance, SW 289, 311, 344.

23. See his 1903 essay "The Definition of the Psychical" (SW 25–59). Pages 52–54 are especially relevant.

24. This view of the past leads Mead to disagree, both here and in *The Philosophy of the Present* (PP 1), with what he takes to be Whitehead's misunderstanding of the way in which memory images figure in present experience: "Whitehead's suggestion that rendering these images sufficiently vivid would spread the specious present is quite beside the mark. No memory image, however vivid, would be anything but a memory image." (SW 345). For the relevant passage in Whitehead's work, see CN 67.

25. MSS 201, 262.

26. A brief discussion of this method appears later in the present chapter.

27. See, for instance: PA 114–15, 215, 281, 325, 329–31, 515, 643–45; PP 35–36, 80–82.

28. See, for instance, essays VII, IX, XI, XIII, and XX in PA. This topic is also discussed in the first of the "Two Unpublished Papers" cited above.

29. For Whitehead's discussion of this method, see PNK 76, 101ff.; CN 60–65, 74ff.

30. Similar observations appear in the second of Mead's "Two Unpublished Papers."

31. See references in n. 27 above, and also the first three supplementary essays in PP.

32. Another example of Mead's use of Whiteheadian concepts in connection with his own functional analysis of conduct can be seen in his employment of Whitehead's notion of the "conveyance" of sense-objects in perception. See essay VIII, "The Mediate Factors in Perception," in PA. For Whitehead's use of this concept, see PNK 88, 186, 193; CN 154.

33. For Whitehead's reference to a "double consciousness of cogredience," see CN 111. The idea of approaching relativity in terms of his own notion of role-taking had occurred to Mead at least as early as 1923. In a letter written during the summer of that year he reports reading C. D. Broad's *Scientific Thought* and feeling "somewhat surer that taking the role of the other is to be recognized as the principle of relativity." Mead to Irene Tufts Mead, June 30, 1923, Mead Papers, box 1a, folder 10.

Chapter 10: "Mead's Social Pragmatism"

1. Mead, "Scientific Method and Individual Thinker," in *Creative Intelligence*, ed. Dewey et al., 176–227, reprinted in SW 171–211.

2. See, for instance, Mead's letters of Sept. 7 and 10, 1920, and Aug. 7, 1923 to Irene Tufts Mead, in Mead Papers, box Ia, folders 6 and 11. See also PA 94–100, 280, 356, 360–64, 514.

3. See Dewey, *Essays in Experimental Logic*, 306, where Dewey uses this phrase in the context of a review of James's *Pragmatism*. It is unfortunate that Mead was not more familiar with the work of Peirce. He might have found especially interesting Peirce's emphasis upon the social dimensions of scientific inquiry and Peirce's social conception of reality.

4. Mead, "The Philosophy of John Dewey" (1935–36), 64–81.

5. Ibid., 68–71, 74, 75, 76.

6. Ibid., 77–79, 80.

7. This story is reported by Rucker in *Chicago Pragmatists*, 19, and by Miller in *George Herbert Mead*, xxi.

8. See Mead Papers, box VII, folder 1, for student notes taken in Mead's course on the philosophy of John Dewey during the winter quarter of 1926, notes for Jan. 4, 1926. A similar point is suggested in Mead's essay, "The Philosophy of John Dewey" (1935–36), 78–79. See also Mead's criticisms of Dewey's *Experience and Nature* in his letter of Sept. 23, 1926, to Irene Tufts Mead, Mead Papers, box Ia, folder 14.

9. Mead's unpublished review of Dewey's *Human Nature and Conduct* is found in Mead Papers Addenda, box 2, folder 4, 5–6.

10. Mead, "The Philosophy of John Dewey" (1935–36), 76.

11. The term "social pragmatism" is also used to characterize Mead's thought by Thayer in his *Meaning and Action*, 264–68.

12. But see PA 205–14, PP 146–49.

13. See, for instance, Supplementary Essay I in PP; Essays II–VI in PA.

Epilogue: "Mead and the Hutchins Controversy"

1. Dean Frederic C. Woodward to G. H. Mead, Nov. 21, 1927, Mead to Woodward, Jan. 23, 1929, Mead to President R. M. Hutchins, Feb. 6 1931, Presidents' Papers ca. 1925–1945, box 106, folder 14.

2. PP vii. It might also be noted here that Mead's final years at Chicago were saddened by the death of Helen Castle Mead, after a long illness, on Christmas Day, 1929. See Mead Papers Addenda, box 1, folder 3.

3. The most complete account of this controversy previously published is found in Adler, *Philosopher at Large*, ch. 7. Adler's recollections and his quotations from correspondence with Hutchins are useful, but he tells the story from his own point of view as a participant, and he makes no use of the departmental memoranda and other documents cited in the present chapter. A brief account of the controversy is also set forth in Ashmore, *Unseasonable Truths*, 85–87. Ashmore's biography reveals several additional facts as background to the present discussion. (1) Like Mead, Hutchins was a graduate of the Oberlin Academy and Oberlin College. (2) From 1907–19, Hutchins's father held essentially the same faculty position in the Oberlin Seminary as that earlier occupied by Mead's father. (3) The Yale University president under whom Hutchins served just prior to his Chicago appointment, and who did not think Hutchins yet mature enough to serve as the president of the University of Chicago, was James Rowland Angell, a former colleague of Mead, Tufts, and Dewey at Chicago. Ibid., 5, 10, 59–60.

4. Adler, *Philosopher at Large*, 127–28.

5. Ibid., 128.

6. See the correspondence between T. V. Smith and R. M. Hutchins in the Presidents' Papers ca. 1925–1945, box 106, folder 14. See also Smith's autobiography, *A Non-Existent Man*, 230–36. Charles Hartshorne, who read a draft of this account in the summer of 1991, questions the accuracy of my view concerning the relationship between Smith and Hutchins. In a personal communication to me, Hartshorne recalls hearing Hutchins refer to Smith as an "idiot" and a "horse dealer" in the years following 1931. Perhaps, then, it was to Mead rather than Smith that Hutchins referred in his letter to Adler in October 1929. But, if so, either Hutchins misunderstood Mead's true sentiments, or else Mead had a radical change of heart about Hutchins's intentions between 1929 and 1931. The reader may be interested in knowing that I also sent drafts of this chapter to Mortimer Adler and E. A. Burtt. Adler did not respond, but Burtt replied as follows: "I have read with care the chapter you sent me. My memory does not include some of

the episodes you mention, but it tells me nothing incompatible with what you say about them." (Personal communication, July 13, 1987.)

7. J. H. Tufts to R. M. Hutchins, memorandum, Oct. 28, 1929, Presidents' Papers ca. 1925–1945, box 106, folder 14.

8. "A Statement from the Department of Philosophy," 1. This document is found in the President's Papers ca. 1925–1945, box 106, folder 14. It is undated but is accompanied by a letter of Mar. 3, 1931, from Dean C. S. Boucher calling it to the attention of the president.

9. Adler, *Philosopher at Large*, 129–30.

10. "A Statement from the Department of Philosophy," 1.

11. Ibid., 130.

12. Ibid.

13. Ibid., 2.

14. Adler admits in his autobiography that he did on at least one occasion while he was still at Columbia make "unmistakably derisive" remarks concerning his Chicago colleagues-to-be. However, he recalls the occasion as a cocktail party in the late spring of 1930. "My remarks were overheard by someone who reported them to friends in the Chicago Philosophy Department. He did not need to embroider or exaggerate this juicy bit of gossip to produce the hostility I deservedly experienced when I arrived in September." Adler, *Philospher at Large*, 133–34.

15. "A Statement from the Department of Philosophy," 2. It should be added here that Tufts's resignation was also motivated in part by health problems involving anemia.

16. Ibid.

17. Adler, *Philospher at Large*, 131–41.

18. Statement by Dean G. J. Laing on "The Situation in the Department of Philosophy" (Mar. 15, 1931), included in a volume called *The Faculty of the Division of the Humanities: December 1930–October 1940*, kept in the Secretary of the Faculties Office at the University of Chicago.

19. Adler, *Philosopher at Large*, 142.

20. "A Statement from the Department of Philosophy," 2.

21. Ibid., 3.

22. I have been unable to find a copy of Hutchins's letter. Unfortunately, the two descriptions of the letter I have found are not wholly in agreement as to its contents. See Laing, "The Situation in the Department of Philosophy," 5–6, and Adler, *Philospher at Large*, 146.

23. Laing, "The Situation in the Department of Philosophy," 6.

24. "Statement of Professors Mead, Burtt and Murphy," 2–3, included in *The Faculty of the Division of the Humanities: December 1930–October 1940*.

25. Quoted in Adler, *Philosopher at Large*, 147.

26. Laing, "The Situation in the Department of Philosophy," 6.

27. Frederic Woodward to R. M. Hutchins, Jan. 22, 1931 (letter), Jan. 28, 1931 (telegram), Presidents' Papers ca. 1925–1945, box 106, folder 14. Columbia University had offered Mead a $10,000 salary for the 1931–32 academic year, whereas Chicago had been paying him only $5,000. But Woodward pointed out in his letter

of Jan. 22, 1931, that Mead's low salary at Chicago was largely the result of the attitude of his long-time chairman, James H. Tufts, who always acted as if he thought
salary was of no concern to Mead. Mead, it should be noted, was independently
wealthy due to his wife's inheritance from the Castle family estate.

28. Laing, "The Situation in the Department of Philosophy," 6.

29. Ibid., 7–8.

30. Woodward's letters and telegrams to Hutchins are contained in the Presidents' Papers ca. 1925–1945, box 106, folder 14. On the reasons for Hutchins's absence from Chicago during this crucial period, see Ashmore, *Unseasonable Truths*,
93–94.

31. This correspondence between Mead and Hutchins is found in the Presidents' Papers ca. 1925–1945, box 106, folder 14.

32. The *Daily Maroon*, University of Chicago, Tues., Apr. 28, 1931; *A Memorial Pamphlet* (privately printed, containing eulogies for G. H. Mead by Edward
Scribner Ames, John Dewey, and James H. Tufts, 1931). Dewey's remarks are also
printed in Dewey, "George Herbert Mead as I Knew Him," 173–77.

Bibliography

I. The Writings of George Herbert Mead: A Chronological Listing

Works Published by Mead during His Lifetime

1. "The Relation of Art to Morality." *Oberlin Review* 9 (1881): 63–64.
2. "Charles Lamb." *Oberlin Review* 10 (1882): 15–16.
3. "De Quincey." *Oberlin Review* 10 (1882): 50–52.
4. "John Locke." *Oberlin Review* 10 (1883), 217–19.
5. "Republican Persecution, Letter to the Editor." *Nation* 39 (1884): 519–20.
6. "The Problem of Psychological Measurement." An abstract of a paper read at the second annual meeting of the American Psychological Association, December 1893. *Proceedings of the American Psychological Association* (1894): 22–23. This abstract also appears in University of Michigan, *University Record* 4 (1894): 21–22.
7. "The Greek Mysteries." An abstract of a paper presented to the Philosophical Society of the University of Michigan in January 1894. University of Michigan, *University Record* 3 (1894): 102.
8. "Herr Lasswitz on Energy and Epistemology." *Psychological Review* 1 (1894): 172–75.
9. Review of Kurd Lasswitz, *Die moderne Energetik in ihrer Bedeutung für die Erkenntnisskritik. Psychological Review* 1 (1894): 210–13.
10. Review of C. L. Morgan, *An Introduction to Comparative Psychology. Psychological Review* 2 (1895): 399–402.
11. "A Theory of Emotions from the Physiological Standpoint." An abstract of a paper read at the third annual meeting of the American Psychological Association in December 1894. *Psychological Review* 2 (1895): 162–64.
12. "Some Aspects of Greek Philosophy." University of Chicago, *University Record* 1 (1896): 42.
13. "The Relation of Play to Education." University of Chicago, *University Record* 1 (1896): 141–45.
14. Review of G. Class, *Untersuchungen zur Phaenomenologie des Ontologie des menchlichen Geistes. American Journal of Theology* 1 (1897): 789–92.
15. "The Child and His Environment." *Transactions of the Illinois Society for Child Study* 3 (1898): 1–11.

16. "The Working Hypothesis in Social Reform." *American Journal of Sociology* 5 (1899): 367–71.

17. Review of Gustave Le Bon, *The Psychology of Socialism. American Journal of Sociology* 5 (1899): 404–12.

18. "Suggestions Towards a Theory of the Philosophical Disciplines." *Philosophical Review* 9 (1900): 1–17.

19. Review of George Simmel, *Philosophie des Geldes. Journal of Political Economy* 9 (1901): 616–19.

20. "A New Criticism of Hegelianism: Is It Valid?" A review of Charles F. D'Arcy, *Idealism and Theology: A Study of Presuppositions. American Journal of Theology,* 5 (1901): 87–96.

21. "The Definition of the Psychical." *Decennial Publications of the University of Chicago,* 1st Ser., 3 (1903): 77–112.

22. "The Basis for a Parents' Association." *Elementary School Teacher* 4 (1903): 337–46.

23. "Image or Sensation." *Journal of Philosophy* 1 (1904): 604–7.

24. "The Relations of Psychology and Philology." *Psychological Bulletin* 1 (1904): 375–91.

25. Review of D. Draghiscesco, *Du Rôle de l'Individu dans le Déterminisme Social* and *Le Problème du Déterminisme Social, Déterminisme biologique et Déterminisme social. Psychological Bulletin* 2 (1905): 399–405.

26. Review of Paul Jacoby, *Études sur la Sélection chez l'Homme. Psychological Bulletin* 2 (1905): 407–12.

27. "Science in the High School." *School Review* 14 (1906): 237–49.

28. "The Imagination in Wundt's Treatment of Myth and Religion." *Psychological Bulletin* 3 (1906): 393–99.

29. "The Teaching of Science in College." *Science* 24 (1906): 390–97.

30. "Concerning Animal Perception." *Psychological Review* 14 (1907): 383–90.

31. "Editorial Note on the School System of Chicago." *School Review* 15 (1907): 160–65.

32. Review of Jane Addams, *The Newer Ideals of Peace. American Journal of Sociology* 13 (1907): 121–28.

33. Review of Henri Bergson, *L'Évolution créatrice. Psychological Bulletin* 4 (1907): 379–84.

34. "The Relation of Imitation to the Theory of Animal Perception." An abstract of a paper presented at the fifteenth annual meeting of the American Psychological Association in December 1906. *Psychological Bulletin* 4 (1907): 210–11.

35. "The Educational Situation in the Chicago Public Schools." *City Club Bulletin* 1 (1907): 131–38.

36. "Educational Aspects of Trade Schools." *Union Labor Advocate* 8 (1908): 19–20.

37. "The Philosophical Basis of Ethics." *International Journal of Ethics* 18 (1908): 311–23.

38. "The Social Settlement, Its Basis and Function." University of Chicago, *University Record* 12 (1908): 108–10.

39. Review of William McDougall, *An Introduction to Social Psychology.* *Psychological Bulletin* 5 (1908): 385–91.

40. Review of Paul Gaultier, *L'Ideal moderne. Psychological Bulletin* 5 (1908): 403–4.

41. "Policy Statement of *The Elementary School Teacher*, Editorial Note." *Elementary School Teacher* 8 (1907–8): 281–84.

42. "Industrial Education and Trade Schools, Editorial Note." *Elementary School Teacher* 8 (1907–8), 402–6.

43. "Resolution on Industrial Education, Editorial Note." *Elementary School Teacher* 9 (1908–9): 156–57.

44. "Industrial Training, Editorial Note." *Elementary School Teacher* 9 (1908–9): 212–14.

45. "Moral Training in the Schools, Editorial Note." *Elementary School Teacher* 9 (1908–9): 327–28.

46. "Industrial Education, the Working-Man, and the School." *Elementary School Teacher* 9 (1908–9): 369–83.

47. "The Problem of History in the Elementary School, Editorial Note." *Elementary School Teacher* 9 (1908–9): 433–34.

48. "Social Psychology as Counterpart to Physiological Psychology." *Psychological Bulletin* 6 (1909): 401–8.

49. "The Adjustment of Our Industry to Surplus and Unskilled Labor." *Proceedings of the National Conference of Charities and Corrections* 34 (1909): 222–25.

50. "Social Consciousness and the Consciousness of Meaning." *Psychological Bulletin* 7 (1910): 397–405.

51. "The Psychology of Social Consciousness Implied in Instruction." *Science* 31 (1910): 688–93.

52. "What Social Objects Does Psychology Presuppose?" An abstract of a paper presented at the eighteenth annual meeting of the American Psychological Association in December 1909. *Psychological Bulletin* 7 (1910): 52–53.

53. "What Social Objects Must Psychology Presuppose?" *Journal of Philosophy* 7 (1910): 174–80.

54. Review of Warner Fite, *Individualism: Four Lectures on the Significance of Consciousness for Social Relations. Psychological Bulletin* 8 (1911): 323–28.

55. Review of B. M. Anderson, Jr., *Social Value, A Study in Economic Theory. Psychological Bulletin* 8 (1911): 432–36.

56. "The Mechanism of Social Consciousness." *Journal of Philosophy* 9 (1912): 401–6.

57. *A Report on Vocational Training in Chicago and Other Cities.* By a subcommittee of the City Club of Chicago, George H. Mead, chairman. Chicago: University of Chicago Press, 1912.

58. "Exhibit of the City Club Committee on Public Education." *City Club Bulletin* 5 (1912): 9.

59. "Probation and Politics." *Survey* 27 (1912): 2003–14. (It is probable, but not certain, that Mead was the author of this essay. See the later editorial reference to Mead in *Survey* 35 [1916]: 614.)

60. "Remarks on Labor Night Concerning Participation of Representatives of Labor in the City Club." *City Club Bulletin* 5 (1912): 214–15.

61. "The Social Self." *Journal of Philosophy* 10 (1913): 374–80.

62. "A Heckling School Board and an Educational Stateswoman." *Survey* 31 (1914): 443–44.

63. "Natural Rights and the Theory of the Political Institution." *Journal of Philosophy* 12 (1915): 141–55.

64. "The Psychological Bases of Internationalism." *Survey* 33 (1915): 604–7.

65. "The Larger Educational Bearings of Vocational Guidance." In *Readings in Vocational Guidance,* edited by Meyer Bloomfield, 43–55. Boston: Ginn and Co., 1915.

66. "Madison: The passage of the University of Wisconsin through the state political agitation of 1914; the survey by William H. Allen and his staff and the legislative fight of 1915, with the indications these offer of the place the state university holds in the community." *Survey* 35 (1915): 349–51, 354–61.

67. "A Rejoinder." *Survey* 33 (1916): 607, 610.

68. "Professor Hoxie and the Community." *University of Chicago Magazine* 9 (1917) 114–17.

69. "The Conscientious Objector." *National Security League, Patriotism through Education Series,* pamphlet no. 33. New York, 1917.

70. "Germany's Crisis—Its Effect on Labor, Parts I and II." Chicago *Herald,* July 26, and 27, 1917.

71. "War Issue to U.S. Forced by Kaiser." Chicago *Herald,* Aug. 2, 1917.

72. "America's Ideals and the War." Chicago *Herald,* Aug. 3, 1917.

73. "Democracy's Issues in the World War." Chicago *Herald,* Aug. 4, 1917.

74. "Josiah Royce—A Personal Impression." *International Journal of Ethics,* 27 (1917): 168–70.

75. "Scientific Method and Individual Thinker." In *Creative Intelligence: Essays in the Pragmatic Attitude,* edited by John Dewey et al., 176–227. New York: Henry Holt and Co., 1917.

76. Review of Edith Abbott and Sophonisba P. Breckinridge, *Truancy and Non-attendance in the Chicago Schools. Survey* 38 (1917): 369–70.

77. "The Psychology of Punitive Justice." *American Journal of Sociology* 23 (1918): 577–602.

78. Review of Thorstein Veblen, *The Nature of Peace and the Terms of Its Perpetuation. Journal of Political Economy* 26 (1918): 752–62.

79. "Social Work, Standards of Living and the War." *Proceedings of the National Conference of Social Work* 45 (1918): 637–44.

80. Letter to Senator Medill McCormick criticizing his opposition to the constitution of the league of nations, quoted in full by the Chicago *Evening Post* in an article entitled "Mead Answers McCormick as to Nations League," Mar. 7, 1919.

81. "The League and the Community." *Bulletin of the Vocational Supervision League,* Apr. 15, 1919, 1.

82. "A Translation of Wundt's *Folk Psychology." American Journal of Theology* 23 (1919): 533–36.

83. "Retiring President's Address." *City Club Bulletin* 13 (1920): 94–95.

84. Articles on "Idea," "Ideal," "Individualism," "Infinity," "Law of Nature," and "Natural Law." In *A Dictionary of Religion and Ethics,* edited by Shailer Mathews and Gerald Birney Smith. New York: Macmillan, 1921.

85. "A Behavioristic Account of the Significant Symbol." *Journal of Philosophy* 19 (1922): 157–63.

86. "Scientific Method and the Moral Sciences." *International Journal of Ethics* 33 (1923): 229–47.

87. Review of E. W. Hobson, *The Domain of Natural Science. Journal of Religion* 4 (1924): 324–27.

88. "Ella Adams Moore." *Bulletin of the Vocational Supervision League,* 1924.

89. "The Genesis of Self and Social Control." *International Journal of Ethics* 35 (1925): 251–77.

90. "The Nature of Aesthetic Experience." *International Journal of Ethics* 36 (1926): 382–92.

91. "The Objective Reality of Perspectives." In *Proceedings of the Sixth International Congress of Philosophy,* edited by Edgar S. Brightman, 75–85. New York: Longmans, Green and Co., 1927.

92. "A Pragmatic Theory of Truth." *University of California Publications in Philosophy* 11 (1929): 65–88.

93. "Bishop Berkely and His Message." *Journal of Philosophy* 26 (1929): 421–30.

94. "National-Mindedness and International-Mindedness." *International Journal of Ethics* 39 (1929): 385–407.

95. "The Nature of the Past." In *Essays in Honor of John Dewey* edited by John Coss, 235–42. New York: Henry Holt and Co., 1929.

96. "Cooley's Contribution to American Social Thought." *American Journal of Sociology* 35 (1930): 693–706.

97. "Philanthropy from the Point of View of Ethics." In *Intelligent Philanthropy,* edited by Ellsworth Faris, Ferris Laune, and Arthur J. Todd, 133–48. Chicago: University of Chicago Press, 1930.

98. "The Philosophies of Royce, James, and Dewey in Their American Setting." *International Journal of Ethics* 40 (1929–30): 211–31.

99. "Dr. A. W. Moore's Philosophy." University of Chicago, *University Record* n.s., 17 (1931): 47–49.

Posthumously Published Writings by Mead

100. *The Philosophy of the Present.* Edited, with an introduction, by Arthur E. Murphy, and prefatory remarks by John Dewey. La Salle, Ill.: Open Court Publishing Co., 1932.

101. *Mind, Self and Society from the Standpoint of a Social Behaviorist.* Edited, with an introduction, by Charles W. Morris. Chicago: University of Chicago Press, 1934.

102. "The Philosophy of John Dewey." *International Journal of Ethics* 46 (1935–36): 64–81.

103. *Movements of Thought in the Nineteenth Century*. Edited, with an introduction, by Merritt H. Moore. Chicago: University of Chicago Press, 1936.

104. *The Philosophy of the Act*. Edited, with an introduction, by Charles W. Morris, in collaboration with John M. Brewster, Albert M. Dunham, and David L. Miller. Chicago: University of Chicago Press, 1938.

105. "Two Unpublished Papers" ("Relative Space-Time and Simultaneity" and "Metaphysics"). Edited with an introduction, by David L. Miller. *Review of Metaphysics* 17 (1964): 511–56.

106. "Mead on the Child and the School." Edited by Darnell Rucker, *School and Society*, 44 (1968): 148–52. (This is the same article Mead published in 1898 as "The Child and His Environment." Rucker was unaware of Mead's publication when he edited what he took to be an unpublished Mead manuscript.)

107. *The Individual and the Social Self*. Edited, with an introduction, by David L. Miller. Chicago: University of Chicago Press, 1982.

Volumes Containing Selections from Mead's Published Writings

Strauss, Anselm, ed. *G. H. Mead on Social Psychology*. Chicago: University of Chicago Press, 1964.

Reck, Andrew J., ed. *G. H. Mead: Selected Writings*. Indianapolis: Bobbs-Merrill, 1964.

Petras, John W., ed. *George Herbert Mead: Essays on His Social Philosophy*. New York: Teachers College Press, 1968.

II. References Cited

Manuscript Collections

Chicago Historical Society Library, Chicago, Ill.
    Mary McDowell and the University of Chicago Settlement Papers
Harvard University, Houghton Library, Cambridge, Mass.
    The Papers of William James
Newberry Library, Chicago, Ill.
    Graham Taylor Papers
University of Chicago, Regenstein Library, Department of Special Collections, Chicago, Ill.
    The Henry Northrup Castle Papers
    The William Rainey Harper Papers
    The George Herbert Mead Papers
    The Elinor Castle Nef Papers
    Presidents' Papers, ca. 1925–1945
    University Presidents' Papers, 1889–1925
University of Illinois at Chicago, Library of Health Sciences, Special Collections Department
    Hull-House Association Papers
    Immigrants' Protective League of Illinois Papers

Published Material

Aboulafia, Mitchell. *The Mediating Self: Mead, Sartre, and Self-Determination.* New Haven: Yale University Press, 1986.

Adler, Mortimer J. *Philosopher at Large: An Intellectual Autobiography.* New York: Macmillan, 1977.

Ames, Edward Scribner. *A Memorial Pamphlet.* Privately printed pamphlet containing funeral eulogies for G. H. Mead by Edward Scribner Ames, John Dewey, and James H. Tufts, 1931.

Angell, James Rowland. Autobiographical Essay. In Carl Murchison, ed. *A History of Psychology in Autobiography,* 3:1–38. New York: Russell & Russell, 1961.

———. "The Province of Functional Psychology." *Psychological Review* 14 (1907): 61–91.

Ashmore, Harry S. *Unseasonable Truths: The Life of Robert Maynard Hutchins.* Boston: Little, Brown and Company, 1989.

Baldwin, James Mark. *Mental Development in the Child and the Race.* New York: Macmillan Co., 1895.

———. *Social and Ethical Interpretations in Mental Development: A Study in Social Psychology.* New York: Macmillan Co., 1897.

Baldwin, John D. *George Herbert Mead: A Unifying Theory for Sociology.* Beverly Hills: Sage Publications, 1986.

Barnard, John. *From Evangelicalism to Progressivism at Oberlin College, 1866–1917.* Columbus: Ohio State University Press, 1969.

Betz, Joseph. "George Herbert Mead on Human Rights." *Transactions of the Charles S. Peirce Society* 10 (1974): 199–223.

Boring, Edwin G. *A History of Experimental Psychology.* 2d ed. New York: Appleton-Century-Crofts, 1950.

Bulmer, Martin. *The Chicago School of Sociology.* Chicago: University of Chicago Press, 1984.

Buroker, Robert L. "From Voluntary Association to Welfare State: The Illinois Immigrants' Protective League, 1908–1926." *Journal of American History* 58 (1971): 643–60.

Buxton, Michael. "The Influence of William James on John Dewey's Early Work." *Journal of the History of Ideas* 45 (1984): 451–63.

Castle, Henry Northrup. *Henry Northrup Castle: Letters.* Edited by George and Helen Mead (London, 1902). Fifty copies of this volume were privately printed for the Castle family. A copy is available in the Regenstein Library at the University of Chicago.

City Club of Chicago. *City Club of Chicago Yearbook.* 1904.

———. *The City Club Bulletin,* vols. 1–24 (1907–31).

Coughlan, Neil. *Young John Dewey.* Chicago: University of Chicago Press, 1975.

Coutu, Walter. "Role-Playing vs. Role-Taking: An Appeal for Clarification." *American Sociological Review* 16 (1951): 180–87.

Cowles, Louise F. "Mrs. Elizabeth Storrs Mead." *Mount Holyoke Alumnae Quarterly* 1 (1917): 75–82.

Davis, Allen F. *Spearheads for Reform: The Social Settlements and the Progressive Movement, 1880–1914.* New York: Oxford University Press, 1967.

Deegan, Mary Jo. *Jane Adams and the Men of The Chicago School, 1892–1918.* New Brunswick: Transaction Publishers, 1988.

Deegan, Mary Jo, and John S. Burger. "George Herbert Mead and Social Reform: His Work and Writings." *Journal of the History of the Behavioral Sciences* 14 (1978): 362–73.

Dewey, John. *The Child and the Curriculum.* Chicago: University of Chicago Press, 1902.

———. "Christianity and Democracy." In *John Dewey: The Early Works,* vol. 4, *1893–1894,* edited by Jo Ann Boydston, 3–10. Carbondale: Southern Illinois University Press, 1971.

———. "Conduct and Experience." In *Psychologies of 1930,* edited by Carl Murchison, 409–22. Worcester: Clark University Press, 1930.

———. *Essays in Experimental Logic.* Chicago: University of Chicago Press, 1916.

———. "George Herbert Mead as I Knew Him." University of Chicago, *University Record* 17 (1931): 173–77.

———. "Introduction to Philosophy: Syllabus of Course 5." In *John Dewey: The Early Works,* vol. 3, *1889–1892,* edited by Jo Ann Boydston, 211–35. Carbondale: Southern Illinois University Press, 1969.

———. "My Pedagogic Creed" (1897). In *John Dewey: The Early Works,* vol. 5, *1882–1898,* edited by Jo Ann Boydston, 84–95. Carbondale: Southern Illinois University Press, 1972.

———. "The Reflex Arc Concept in Psychology" (1896). Reprinted in *John Dewey: The Early Works,* vol. 5, *1882–1898,* edited by Jo Ann Boydston, 96–109. Carbondale: Southern Illinois University Press, 1972.

———. *The School and Society.* Chicago: University of Chicago Press, 1899.

———. "The Theory of Emotion." (1894). Reprinted in *John Dewey: The Early Works,* vol. 4, *1893–1894,* edited by Jo Ann Boydston, 152–69. Carbondale: Southern Illinois University Press, 1971.

———. Two reviews of James Mark Baldwin, *Social and Ethical Interpretations in Mental Development.* In *John Dewey: The Early Works,* vol. 5, *1882–1898,* edited by Jo Ann Boydston, 385–422. Carbondale: Southern Illinois University Press, 1972.

Dewey, Richard. "Charles Horton Cooley: Pioneer in Psychosociology." In *An Introduction to the History of Sociology,* edited by Harry Elmer Barnes, 833–52. Chicago: University of Chicago Press, 1948.

Diner, Steven J. *A City and Its Universities: Public Policy in Chicago, 1892–1919.* Chapel Hill: University of North Carolina Press, 1980.

Dykhuizen, George. *The Life and Mind of John Dewey.* Carbondale: Southern Illinois University Press, 1973.

Fairchild, James H. "Professor [Hiram] Mead." *Oberlin Review* 8 (May 28, 1881): 212–14.

Faris, Robert E. L. *Chicago Sociology, 1920–1932.* San Francisco: Chandler Publishing Co., 1967.

Habermas, Jürgen. *The Theory of Communicative Action,* vol. 2. Translated by Thomas McCarthy. Boston: Beacon Press, 1988.

Hall, G. Stanley. "Philosophy in the United States." *Mind* 4 (1879): 89–105.

Heidbreder, Edna. "Functionalism." In *Schools of Psychology,* edited by David L. Krantz. New York: Appleton-Century-Crofts, 1969.

Herrick, Mary J. *The Chicago Schools: A Social and Political History.* Beverly Hills: Sage Publications, 1971.

Hull-House Bulletin, vols. 2–3.

James, William. *The Principles of Psychology.* New York: Henry Holt and Co., 1890.

Joas, Hans, ed. *Das Problem der Intersubjektivität: Neuere Beiträge zum Werk George Herbert Meads.* Frankfurt am Main: Suhrkamp, 1985.

———. *G. H. Mead: A Contemporary Re-examination of his Thought.* Translated by Raymond Meyer. Cambridge: MIT Press, 1985.

Joeckel, Carleton Bruns, and Loen Carnovsky. *A Metropolitan Library in Action.* Chicago: University of Chicago Press, 1940.

Kolb, William L. "A Critical Evaluation of Mead's 'I' and 'me' Concepts." *Social Forces,* 22 (1944): 291–96. Reprinted in *Symbolic Interaction: A Reader in Social Psychology,* edited by Jerome G. Manis and Bernard N. Meltzer, 241–50. Boston: Allyn and Bacon, 1967.

Lauer, Robert H., and Linda Boardman. "Role-Taking: Theory, Typology, and Propositions." *Sociology and Social Research* 55 (1971): 137–48.

Leavitt, Frank M. Review of *A Report on Vocational Training in Chicago and in other Cities. American Journal of Sociology* 18 (1912–13): 402–4.

Lewis, J. David, and Richard L. Smith. *American Sociology and Pragmatism: Mead, Chicago Sociology, and Symbolic Interaction.* Chicago: University of Chicago Press, 1980.

Mayhew, Katherine Camp, and Anna Camp Edwards. *The Dewey School.* New York: Atherton Press, 1966.

McCaul, Robert L. "Dewey and the University of Chicago." *School and Society* 89 (1961): 152–57, 179–83, 202–6.

———. "Dewey's Chicago." *School Review* 67 (1959): 258–80.

Mead, Henry C. A. "Biographical Notes." In George Herbert Mead, *The Philosophy of the Act.* Edited by Charles W. Morris. Chicago: University of Chicago Press, 1938, lxxv–lxxix.

Miller, David L. *George Herbert Mead: Self, Language, and the World.* Austin: University of Texas Press, 1973.

Nef, Elinor Castle. *Letters & Notes: Volume I.* Edited by John U. Nef. Los Angeles: Ward Ritchie Press, 1953.

———. *My Mother's Reminiscences.* Chicago: privately printed, 1954.

Public Education Association of Chicago. *Bulletins* 1–4 (1916).

Reck, Andrew J. "The Influence of William James on John Dewey in Psychology." *Transactions of the Charles S. Peirce Society* 20 (1984): 87–118.

Rochberg-Halton, Eugene. *Meaning and Modernity: Social Theory in the Pragmatic Attitude.* Chicago: University of Chicago Press, 1986.

Royce, Josiah. "The External World and the Social Consciousness." *Philosophical Review* 3 (1894): 513–45.

———. "Self-Consciousness, Social Consciousness, and Nature." *Philosophical*

Review 4 (1895): 465–85, 577–602. Reprinted in *Studies of Good and Evil* (1898).

————. "Some Observations on the Anomalies of Self-Consciousness." *Psychological Review* 2 (1895): 433–57, 574–84. Reprinted in *Studies of Good and Evil* (1898).

————. *Studies of Good and Evil.* New York: D. Appleton and Co., 1898.

Rucker, Darnell. *The Chicago Pragmatists.* Minneapolis: University of Minnesota Press, 1969.

Scheffler, Israel. *Four Pragmatists: A Critical Introduction to Peirce, James, Mead, and Dewey.* New York: Humanities Press, 1974.

Schwalbe, Michael L. "Toward a Sociology of Moral Problem Solving." *Journal for the Theory of Social Behavior* 20 (1990), 131–55.

Shalin, Dmitri N. "G. H. Mead, Socialism, and the Progressive Agenda." *American Journal of Sociology* 93 (1988): 913–51.

————. "Mead, Behaviorism and Indeterminacy." *Symbolic Interaction* 12 (1989): 37–41.

Singer, Beth J. "Rights and Norms," a paper presented at the international conference on Frontiers in American Philosophy, Texas A & M University, June 1–4, 1988.

Smith, T. V. *A Non-Existent Man.* Austin: University of Texas Press, 1962.

Taylor, Frank J., Earl M. Welty, and David W. Eyre. *From Land and Sea: The Story of Castle & Cooke of Hawaii.* San Francisco: Chronicle Books, 1976.

Thayer, H. S. *Meaning and Action: A Critical History of Pragmatism.* Indianapolis: Bobbs-Merrill Co., 1968.

Tufts, James H. Short reviews of current social psychological literature, *Psychological Review* 2 (1895): 305–9, 407–8, 616–8; 4 (1897): 316–18; 6 (1899): 533–36.

————. Review of James Mark Baldwin, *Social and Ethical Interpretations in Mental Development. Psychological Review* 5 (1898): 313–21.

Tugendhat, Ernst. *Self-Consciousness and Self-Determination.* Cambridge: MIT Press, 1986.

University of Chicago. *Daily Maroon.*

————. *The Faculty of the Division of the Humanities: December 1930–October 1940.* This volume is kept in the Secretary of the Faculties Office at the University of Chicago.

————. *Register of the University of Chicago.*

University of Chicago Settlement. *A Study of Chicago's Stockyards Community,* 3 volumes: vol. 1, *Opportunities in School and Industry for Children of the Stockyards District,* by Ernest L. Talbert; vol. 2, *The American Girl in the Stockyards District,* by Louise Montgomery; vol. 3, *Wages and Family Budgets in the Chicago Stockyards District,* by John C. Kennedy. Chicago: University of Chicago Press, 1912–14.

University of Michigan. *Calendar of the University of Michigan, 1891–94.*

————. *Michigan Daily.*

Watson, John B. Autobiographical essay. In *A History of Psychology in Autobiog-*

raphy, edited by Carl Murchison, 3:271–81. New York: Russell & Russell, 1961.

———. "Psychology as the Behaviorist Views It." *Psychological Review* 20 (1913): 158–77.

Welchman, Jennifer. "From Absolute Idealism to Instrumentalism: The Problem of Dewey's Early Philosophy." *Transactions of the Charles S. Peirce Society* 25 (1989): 407–19.

Wenzel, Harald. *George Herbert Mead zur Einführung.* Hamburg: Junius Verlag, 1990.

White, Morton G. *The Origin of Dewey's Instrumentalism.* New York: Columbia University Press, 1943.

Whitehead, Alfred North. *An Enquiry Concerning the Principles of Natural Knowledge.* Cambridge: Cambridge University Press, 1919.

———. *The Concept of Nature.* Cambridge; Cambridge University Press, 1920.

———. *The Principle of Relativity.* Cambridge; Cambridge University Press, 1922.

Wilson, Howard E. *Mary McDowell, Neighbor.* Chicago: University of Chicago Press, 1928.

Index

Abbott, Grace, 104
Addams, Jane, 100, 104
Adler, Mortimer J., 184, 185, 186, 187, 188,
    189, 191, 192, 212*nn3,6*, 213*n14*
Alexander, Samuel, 140, 141, 147
Ames, Edward Scribner, 185, 193, 201*n1*
Ames, Van Meter, 209*n5*
Angell, James Burrill, 25, 38
Angell, James Rowland, 37, 38, 60, 69, 71,
    212*n3*
Animal behavior, 43, 44, 56, 57, 60–61,
    81–82, 85–87, 97, 153, 168, 170
Ann Arbor, Mich.: Mead at, 27–34
Ashmore, Harry S., 212*n3*
Attitudes: and consciousness of meaning,
    60; defined, 79, 83

Baldwin, James Mark, 45, 46, 58, 59, 85
Behaviorism, 66, 78, 140, 143, 161, 162; and
    Mead's *Mind, Self and Society,* 67–77
    passim; social, 70–71
Behaviorist tradition: Mead and the, 74–77
Bergson, Henri, 138, 139, 140, 141, 147, 151,
    209*nn3,4*
Berlin, Germany: Mead's studies at, 21–26
Berlin Heights, Ohio: Mead teaching school
    at, 6–8
Blaine, Mrs. Anita McCormick, 103
Bond, William Scott, 102
Boring, E. G., 74
Bowen, Francis, 13
Breckinridge, Sophinisba P., 104
Brogan, Albert P., 191, 192
Buchanan, Scott, 184, 185, 186, 189, 190,
    191, 192
Bulkley, Julia E., 201*n1*

Bureau of Vocational Guidance, 113
Burtt, E. A., 185, 186, 191, 192, 193, 212*n6*

Castle, Dorothy, 21, 34, 35
Castle, Elinor, 35, 200*n38*
Castle, Frida Stechner, 21, 22
Castle, Helen. *See* Mead, Helen Castle
Castle, Henry Northrup: correspondence
    with Mead, 1; and Mead, at Oberlin Col-
    lege, 2–6; in Honolulu, 6, 10, 13, 20, 21,
    35, 197*n46*; study of philosophy in Berlin,
    10–11; at Harvard Law School, 11–13;
    with Mead, in Germany, 20–21; with
    Mead, at Ann Arbor, 34; death of, 35;
    mentioned, 7, 8, 9, 14, 15, 17, 18, 22, 24,
    25, 27, 30, 32, 36, 37, 197*n33*
Castle, Mabel Wing, 34, 35, 200*n35*
Castle, Samuel Northrup, 35
Castle & Cooke Company of Hawaii, 2
Chicago, Ill.: stockyards neigborhood, 102,
    112; public library service, and Mead, 106
Chicago Physiological School: Mead and,
    202*n9*
Christianity: Mead and, 6, 7, 8, 21, 22, 33,
    100–101, 115, 126
Chocorua, N.H.: Mead at, 15–18, 198*n58*
Citizens Committee: and 1910 garment
    workers' strike, 104–5
City Club of Chicago, 105–8
Common world, 145, 150, 157–58, 178–79,
    180, 181, 182
Cooley, Charles Horton, 58, 199*n19*
Cooley, Edwin G., 109

Democracy: and vocational education,
    111; war, international-mindedness, and,
    122–26

Dewey, John: and Mead, at Ann Arbor, 25, 27–34, 36; 1892 course syllabus, 27–30; influence on Mead, 27, 32, 36, 37, 38–42, 69–70, 108–9, 111; essay on the reflex arc concept, 28, 39, 49–50, 51, 52, 53, 57, 68, 69, 70, 71, 72, 76, 171; and Mead, at Chicago, 37–44, 46, 49; experimental elementary school, 39–40, 46, 109, 163; remarks about Mead, 48, 193–94; and behaviorism, 74, 75; and Hull-House, 100; pragmatism of, 161, 162, 163–66; and social psychology, 165; mentioned, 60, 99, 118, 130, 139, 142, 169, 176, 177, 178, 182, 197n33
Dewey, Mrs. John, 34
Dilthey, Wilhelm, 22, 24, 25
Distance and contact experience, 56–57, 139, 142, 170–71, 172
Doering, O. C., 106
Dualism: psychophysical, 29–30, 52, 69, 71, 72, 74, 140, 142, 143, 144, 149
Dummer, Mrs. Ethel, 103

Ebbinghaus, Hermann, 21
Eddington, Arthur, 139, 157
Educational theory and reform, 39–40, 99, 106–7, 108–14
Edwards, Jonathan, 3, 5
Einstein, Albert, 139, 157, 210n6
Ellis, John M., 4, 5
Emergence: passage, temporality, and, 146–49; and temporality, 154–57; and the human mind, 159, 168–69; mentioned, 141, 158
Emotions: theory of, 33, 38
Ethics and social psychology: Mead's later works on, 131–36
Everett, Charles Carroll, 16
Evolution, 25, 42, 118, 130, 141, 162, 163, 167–68, 181

Fairchild, James H., 4, 5
Faris, Ellsworth, 47, 203n34
Fichte, Johann Gottlieb, 24
Ford, Franklin, 30
Foster, George Burman, 115
Free will, 5, 7
Freund, Ernst, 104
Functionalism: Mead's early, 49–54; and perception, 55, 57, 58; and behaviorism,

68, 70–77 passim; and Mead, at Chicago, 68–70; Mead's alleged rejection of, 70–74; and moral psychology, 116–20; mentioned, 65, 66, 154, 166

Game, 96
Generalized other, 93, 95, 96, 98, 133, 135, 181
Germany: Mead's studies in, 20–26
Gestures: conversation of, 59–60, 61, 63, 82, 84, 85, 91, 93, 95, 166; vocal, 61, 82, 83, 84, 86; and taking the attitude of the other, 82–84; mentioned 75–76, 166
Gibbens, Margaret, 16, 18
God, 31, 156
Green, T. H., 15

Hall, Everett W., 185
Hall, G. Stanley, 20–21, 198n3
Hamilton, William, 3, 5, 15
Harper, William Rainey, 38, 100, 201n3
Hartmann, Eduard von, 28
Hartshorne, Charles, 185, 212n6
Harvard: Mead at, 12–19, 197n50
Heaven, kingdom of: Mead on, 31, 33
Hegelianism: and Dewey, 27, 28, 30, 32, 33, 39, 163–64; and Mead, 32, 33, 39, 42, 46, 50, 101, 117, 130
Heidbreder, Edna, 69
Heinze, Max, 20
Henderson, Charles R., 102, 103, 104
Hull, Mrs. M. D., 103
Hull-House: Dewey and, 100; Mead and, 100, 206n2
Hutchins, Robert Maynard, 183–93 passim, 212nn3,6
Hypotheses: and social reform, 41, 42; and reconstructive thought, 54, 120, 122, 128, 129, 135, 149; and pragmatism, 162, 164; and scientific inquiry, 177, 178, 180–81

"I" and "Me" concepts: introduction of, 54–55; and social self, 62–66
Images: memory, 61, 63, 65, 88–89
Imitation: indirect, 89–92
Immigrants: and the University of Chicago Settlement, 99–105
Immigrants' Protective League, 104
Impulses or instincts: social, 41, 42, 58, 61, 80, 83, 84, 86, 88, 91, 125; imitative, 58–

59, 85, 88, 90; defined, 80; hostile, 125; as phase of conduct, 169–70; contrasted, 204n8

Inhibition, 50, 51–52, 60, 94, 164

Intelligence: reflective, 39, 53–54, 94–95, 127, 177, 180, 181

Internationalism: war, democracy, and, 122–26

Introspection: as a method in psychology, 69, 73

Introspective self-consciousness: social genesis of, 61–62; and the "I" and "me," 62–66

James, Harry, 16

James, William: and Mead, at Chocorua, 15–18, 198n58; *Principles of Psychology*, 17, 28, 53, 54; pragmatism of, 161, 162–63; mentioned, 38, 51, 71, 125, 169, 184

James, Mrs. William, 16

Jesus Christ, 33, 134

Joas, Hans, 124, 198n2, 208n4

Kant, Immanuel, 6, 7, 9, 10, 11, 18, 19, 23, 24, 25, 26, 132

Knowledge: and pragmatism, 162, 163, 164; and science, 177–78

Laing, G. J., 191

League of Nations, 107–8

Leipzig, Germany: Mead's studies at, 20–21

Lewis, J. David, 195n12

Lillie, W. T., 203n1

Lloyd, Alfred, 27

McCormick, A. A., 104

McCormick, Sen. Medill, 107

McCosh, James, 4

McDougall, William, 58

McDowell, Mary E., 100, 103

McGill, V. J., 184

Mack, Julian W., 104

McKeon, Richard, 184, 185, 186, 189, 190

Manipulation: as phase of conduct or experience, 57, 153, 170, 172–73, 175

Mead, Elizabeth Storrs (mother of GHM), 1, 6, 11

Mead, Helen Castle (wife of GHM), 4, 11, 13, 22, 25, 30, 35–36, 212n2

Mead, Henry Castle Albert (son of HCM and GHM), 33, 193

Mead, Hiram (father of GHM), 1

Mead, Irene Tufts (daughter-in-law of GHM), 46, 198n58

Mechem, Floyd R., 102

Merriam, Charles R., 103, 107

Milikan, Robert A., 102

Mill, John Stuart, 132

Miller, David L., 70, 71, 195n12, 210n11

Miller, John S., 107

Mind: and objective relativism, 140–46; and nature, 159

Minkowski space-time, 153, 157, 158

Moore, Addison W., 201n1

Moral psychology: and moral consciousness, 101–2, 118–20, 121; early functionalist, 116–20

Moral reconstruction: and scientific intelligence, 101, 116, 118, 120, 122, 132; and moral problems, 117–22, 127–36 passim; and scientific method, 126–31; and critical moral reflection, 133–36

Morality: and the social self, 120–22; and social psychology, 131–36

Morgan, Lloyd, 141, 147

Morris, Charles W., 71, 131, 203n1, 204n9

Munk, Hermann, 24

Murphy, Arthur E., 159, 165, 166, 183, 185, 191, 192, 193, 209n4

Nicholes, Anna E., 104

Novelty: in experience, 53–54, 63, 65, 147, 149, 155, 159

Oberlin College: Mead at, 2–6; mentioned, 36, 197n50

Objective relativism: and the place of mind in nature, 140–46; and post-Newtonian physics, 175

Other, taking the attitude of: terminological considerations, 78–80; and the conversation of gestures, 80–84; rudimentary form of, 80, 82–84, 89; and self-stimulation, 82–84; anticipatory function of, 83, 90–92; and the problem of socialization, 84–92; and memory images, 88–89; applications of the concept of, 92–98; reflexive function of, 92–93, 95–96; appropriative function of,

Other (*continued*)
93; and generalized others, 93; advanced
level of, 97; and common world, 145, 157,
158, 159, 175, 176; mentioned, 64, 65, 77,
92–93, 145, 153, 167, 173, 178, 181

Palmer, George Herbert, 13, 14, 15, 16, 184
Parallelism: psychophysical. *See* Dualism
Passage: emergence and temporality, 146–
49
Past, present, and future, 146–49, 155
Paulsen, Friedrich, 21, 24
Peirce, Charles S., 161–62, 211*n*3
Perceptual objects: physical, 55–57, 62,
76–77, 142–43, 171–73; and the social
genesis of consciousness, 55–62; social,
58, 62, 76–77, 95–96, 172
Perspectives, 80, 141–42, 143, 145–46, 150,
151, 152, 156, 157, 158, 159, 175, 178
Pfleiderer, Otto, 22
Ph.D.: Mead's projected dissertation for,
24, 25–26; Mead's lack of, 26, 38
Physiological psychology, 15, 21, 22, 23, 25,
27, 31–32, 33, 61, 70, 200*n*35
Play: and game, 96
Plimpton, Nathan C., 102
Poets: English, 2, 9, 193
Pond, Allen B., 104, 106
Porter, Noah, 2, 3, 4
Pragmatism: Mead on, 161–66
Psychical or subjective consciousness: re-
constructive function of, 48, 51–54, 55,
63

Queen, S. A., 195*n*12

Reason: and rationality, 133–36
Reck, Andrew J., 70, 71
Relativity: theory of, 139, 157, 158, 159, 165,
174, 209*n*5
Role: defined, 79. *See also* Other, taking the
attitude of
Royce, Josiah, 12, 13, 14, 15, 16, 18–19, 24,
38, 45, 46, 58, 59, 60, 85, 184

Santayana, George, 16, 184
Schelling, F. W. J., 24
Schmoller, Gustav, 24
Schopenhauer, Arthur, 21
Scientific knowledge: growth of, 145–46,

176–82; and scientific data, 145–46,
179–80; and the past, 155–56
Scientific method: and Hegelianism, 39; and
social reform, 41, 42, 101–2; and moral
problems, 117–18, 120; and moral recon-
struction, 126–31; and hypotheses, 177,
178
Scottish philosophy, 3, 4, 9, 18
Secularism, 22, 34, 115, 126–27, 137
Self: and social genesis of self-conscious-
ness, 44–45, 95–96; as social object, 58,
61–62, 172; the social, 62–66; social
structure of, 96–97
Seydel, Rudolf, 20
Shalin, Dmitri N., 205*n*4, 208*n*51
Shoop, John D., 106
Smith, Richard L., 195*n*12
Smith, T. V., 185, 212*n*6
Social act, 58–9, 61, 70, 75, 76, 81, 93
Social genesis: of consciousness and percep-
tual objects, 55–62
Social objects, 58, 60, 62, 63, 98
Social organization: human, 97–8; and
nonhuman species, 97
Social pragmatism: Mead's constructive,
166–82
Social process: human, 29, 31, 32, 33, 40,
42, 67, 73, 94, 95, 123, 127, 130, 134, 150,
163, 167–69, 181
Social psychology: beginnings of Mead's
interest in, 43–47
Social reform: Mead's early writings on,
40–42; piecemeal and experimental
approach to, 40–41, 99, 130, 136–37;
University of Chicago Settlement and
immigrants, 100–105; and social sur-
vey research, 102–3; and City Club of
Chicago, 105–8
Social self: and morality, 120–22
Socialism, 22, 23, 124
Sociality: in nature, 157, 158, 159
Socrates, 134
Space: perception of, 9, 23–24, 26
Spatiotemporal structures: of experience,
118, 142–43, 146–49, 153, 155, 172–73; of
scientific world, 154, 157, 174–76
Spencer, Herbert, 28
Stages of the act: consummation, 76, 171,
172; manipulation, 76, 170; perception,
76, 170; impulse, 169–70

Stimulus and response: and psychological functionalism, 49–50, 75–76; mediation of stimulus by response, 50, 76–77, 89, 96, 171; anticipatory responses, 59, 81, 82; social, 59, 61, 70, 94–95; self-stimulation, 64, 82–89 passim, 91, 173; and behaviorism, 75

Stout, G. F., 57

Strong, Charles A., 201*n1*

Surveying: railroad, 9–10

Swing, Albert, 25

Swing, Alice Mead, 25

Symbols: significant, 93–94, 95, 133, 167, 180

Taylor, Graham, 104

Teaching: surveying, tutoring, and, 6–12; at University of Michigan, 27–34, 43, 200*n33*; at University of Chicago, 34–35, 43, 44, 46–7, 201*n3*, 213*n27*

Thought: reconstructive function of, 39, 94, 145; mediated by symbols, 94–95; social structure of, 94–95; and internalized conversation of gestures, 95

Truth: and scientific inquiry, 178

Tufts, James H., 37–38, 46, 183, 184, 185, 186, 187, 188, 189, 193, 213*nn15,27*

Universe of discourse, 93–94, 135, 136, 139

University of Chicago Settlement: and the immigrants, 99–105; mentioned, 112

University of Michigan: Mead at, 27–34

Values: naturalistic view of, 118, 121, 130–

31, 137, 143–44, 164, 171; moral, 122, 133, 135, 136; incommensurable, 128–29

Vincent, George E., 46

Vocational education: Mead's research and writing on, 106, 110–14

Vocational guidance: Mead's writing on, 113–14

Vocational Supervision League, 114

Waldeyer, Wilhelm, 21

War: democracy, international-mindedness, and, 122–26; moral equivalent of, 125–26

Watson, John B., 43, 67, 68, 73, 74, 75, 77

Whitehead, Alfred North: beginnings of Mead's interest in, 138–40; and cogredience, 141; and consentient sets, 141, 175; and objective relativism, 141–44, 149, 151, 152, 175; and percipient events, 141, 143, 174, 175; and perspectives, 141, 142, 143, 151, 152–56, 175, 178; and eternal objects, 144, 156; and ingression, 144, 156; and mind, 144; and common world, 145; influence seen in Mead's posthumously published works, 149–59; and extensive abstraction, 151, 154, 156; mentioned, 210*nn11,12*, 211*nn32,33*

Wilson, Woodrow, 123, 124

Woodward, Frederic C., 192

World: problematic and unproblematic features of, 51–53, 54, 136, 177–80; that is there, and scientific inquiry, 178, 180

World War I, 99, 122–25, 126

Wundt, Wilhelm, 16, 20, 59, 73

Young, Ella Flagg, 106

GARY A. COOK is a professor of philosophy and chair of the Department of Philosophy and Religion at Beloit College, Beloit, Wisconsin. His previous publications include articles in the *Journal of General Education*, the *Journal of the History of the Behavioral Sciences*, and *Transactions of the Charles S. Peirce Society*.